Global History and Geography

Readings and Documents

Norman Lunger

AMSCO SCHOOL PUBLICATIONS, INC.
315 Hudson Street / New York, N.Y. 10013

Design and Composition: Nesbitt Graphics
Cover Design: Nesbitt Graphics
Photo Research: Linda Sykes

Please visit our Web site @ www.amscopub.com

When ordering this book, please specify:
R 762 **P** or
GLOBAL HISTORY: READINGS AND DOCUMENTS

ISBN: 1-56765-656-0 / *NYC Item 56765-565-X*

Printed in the United States of America

1 2 3 4 5 6 7 07 06 05 04 03 02

NORMAN LUNGER, Writer, Editor, Reporter; Author of *Reviewing American History* (Amsco), Coauthor of *Global Geography* (Amsco) and *Global Issues* (Amsco)

Contributing Writer: **Lillian Forman**, Social Studies Writer and Researcher

Question Writers

Steven A. Shultz, Social Studies Coordinator, Rocky Point Public Schools, New York

Ross Bloomfield, Social Studies Teacher, John Adams High School, New York

Consultants

Dominick J. Camastro, Lead Teacher, Social Studies, Erasmus Campus: High School for Business and Technology, Brooklyn, New York

Carol J. Gómez, Former Assistant Principal (Supv.) for Social Studies, New York City School System; New York City Social Studies Supervisors' Association Executive Board

Steven P. Juliano, Teacher of Social Studies, William H. Maxwell High School, Brooklyn, New York

Sol Levine, Retired Superintendent, Beverly Hills (CA) Unified School District

Mary Ann Pluchino, Global Studies Teacher, Kings Park High School, Kings Park, New York

Steven C. Wolfson, Former Assistant Principal (Supr.) for Social Studies, Fort Hamilton High School, Brooklyn, New York; Social Studies Consultant, New York City Board of Education

To the Student

Welcome to *Global History and Geography: Readings and Documents.* The documents we have chosen for this book are only a tiny fraction of all the original materials from the past that we who live in the 21st century can find in books, in museums, on tape, film, and disk, and on the Internet, to mention just the major sources. Since recorded history began, over 5,000 years ago, humans have been documenting everything about themselves: their names and those of their family members, the kinds of work they did, the names of their leaders, the property they owned, how their crops and animals fared. People also began early on to record their thoughts, feelings, wishes, beliefs, and wants. They made records of their laws and the major events in the lives of their people, so that those who came later would know and remember them and pass them on to the next generation. They wrote about their friends and their enemies, about peace and war.

Many of the places, people, and subjects you will read about in this book may seem strange to you at first. That's normal. The names, places, and societies are often very different from the ones you have encountered in your daily lives. Once you get past the surface differences, which can be great, you will see that people in the past had many, even most, of the wants, needs, and hopes that we do today. They questioned why things happened when they did—for instance, why the seasons changed, why their lives were sometimes very good and sometimes very hard, what goals they should seek in life. They also wanted to know how everything around them got started. Who or what made them what they were? How should they behave toward others? What should they believe or not believe? People have been asking these questions for thousands of years, and they continue to do so today.

This book is arranged into chronological units like those in the Amsco textbook *Global History and Geography: The Growth of Civilizations.* Many of the global areas and civilizations in the text are represented in this book. We have included documents by or about people of the past whose thoughts and actions greatly influenced the lives of others. We have also included documents about average people, who left interesting records of their lives and times. You will read about the laws and codes that people enacted, what they studied and where they traveled, and their hopes and dreams for the future. In the documents of the past, you will begin to see parallels to the present, to similar ideas, to encounters between people and groups with vastly different beliefs and ways of life. You may be reminded of events that are occurring today. You will read about examples of historical conflicts, and the ways that people have resolved them.

One of the famous sayings about history is this: Those who do not remember the lessons of the past are destined to repeat them. We hope that you will find the documents have given you many things to remember.

To the Teacher

Global History and Geography: Readings and Documents is a book of 115 original readings and visual documents that span the course of recorded history from about 2000 B.C. to the present. These works are correlated to the New York State curriculum for global history and geography and to the Amsco textbook *Global History and Geography: The Growth of Civilizations.* The subjects and topics of the documents in this book were chosen to fit into and complement the organizational framework of the textbook. Many come from sources recommended in the New York State global history and geography curriculum guide. (See the "Connections" column in the syllabus.) The eight units in this book cover topics and time periods in the eight units of the textbook. The documents in each unit may be used along with the unit of the same number in the textbook.

One of the major purposes of this book is to give students practice in reading and understanding original documents. Many high school history examinations, as well as Advanced Placement examinations, now require students to read and answer questions about original materials—both written and visual—and then write an essay on a topic related to the documents. For example, students in New York State take a required Regents examination after their two-year global history and geography course. One of the components of this exam is a document-based question. This question contains excerpts from seven or eight original text and visual documents. Students are required to read and study the documents, answer comprehension questions after each document, and then use at least four of the documents as the basis for an original essay, whose subject is determined by the exam.

Each document in this book has an introduction that describes the culture, time period, and persons in the document. Some introductions discuss the writer or creator of the document. Many documents are first-hand accounts of the writer's experience. Others, which were written years or centuries after the events they describe, are accepted by authorities as accurate historical statements. Many documents are followed by explanatory sections that round out the content of the document and place it in a larger historical context.

The documents in this book emphasize the special contributions to human experience and knowledge that people in different societies have made over the millennia. The exchange of products, ideas, and beliefs among the world's people also receives prominent emphasis. Ranging from the earliest Sumerian and Egyptian tales to present-day documents about globalization, the environment, and women's rights, the documents include excerpts from religious texts and classical narratives; writings about political, social, and human rights; laws and codes of justice and personal behavior; diary entries and memoirs; poems and folktales; and historical and contemporary illustrations, including works of art, photographs, and other graphic materials.

The text documents are presented substantially as they appeared in our sources. While they have not been rewritten to make them easier, sections that are not relevant have been omitted. In some cases, our "document" is an abridgment of many pages of text. All places in the text where material has been deleted are indicated with ellipses. To make comprehension easier for students, difficult or obscure words are either glossed in brackets or replaced by easier ones, also in brackets. In some cases, when a bracketed explanation would hinder the reading of the text, brief footnotes are used. Editorial comments in the documents are clearly noted.

Review questions follow each document. These questions will help students focus on important facts and concepts. They are similar in purpose to the "scaffolded" questions that follow each document in the New York State Regents examination's document-based question. Some review questions may also be used for class discussion or student research. You may wish to assign "mini"document-based questions about several related documents in a unit, or about documents in different units that discuss similar topics or contain similar concepts or ideas.

A separate answer key is available for the review and document-based questions.

Contents

Unit I The Ancient World: Civilizations and Religion (4000 B.C.–A.D. 500)

Unit II Expanding Zones of Exchange and Encounter (A.D. 500–1200)

Unit III Global Interactions (1200–1650)

Unit IV The First Global Age (1450–1770)

Unit V An Age of Revolutions (1600–1914)

Unit VII The World Since 1945

Unit VIII Global Connections and Interactions

The Ancient World: Civilizations and Religion

(4000 B.C.–A.D. 500)

A Sumerian Schoolboy's Tale

The world's first known writing system developed in the area of Mesopotamia known as Sumer sometime around 3300 B.C. People known as scribes used hand tools to press wedge-shaped symbols called cuneiform into tablets of wet clay. Sumerian boys prepared for the life of a scribe by going to school. A scribe might be a clerk who kept business or government records. Or he might be a scholar who studied serious subjects, wrote stories and poems, or ran a school for other scribes. The role of scribe seems to have been closed to Sumerian women, and there are no records of schools for girls in Sumer.

The following document is an essay written by a Sumerian scribe and schoolteacher about 2000 B.C. It seems to have been a popular essay, for many copies were made. Scholars have recovered and studied bits and pieces of 21 different copies, and they have assembled the pieces into a nearly complete text.

AUTHOR: Schoolboy, where did you go from earliest days?

STUDENT: I went to school.

AUTHOR: What did you do in school?

STUDENT: I recited my tablet, ate my lunch, prepared my [new] tablet, wrote it, finished it; then they assigned me my oral work, and in the afternoon they assigned me my written work.

When school was dismissed, I went home, entered the house, and found my father sitting there. I told my father of my written work, then recited my tablet to him, and my father was delighted. . . .

When I awoke early in the morning, I faced my mother and said to her, "Give me my lunch, I want to go to school." My mother gave me two rolls and I went to school.

In school the monitor in charge said to me "Why are you late?" Afraid and with pounding heart, I entered before my teacher and made a respectful curtsy.

> [The student misbehaved—by talking in class, standing up at the wrong time, leaving the school grounds, and making careless copies. For each offense, he was beaten with a cane. When the student returned home, he asked his father to invite the teacher to dinner.]

The teacher was brought from school, and after entering the house he was seated in the seat of honor [and given a good dinner]. The schoolboy attended and served him, and whatever he had learned of the art of tablet-writing he unfolded to his father.

> [The father then dressed the teacher in a new garment, gave him a gift, and put a ring on his hand.]

TEACHER TO STUDENT: Young man, because you did not neglect my word, did not forsake it, may you reach the [top] of the scribal art, may you achieve it completely. . . . Of your brothers may you be their leader, of your friends may you be their chief, may you rank the highest of the schoolboys. . . . You have carried out well the school's activities, you have become a man of learning.

Review Questions

1. What was meant in the story by a "tablet"?
2. What were the student's responsibilities in school?
3. Why was the teacher invited to the student's home?
4. a. How did the student's family treat the teacher?
   b. How did the teacher respond?
5. How was the Sumerian school different from a school today?
6. How was the Sumerian school similar to a present-day school?

The Great Flood, From *The Epic of Gilgamesh*

After the decline of Sumerian civilization, other groups dominated Mesopotamia. Sometime after 1800 B.C., one of those groups, known as Akkadians, produced a literary work called *The Epic of Gilgamesh*. It relates the deeds, real and imagined, of an ancient Mesopotamian king named Gilgamesh. Written in cuneiform characters on clay tablets, the tale was often rewritten over a period of many centuries. One of its most famous sections describes an immense flood sent by a group of gods who wanted to destroy the human race.

In this section, Gilgamesh hears the tale of the flood firsthand from Utanapishtim, who had been warned of the coming flood by a trickster god named Ea. Utanapishtim survived the flood by building an immense boat in which he, his wife, and their animals took refuge. In recognition of Utanapishtim's devotion to Ea, the gods granted him and his wife the gift of eternal life—meaning that they will live forever. (Question marks in parentheses indicate that a word is the editor's best guess about the meaning of the text.)

Utanapishtim spoke to Gilgamesh, saying:
"I will reveal to you, Gilgamesh, a thing that is hidden,
a secret of the gods I will tell you!
Shuruppak, a city that you surely know,
situated on the banks of the Euphrates.
that city was very old, and there were gods inside it.
The hearts of the Great Gods moved them to inflict the
Flood. . . .
Ea,[1] Clever Prince(?), [*said to Utanapishtim*] . . .
Tear down the house and build a boat! . . .
Spurn possessions and keep alive living beings!

[1]**Ea**—god of the underground freshwater sea called the Apsu; a trickster

Make all living beings go up into the boat.
The boat which you are to build,
its dimensions must measure equal to each other:
its length must correspond to its width. . . . '
I understood and spoke to my lord, Ea:
'My lord, thus is the command which you have uttered
I will heed and will do it.' . . .

[Utanapishtim describes how workers brought tools and material and how the boat was built.]

The boat was finished by sunset.
The launching was very difficult.
They had to keep carrying a runway of poles front to back,
until two-thirds of it had gone into the water(?). . . .
Whatever silver I had I loaded on it,
whatever gold I had I loaded on it.
All the living beings that I had I loaded on it,
I had all my [relatives] go up into the boat,
all the beasts and animals of the field and the craftsmen I had go up. . . .
Just as dawn began to glow
there arose from the horizon a black cloud. . . .
The . . . land shattered like a . . . pot.
All day long the South Wind blew . . . ,
blowing fast, submerging the mountain in water,
overwhelming the people like an attack.
No one could see his fellow, . . .
The gods were frightened by the Flood,
and retreated . . . . cowering like dogs . . . by the outer wall. . . .
When the seventh day arrived, the storm was pounding,
the flood was a war—struggling with itself like a woman . . . (in labor).
The sea calmed, fell still, the whirlwind (and) flood stopped up.
I looked around all day long—quiet had set in
and all the human beings had turned to clay!

The terrain was as flat as a roof.
I opened a vent and fresh air (daylight?) fell upon the side of my nose.
I fell to my knees and sat weeping, . . .
I looked around for coastlines in the expanse of the sea,
and at twelve leagues there emerged a region (of land).
On Mt. Nimush[2] the boat lodged firm,
Mt. Nimush held the boat, allowing no sway. . . .
When a seventh day arrived
I sent forth a dove and released it.
The dove went off, but came back to me;
no perch was visible so it circled back to me.
I sent forth a swallow and released it.
The swallow went off, but came back to me;
no perch was visible so it circled back to me.
I sent forth a raven and released it.
The raven went off, and saw the waters slither back.
It eats, it scratches, it bobs, but does not circle back to me.
Then I sent out everything in all directions and sacrificed (a sheep). . . .
The gods smelled the [aroma] . . .
and collected like flies over a (sheep) sacrifice. . . ."

Review Questions

1. Who brought about the great flood?
2. Why was Utanapishtim told to "tear down the house" and "build a boat"?
3. Why was Utanapishtim told to "spurn possessions and keep alive living beings"?
4. Who went into the boat once it was finished?
5. What happened at dawn the next day?
6. How did Utanapishtim know when the floodwaters had begun to recede?
7. Why do you think Utanapishtim told Gilgamesh this story?

---

[2]**Mt. Nimush**—reference to a mountain peak in what is now eastern Iraq

The Great Flood, From the Torah

The story of a great flood similar to the one in Mesopotamia figures in Jewish scriptures, or sacred writings. The written story dates to about the 9th century B.C. and appears in Genesis, the first book of the Bible. (Genesis and the four books that follow are known to Jews as the Torah.)

Again, the flood occurs by the order of a god. Because the Jews were monotheistic, there is only one God involved in the story. Judging that the human race has become evil, God decides to send a great flood to destroy life. But God spares Noah because he is a righteous (good) man. God tells Noah to build a large boat, or ark, and to bring his large family and pairs of animals onto the ark. When the flood waters go down, Noah and his family are the only humans left. They become the ancestors of all succeeding generations of humans.

Eventually, the Genesis story of the flood became part of the scriptures of Christians. Muslims too honor the story; they consider Noah to be one of their own prophets. (A prophet is a divinely inspired person—one who spreads God's word to people at large.)

The numbers show the beginnings of chapters in Genesis.

6

. . .When God saw how corrupt the earth was, for all flesh had corrupted its ways on earth, God said to Noah, "I have decided to put an end to all flesh, for the earth is filled with lawlessness because of them: I am about to destroy them with the earth. Make yourself an ark of . . . wood. . . . For My part, I am about to bring the Flood-waters upon the earth—to destroy all flesh under the sky in which there is breath of life; everything on earth shall perish. But I will establish My covenant [contract, agreement] with you, and you shall enter the ark, with your sons, your wife, and your sons' wives. And of all that lives, of all flesh, you shall take two of each into the ark to keep alive with you; they shall be male and female. From birds of every kind, cattle of every kind, every kind of creeping thing on earth, two of each shall come to you to stay alive. For your part, take of everything that is eaten and store it away, to serve as food for you and for them." Noah did so; just as God commanded him, so he did.

7

Then the LORD said to Noah, "Go into the ark, with all your household, for you alone have I found righteous before Me in this generation. Of every clean animal[1] you shall take seven pairs, males and their mates, and of every animal which is not clean, two, a male and its mate; of the birds of the sky also, seven pairs, male and female, to keep seed alive upon all the earth. For in seven days' time I will make it rain upon the earth, forty days and forty nights, and I will blot out from the earth all existence that I created." And Noah did just as the LORD commanded him. . . .

In the six hundredth year of Noah's life, in the second month, on the seventeenth day of the month, on that day

All the fountains of the great deep burst apart,
And the floodgates of the sky broke open.

That same day Noah and Noah's sons, Shem, Ham, and Japheth, went into the ark, with Noah's wife and the three wives of his sons—they and all beasts of every kind, all cattle of every kind, all creatures of every kind that creep on the earth, and all birds of every kind, every bird, every winged thing. They came to Noah into the ark, two each of all flesh in which there was breath of life. Thus they that entered [were] male and female of all flesh, as God had commanded him. And the LORD shut him in.

The Flood continued forty days on the earth, and the waters increased and raised the ark so that it rose above the earth. The waters swelled and increased greatly upon the earth, and the ark drifted upon the waters. When the waters had swelled much more upon the earth, all the highest mountains everywhere under the sky were covered. . . . All existence on earth was blotted out—man, cattle, creeping things, and birds of the sky; they were blotted out from the earth. Only Noah was left, and those with him in the ark.

---

[1]**clean animal**—an animal used in religious sacrifices

8

And when the waters had swelled on the earth one hundred and fifty days, God remembered Noah and all the beasts and all the cattle that were with him in the ark, and the waters subsided. The fountains of the deep and the floodgates of the sky were stopped up, and the rain from the sky was held back; the waters then receded steadily from the earth. At the end of one hundred and fifty days the waters diminished, so that in the seventh month, on the seventeenth day of the month, the ark came to rest on the mountains of Ararat[2]. The waters went on diminishing until the tenth month; in the tenth month, on the first of the month, the tops of the mountains became visible.

At the end of forty days, Noah opened the window of the ark that he had made and sent out the raven; it went to and fro until the waters had dried up from the earth. Then he sent out the dove to see whether the waters had decreased from the surface of the ground. But the dove could not find a resting place for its foot, and returned to him to the ark, for there was water all over the earth. So putting out his hand, he took it into the ark with him. He waited another seven days, and again sent out the dove from the ark. The dove came back to him toward evening, and there in its bill was a plucked-off olive leaf! Then Noah knew that the waters had decreased on the earth. He waited still another seven days and sent the dove forth; and it did not return to him any more.

In the six hundred and first year, in the first month, on the first of the month, the waters began to dry from the earth; and . . . Noah saw that the surface of the ground was drying. And in the second month, on the twenty-seventh day of the month, the earth was dry.

God spoke to Noah, saying, "Come out of the ark, together with your wife, your sons, and your sons' wives. Bring out with you every living thing of all flesh that is with you: birds, animals, and everything that creeps on earth; and let them swarm on the earth and be fertile and increase on earth." So Noah came out, together with his sons, his wife, and his sons' wives. Every animal, every creeping thing, and every bird, everything that stirs on earth came out of the ark by families.

---

[2]**Ararat**—a twin-peaked mountain in what is now eastern Turkey

Then Noah built an altar to the LORD and, taking of every clean animal and of every clean bird, he offered burnt offerings on the altar. The LORD smelled the pleasing odor, and the LORD said to Himself: "Never again will I doom the earth because of man, since the [workings] of man's mind are evil from his youth; nor will I ever again destroy every living being, as I have done.

So long as the earth endures,
Seedtime and harvest,
Cold and heat,
Summer and winter,
Day and night
Shall not cease."

9

God blessed Noah and his sons, and said to them, "Be fertile and increase, and fill the earth."

Review Questions

1. Why did God send a flood to cover the earth?
2. Why were Noah and his family saved?
3. Why were a male a female of each species taken aboard the ark?
4. How did Noah learn when it was safe to leave the ark?
5. How does the portrayal of the gods or God differ in the stories of Noah and Utanapishtim?

The Code of Hammurabi

Hammurabi, the ruler of Babylon, compiled one of the first written law codes in about 1750 B.C. The code reveals a stern ruler who wished to strengthen the power of the central government, keep order in his realm, and maintain the hierarchical (rigidly structured) nature of society. At the same time, it showed his desire to give some protection to his less privileged subjects—commoners, women, and slaves.

The code was inscribed on a seven-foot-high stone pillar. At its top, a relief lends the weight of divine authority to the laws by showing Hammurabi standing before the sun god.

The following laws from Hammurabi's code reveal almost as much about the society that he ruled as it does about his concept of justice.

1. If a man weave a spell and bring a charge of murder against another man and has not justified himself, the accuser shall be put to death.
2. If a man has put a spell upon another man, and has not justified himself, the one who is charged with [witchcraft] shall go to the holy river, he shall plunge into the holy river, and if the holy river overcomes him, his accuser shall take his estate. If the holy river shows that man to be innocent and has saved him, he who charged him with [witchcraft] shall be put to death and the man who plunged into the river shall take the estate of him who brought the charge against him.
8. If a man has stolen ox or sheep or ass or pig, whether from the temple or from the palace, he shall pay thirty [times the value of the stolen goods]; if he stole from a commoner, he shall [pay] ten [times its value]. If the thief cannot pay, he shall be put to death.

From B. Tierney, ed., *Western Societies: A Documentary History*, vol. 1. New York, Alfred A. Knopf.

15. If a man has helped a male or female palace slave, or a commoner's male or female slave, to escape out of the city gate, he shall be put to death.

21. If a man has broken into a house, he shall be killed before the [gap] and walled in it.

23. If the robber has not been caught, the man who has been [robbed] shall [tell] before the god what he has lost, and the city and governor in whose territory the robbery took place shall make good to him his loss.

53. If a man has neglected to strengthen the dyke of his canal, and a [gap] has opened in his dyke, and the waters have [damaged] the meadow, the man in whose dyke the [gap] has opened shall make good the corn that he caused to be lost.

110. If a nun, a lady of god, who is not living in a convent, has opened the door of a wine shop or entered the wine shop for a drink, that woman shall be burned.

117. If a debt came due against a man, and he has given his wife, his son, his daughter for the money, or handed himself over to work off the debt, for three years they shall work in the house of their buyer or exploiter. In the fourth year they shall be set free.

129. If the wife of a man has been caught lying with another man, they shall bind them and throw them into the waters.

Review Questions

1. What evidence in the Code of Hammurabi indicates that Babylonian justice was based on an individual's social class?
2. How did the code tend to punish crimes against property?
3. How did the code tend to punish crimes against persons?
4. Why was the code carved onto a stone pillar?
5. How does the Code of Hammurabi compare to today's laws?

The Birth of Hatshepsut

Hatshepsut was ancient Egypt's only independently ruling female pharaoh. She ruled for 21 years, from about 1508 to 1487 B.C. During that time she built many magnificent monuments, including a majestic temple set into the side of a cliff near Thebes, Egypt's ancient capital. She also sponsored an expedition by sea to "God's Land" or Punt (perhaps located on the coast of eastern Africa, in present-day Somalia). The expedition brought back such treasures as gold, ivory, ebony, and 31 living myrrh trees, which were planted near the entrance of her temple.

Ancient Egypt had no provision for female pharaohs in its laws or customs, but unusual circumstances brought Hatshepsut to power. She was the daughter of Pharaoh Thutmose I and the wife of Pharaoh Thutmose II, who was also her half-brother. (Royal marriages between sisters and brothers were common in ancient Egypt.) When Thutmose II died, his only son—Hatshepsut's stepson and nephew—was still an infant. Therefore, Hatshepsut took over as regent. (A regent is an adult who rules temporarily until the next monarch reaches adulthood.) Before long, however, she began ruling in her own name.

In order to rule as pharaoh, Hatshepsut had herself officially declared a man. On some ceremonial occasions, she put on a fake beard and wore the traditional clothing and headgear of male pharaohs. She also adopted many of the honorary titles used by male pharaohs.

Like other Egyptian rulers, Hatshepsut presented herself as a direct descendant and representative of the god Amun (sometimes called Amun-Re, meaning he was a form of the sun god Re). The following document is based on information found in reliefs (sculptures in which the design is raised slightly from the background) that are part of Hatshepsut's temple near Thebes. According to the document, her birth resulted from a union between the god Amun and Iahmes, the wife of Pharaoh Thutmose I.

Amun summoned the [other gods] in heaven to him and proclaimed to them his decision to [father] for the land of Egypt a new king, and he promised to the gods all good through it. As successor, Hatshepsut was chosen the unique woman; the royal office for her was claimed. . . .

Amun charged Thoth, the god of wisdom and messenger, to seek Queen Iahmes, the wife of the reigning king, whom he selected as the future mother of the successor, and Thoth answered him as follows: "This young woman is a princess. She is called Iahmes. She is more beautiful than all the women in the whole land. She is the wife of the king, the king of Upper and Lower Egypt, Tuthmosis I,[1] and his majesty is still a youth. Go therefore to her. . . ."

There came the ruling god, Amun, Lord of the throne of the Two Lands,[2] after he had assumed the form of the majesty of her husband, the king of Upper and Lower Egypt, Tuthmosis I. He found her as she rested in the innermost [area] of her palace. . . .

Amun, the lord of the throne of the Two Lands spoke to her, "Hatshepsut is thus the name of this your daughter. . . . She will exercise the splendid kingship in the whole land. My glory will belong to her, my authority will belong to her, and my crown will belong to her. She will rule the Two Lands. I will surround her every day with my protection in common with the god of the respective day."

After Amun attended the queen, determined the name of the child, and promised her the lordship over Egypt, he spoke with the creator god Khnum who would form the child on the potter's wheel from mud. Thereby, he commissioned him to create for the child a [soul]. And Khnum answered him:

"I form this your daughter prepared for life, prosperity, and health, for food, nourishment, for respect, popularity, and all good. I distinguish her form from the gods [only] in her great dignity of king of Upper and Lower Egypt."

Then, according to the divine instruction, Khnum created the royal child Hatshepsut and her [soul] on the potter's wheel, and the goddess of birth, the frog-headed Heket, [gave] life to her. Khnum spoke in addition, "I form you with this divine body. . . . I have come

---

[1]**Tuthmosis**—another way to write Thutmose
[2]**The Two Lands**—Upper and Lower Egypt

to you to form you completely as all gods, give to you all life and prosperity, give to you enduring . . . joy . . . and give to you all health, deliver to you all flat lands and all mountain lands as well as all subjects, give to you every food and nourishment and cause that you appear on the throne of Horus[3] like [the sun god] Re [himself]. I cause that you stand as the head of all the living when you appear as king of Upper and Lower Egypt. Thus, as your father Amun-Re who loves you has commanded it."

Khnum's divine companion Heket concluded with speeches of blessing and gave the child with her word, life enduring, and happiness in all eternity. . . .

Khnum, the creator god, and his divine companion Heket conducted the pregnant queen to . . . the birthplace and there pronounced their blessings. Khnum spoke to her, "I surround your daughter with my protection. You are great, but the one who opens your womb will be greater than all kings till now. . . ." Thus spoke Khnum, the potter . . . and Heket, the deliverer.

Review Questions

1. a. Who was Amun?
   b. What did Amun promise Iahmes?
2. What was the relationship between Amun and Hatshepsut?
3. What role did the god Khnum play in the birth of Hatshepsut?
4. What role did the goddess Heket play in the birth of Hatshepsut?
5. Why did Hatshepsut portray herself as a descendant of the god Amun?
6. Why was the story of Hatshepsut's birth depicted on the walls of her temple?

[3]**Horus**—a major Egyptian god, the personal god of Egyptian pharaohs

Women and Marriage in Ancient China

Most Chinese women had little status and few rights or privileges. Occasionally, however, women who belonged to the nobility attained a measure of power and respect. One example was Fu Hao, a wife of Wu Ding, who ruled China in the 13th century B.C. during the Shang Dynasty. Fu Hao owned land, led armies in battle, and became well known. Her tomb was filled with valuable objects, including hundreds of bronze items weighing a ton and a half in all.

These two poems deal with the role of women in ancient China. The first is a general lament about the low status of women in Chinese society. The second deals with the Chinese custom of arranged marriages, in which a woman's family chooses her husband with little or no consideration of her own wishes. Arranged marriages were common in most parts of the world until relatively recent times.

A. "Woman"

by Fu Hsüan (A.D. 217–278)

How sad it is to be framed in woman's form!
Nothing on earth is held so cheap.
A boy that comes to a home
Drops to earth like a god that chooses to be born.
His bold heart braves the Four Oceans,
The wind and dust of a thousand miles.
No one is glad when a girl is born;
By *her* the family sets no store.
When she grows up, she hides in her room
Afraid to look a man in the face.
No one cries when she leaves her home—
Sudden as clouds when the rain stops.
She bows her head and composes her face,

Her teeth are pressed on her red lips.
She bows and kneels countless times,
She must humble herself even to the servants.
While his love lasts he is as distant as the stars;
She is a sunflower, looking up to the sun.
Soon their love will be severed[1] more than water from
fire;
A hundred evils will be heaped upon her.
Her face will follow the year's changes;
Her lord will find new pleasures.
They that were once like substance and shadow
Are now as far as Hu[2] and Ch'in.[3]
Yes, Hu and Ch'in shall sooner meet
Than they, whose parting is like Shen and Ch'en.[4]

B. "Lament of Hsi-chün"

(Hsi-chün was a real-life Chinese princess. In about 110 B.C. her family married her to a nomad king for political reasons. The author of this poem is unknown.)

My people have married me
In a far corner of Earth:
Sent me away to a strange land,
To the king of the Wu-sun.[5]
A tent is my house,
Of felt[6] are my walls;
Raw flesh my food
With mare's milk[7] to drink.
Always thinking of my own country,
My heart sad within.
Would I were a yellow stork
And could fly to my old home!

---

[1]**severed**—cut apart
[2]**Hu**—land of barbarians
[3]**Ch'in (Qin)**—China
[4]**Shen and Ch'en**—morning and evening star
[5]**Wu-sun**—nomadic people living in central Asia
[6]**felt**—soft cloth of wool and fur, used for nomads' tents
[7]**mare's milk**—milk of a female horse

Review Questions

A. "Woman"

1 How did ancient Chinese families feel about the birth of girls as opposed to the birth of boys?

2. How did opportunities differ for males and females in ancient China?

B. "Lament of Hsi-Chün"

1. Who chose the man Hsi-Chün would marry?
2. Why do you think Hsi-Chün's family decided she should marry the king of the Wu-Sun?
3. How did Hsi-Chün feel about her marriage?
4. How did Hsi-Chün's life change after marriage?

Athenian Democracy: A Golden Age

The Age of Pericles in the 5th century B.C. marked the high point in the power and glory of the small Greek city-state of Athens. Under the leadership of Pericles, Athenian democracy reached its fullest expression, and Athens experienced a "golden age" in which sculpture, literature, and painting flourished.

Born about 490 B.C., Pericles became a prominent figure in the democratic faction in Athens. The leader of the rival aristocratic faction at the time was a man named Cimon (pronounced as if it were spelled "Simon"). Eventually, Pericles won out over Cimon. For more than 30 years, until his death in 429 B.C., Pericles was Athens' most prominent political leader and statesman. He also directed Athens' foreign policy, and played a key role in the Peloponnesian War that broke out in 431. This war pitted Athens and its empire against the city state of Sparta and its Greek allies. Crowded with wartime refugees, Athens suffered a plague in which one-third of its people died—including eventually Pericles. The war lasted for 27 years. In the end, Sparta won the war and Athens' power and influence declined.

The following document is by a Greek writer named Plutarch, who lived from about A.D. 50 to 120. Plutarch is famous for a series of biographies he wrote of important historical figures. Until recent times, his *Parallel Lives* were the main source of knowledge about ancient Greek and Roman leaders.

A. Pericles

[T]he man who was closest to Pericles and had most to do with giving him dignity of manner . . . was [the philosopher] Anaxagoras. . . .

Pericles had great esteem for this man, and became deeply absorbed in his . . . philosophy and profound speculations. Thus he acquired both solemnity of spirit and a lofty style of speech, free from vulgarity and spiteful buffoonery; also a gravity of countenance that did not break out into laughter, a gentleness of [manner] and a quietness of tone that no emotion disturbed while he was speaking, as well as other qualities that impressed and astonished his hearers. Once, he sat silently in the [marketplace] all day, working at some important business, while a low, worthless fellow was [insulting] and abusing him. Toward evening he went calmly home, with the man following and heaping every kind of insult on him. When about to enter his own door, he ordered one of his servants, since it was dark, to take a torch and escort the man to his house. . . .

As a young man, Pericles shrank very much from facing the people, for in appearance he was thought to resemble the tyrant [despotic ruler] Pisistratus. His voice, too, was sweet and his tongue fluent and quick in conversation, so the older men were struck by the likeness. Also, he was wealthy, of distinguished [family] and had extremely powerful friends, so that he was afraid of being ostracized[1] and kept out of politics, even though in military service he proved himself brave and daring. Accordingly, . . . Pericles devoted himself to the people, taking the side of the poor and the many against the rich and the few, contrary to his own natural bent, which was far from democratic. He apparently dreaded [arousing] the suspicion of playing tyrant, so when he saw that Cimon[2] took the aristocratic side and was very popular with the [conservatives], he began making [advances] to the people, thereby obtaining safety for himself and power to oppose Cimon.

. . . Pericles was careful about his words, and always when he ascended the [platform] to speak, he prayed to the gods that nothing unfit for the occasion might fall unintentionally from his lips. He left no writings behind him except the laws he sponsored, and very few of his sayings are recorded. . . .

From the beginning, as we have said, measured as he was against the famous Cimon, Pericles set about winning the people's affection. He had not the wealth and resources of Cimon by which to attract the poor, offering a dinner every day to any Athenian who needed one, clothing aged persons, and taking down fences from his estates

[1]**ostracized**—ordered to leave Athens for a period of ten years
[2]**Cimon**—Athenian general, supporter of aristocracy; ostracized in 461 B.C.

so that anyone who wished might pick the fruit. So, unable to compete on these popular lines, Pericles turned to distributing the people's own property. . . . And soon by his funds for spectacles, jurors' fees, and other large payments and expenditures, he had bribed the whole population, and was able to use them against the [aristocratic] council. . . . He himself was not a member of that body. . . . For this reason, Pericles, when he had gained strength with the people, organized a party against the council. . . . [I]t was deprived of most of its judicial powers, while Cimon, on a charge of being a friend of Sparta and a hater of the people, was banished by ostracism. . . .

Pericles . . . surrendered the reins [of government] to the people and planned his policy to please them, constantly arranging some kind of pageant or festival or procession in the city, thus entertaining them with refined amusements. Every year, too, he sent sixty [ships] out on a cruise, and many citizens sailed around on them for eight months with pay, at the same time learning and practicing the art of seamanship. Besides this, he sent [thousands of settlers out to start colonies]. . . . All these things he did in order to relieve the city of a mob of lazy and idle agitators, provide for the wants of the needy, and establish formidable [military bases] near the allies of Athens to prevent revolt.

But what brought the greatest pleasure and beauty to Athens and the most astonishment to the rest of the world, and now alone bears witness for [Greece] that the tales of her ancient power and glory were not fables, was Pericles' building of shrines. Yet for that, more than for all his other public enterprises, his enemies [condemned] him [for using money that they said belonged to the Greek city-states in common]. . . . But Pericles told the people that they owed no account of the money to their allies, so long as they carried on the war for them and defended them from the Persians. . . .

[S]ince he did not wish the unwarlike mass of common workmen to go without a share in the city's revenues, nor yet to be paid for idleness, he proposed to the people plans for great [buildings] and designs for elaborate works, which would take a long time to complete. Thereby, those who stayed at home would have as good a claim to a share of the public funds as the sailors, garrison troops, and active sailors. . . . [A]s each craft, like a commander at the head of an army, employed a number of unskilled and ignorant laborers, like tools or bodies for subordinate service, the city's wealth would be divided and dispersed to meet the needs of people of every age and ability.

The buildings rose, towering in size and matchless in contour and grace, for the workmen strove to outdo themselves in the perfection of their handiwork. Most remarkable was the speed with which they were built. Each one of them, men thought, would take many succeeding generations to complete, but all were finished during [Pericles' rule]. . . . Certainly, ease and speed of execution do not usually produce a work of permanent value or faultless beauty, whereas time spent in painstaking labor makes for lasting quality. For this reason the works of Pericles are all the more wonderful; they were quickly created, and they have lasted for ages. In beauty each one appeared [aged and important] as soon as it was finished, but in freshness and vigor it looks even now new and lately built. They bloom with an eternal freshness that seems untouched by time, as though they had been inspired by an unfading spirit of youth.

B. Aspasia

Because public life was closed to women in ancient Greece, women with strong personalities or exceptional talents made their mark in other ways. Plutarch's biography of Pericles mentions one such woman—Aspasia. Aspasia was an educated woman whose circle of acquaintances included the philosopher Socrates. She lived as Pericles's wife, although he did not officially marry her. She was a foreigner from the Greek city-state Miletus along the coast of what is now Turkey, and scholars believe that Athenian law forbade marriage between Athenian citizens and foreigners.

The following excerpt gives a glimpse of Aspasia's life in Athens. Because Plutarch was writing some 500 years after Aspasia's time, his knowledge of her was limited by the nature of his sources of information. For example, most references to her in the Greek literature known to Plutarch came from Pericles's political enemies. Even today, few of the details of Aspasia's life are known for certain.

. . . Pericles got a resolution passed for a [military campaign] against Samos[3] on the charge that, though ordered to stop their war on the Milesians,[4] they were not obeying. And as it was thought that he began this attack on the Samians to please Aspasia, here may be a good place to speculate about that woman, and the extraordinary skill and power she had, to wind about her finger the first statesman of the day and set the philosophers to discussing her in lofty terms and at great length. That she was a Milesian by birth . . . is generally agreed.

[S]ome say that Pericles prized Aspasia for her political wisdom. Socrates himself came sometimes with his friends to her house, and those who knew her well on occasion brought their wives to hear her in her house. . . . [According to Plato] she had the reputation of meeting with many Athenians to discuss rhetoric.[5] But the feeling that Pericles had for her seems to have been love. . . . [After separating from his wife, Pericles] himself took Aspasia and loved her intensely. Every day, it is said, when he went out or came in . . . , he greeted her with a kiss. . . .

Review Questions

A. Pericles
1. What kind of person was Pericles, according to Plutarch?
2. How did Pericles become popular with the Athenian people?
3. How did Pericles distribute the wealth of Athens?
4. What leadership qualities did Pericles possess?
5. What did Plutarch say was Pericles' most lasting achievement?

B. Aspasia
1. How did Pericles feel about Aspasia?
2. What influence did Aspasia have over Pericles?
3. What qualities made Aspasia influential?
4. What opportunities for women existed in ancient Greece?

---

[3]**Samos**—Greek city-state that revolted against Athens
[4]**Milesians**—residents of Miletus, Aspasia's birthplace
[5]**rhetoric**—the art of speaking and writing persuasively, highly prized by the ancient Greeks

Britain's Warrior Queen Takes on the Romans

In A.D. 43–47, a Roman army landed in the British Isles, conquered various British tribes, and turned eastern and southeastern England into the Roman province of Britain. To the Romans, the Britons were barbarians. That is, they were backward peoples who needed the guiding hand of civilized Rome. But the Britons fiercely resented their new foreign rulers.

In A.D. 60, a warrior queen named Boudicca (pronounced bu-DIK-a) led a bloody attempt to overthrow Roman rule and drive the Romans away. She was the wife of the king of the part of present-day England known as Norfolk, northeast of London. Her husband had kept his kingdom semi-independent by paying a yearly tribute to the Romans. After he died in the year 60, however, the Romans responded by trying to take over his kingdom. Boudicca led the Britons' resistance.

In the following excerpt, a Roman historian describes what happened next.

. . .[T]he person who was chiefly instrumental in rousing the natives and persuading them to fight the Romans, the person who was thought worthy to be their leader and who directed the conduct of the entire war, was Boudicca, a Briton woman of the royal family and possessed of greater intelligence than often belongs to women. This woman assembled her army, to the number of some 120,000, and then ascended a [platform] which had been constructed of earth in the Roman fashion. In stature she was very tall, in appearance most terrifying, in the glance of her eye most fierce, and her voice was harsh; a great mass of the tawniest hair fell to her hips; around her neck was a large golden necklace; and she wore a [gown] of [many] colors over which a thick [cloak] was fastened with a brooch. This was her invariable attire. She now grasped a spear to aid her in terrifying all beholders and spoke as follows:

"You have learned by actual experience how different freedom is from slavery. Hence, although some among you may previously, through ignorance of which was better, have been deceived by the alluring promises of the Romans, yet now that you have tried both, you have learned how great a mistake you made in preferring an imported despotism to your ancestral mode [way] of life, and you have come to realize how much better is poverty with no master than wealth with slavery. For what treatment is there of the most shameful or grievous sort that we have not suffered ever since these men made their appearance in Britain? Have we not been robbed entirely of most of our possessions, and those the greatest, while for those that remain we pay taxes? Besides pasturing and tilling for them all our other [lands], do we not pay a yearly tribute for our very bodies? How much better it would be to have been sold to masters once [and] for all than, possessing empty titles of freedom, to have to ransom ourselves every year! How much better to have been slain and to have perished than to go about with a tax on our heads! . . .

"But, to speak the plain truth, it is we who have made ourselves responsible for all these evils, in that we allowed them to set foot on the island in the first place instead of expelling them at once as we did their famous Julius Caesar, . . . As a consequence, although we inhabit so large an island . . . and although we possess a veritable world of our own and are so separated by the ocean from all the rest of mankind that we have been believed to dwell on a different earth and under a different sky, . . . we have been despised and trampled underfoot by men who know nothing else than how to secure gain. . . .

"Have no fear whatever of the Romans; for they are superior to us neither in numbers nor in bravery. And here is the proof: [The queen describes the Roman soldiers' dependence on armor and fortifications.] But these are not the only respects in which they are vastly inferior to us: . . . they cannot bear up under hunger, thirst, cold, or heat, as we can. They require shade and covering, they require kneaded bread and wine and oil, and if any of these things fails them, they perish; for us, on the other hand, any grass or root serves as bread, the juice of any plant as oil, any water as wine, any tree as a house. Furthermore, this region is familiar to us and is our ally, but to them it is unknown and hostile. As for the rivers, we swim them naked, whereas they do not get across them easily even with boats. Let us, therefore, go against them trusting boldly to good fortune. Let us show them that they are hares and foxes trying to rule over dogs and wolves."

When she had finished speaking, she employed a species of divination,[1] letting a [rabbit] escape from the fold of her dress; and since it ran on what they considered the [favorable] side, the whole multitude shouted with pleasure, and Boudicca, raising her hand toward heaven, said: "I thank thee, Andraste,[2] and call upon thee as woman speaking to woman; for I rule over no burden-bearing Egyptians . . . nor over trafficking Assyrians . . . , much less over the Romans themselves . . . ; nay, those over whom I rule are Britons, men that know not how to till the soil or ply a trade, but are thoroughly versed in the art of war and hold all things in common, even children and wives, so that the latter possess the same valor as the men. As the queen, then, of such men and of such women, I . . . pray thee for victory, preservation of life, and liberty against men insolent, unjust, insatiable, impious—if, indeed, we ought to term these people men who bathe in warm water, eat artificial dainties, drink unmixed wine, anoint themselves with myrrh, sleep on soft couches, . . . and are slaves to [Nero,] a lyre-player and a poor one too. Wherefore may this . . . Nero reign no longer over me or over you men. . . ."

At first, the uprising seemed a success. The Britons massacred thousands of Romans and burned important Roman-held cities. But the Roman governor, who had been away at war, returned and defeated the Britons. Boudicca, says Dio Cassius, "fell sick and died."

Review Questions

1. How did Boudicca come to lead an uprising against the Britons?
2. Why did Boudicca believe that the Britons should revolt against Rome?
3. Why did Boudicca believe that the Britons could defeat the Romans?
4. What advantage did Boudicca's army have over the Roman invaders?
5. Which of the two women–Boudicca or Aspasia (Document 7)–showed greater leadership qualities? How do you justify your choice?

---

[1]**divination**—seeking knowledge of the future in natural events

[2]**Andraste**—a goddess worshiped by the Britons

The Roman Emperor Nero

Ancient Rome evolved from a small city-state into a republic with relatively democratic institutions. The republic lasted from 509 to 30 B.C. It collapsed in civil wars, giving way to the rule of dictators and emperors. Rome's first emperor was Caesar Augustus, who ruled from 27 B.C. to A.D. 14. Imperial Rome remained powerful for hundreds of years. Its emperors varied greatly. Some were relatively wise and public-spirited, while others were cruel and irresponsible. Of the latter sort was Nero, who became emperor in the year 54, when the emperor Claudius, his adoptive father, died. Nero was 17 years old at the time.

The following account of Nero's life is by a Roman historian, Suetonius, born a year after Nero died. Nero is one of a dozen Roman rulers whose biographies Suetonius collected in his book *The Twelve Caesars*.

Nero started off with a parade of virtue. . . . [H]e promised to model his rule on the principles laid down by Augustus, and never missed an opportunity of being generous or merciful, or of showing what a good companion he was. He lowered, if he could not abolish, some of the heavier taxes. . . . Moreover, he presented the [representatives of the common people] with forty gold pieces each; settled annual salaries on distinguished but impoverished senators—to the amount of 5,000 gold pieces in some cases—and granted the Guards battalions a free monthly issue of grain. If asked to sign the usual execution order for a [criminal] he would sigh: "Ah, how I wish that I had never learned to write!" He seldom forgot a face, and would greet men of whatever rank by name without a moment's hesitation. Once, when the Senate passed a vote of thanks to him, he answered: "Wait until I deserve them!" He . . . often gave public [speeches]. Also, he recited his own poems, both at home and in the Theater: a performance which . . . delighted everyone. . . .

He gave an immense variety of entertainments—coming-of-age parties, chariot races in the Circus, stage plays, a gladiatorial show. . . .

He . . . actually raced four-camel chariots! At the Great Festival, as he called the series of plays devoted to the hope of his reigning forever, parts were taken by men and women of [both aristocratic and common background], and one well-known knight rode an elephant down a sloping tight-rope. . . . Throughout the Festival all kinds of gifts were scattered to the people—1,000 assorted birds daily, and quantities of food parcels; besides vouchers for corn, clothes, gold, silver, precious stones, pearls, paintings, slaves, transport animals, and even trained wild beasts—and finally for ships, blocks of city tenements, and farms.

. . . The gladiatorial show took place in a wooden theater, . . . which had been built in less than a year; but no one was allowed to be killed during these combats, not even criminals. He did, however, make 400 senators and 600 knights, many of them rich and respectable, do battle in the arena; and some had to fight wild beasts and perform various duties about the ring. . . .

I have separated this catalog of Nero's less atrocious acts—some forgiveable, some even praiseworthy—from the others; but I must begin to list his follies and crimes.

Music formed part of his childhood curriculum, and he early developed a taste for it. Soon after his accession [becoming emperor], he summoned Terpnus, the greatest lyre-player of the day, to sing to him when dinner had ended, for several nights in succession, until very late. Then, little by little, he began to study and practice himself, and conscientiously undertook all the usual exercises for strengthening and developing the voice. . . . Ultimately, though his voice was still feeble and husky, he was pleased enough with his progress to nurse theatrical ambitions, and would quote to his friends the Greek proverb, "Unheard melodies are never sweet." His first stage appearance was at Naples where, disregarding an earthquake which shook the theater, he sang his piece through to the end. [The theater later collapsed, just after the audience had gone home.]

It might have been possible to excuse his insolent, lustful, extravagant, greedy or cruel early practices (which were, I grant more furtive than aggressive), by saying that boys will be boys; yet at the same time, this was the true Nero, not merely Nero in his adolescence. As soon as night fell he would snatch a hat or cap and make a round of the taverns, or prowl the streets in search of mischief—

and not always innocent mischief either, because one of his games was to attack men on their way home from dinner, stab them if they offered resistance, and then drop their bodies down the sewers. He would also break into shops, afterwards opening a miniature market at the Palace with the stolen goods. . . . During these escapades he often risked being blinded or killed—once he was beaten almost to death by a senator whose wife he had molested. . . .

Gradually Nero's vices gained the upper hand: he no longer tried to laugh them off, or hide, or deny them, but turned quite [bold]. . . .

The over-watchful, over-critical eye that [his mother] kept on whatever Nero said or did proved more than he could stand. . . . He tried to poison her three times, but she had always taken the antidote in advance; so he rigged up a machine in the ceiling of her bedroom which would dislodge the panels and drop them on her while she slept. However, someone gave the secret away. Then he had a collapsible cabin-boat designed which would either sink or fall in on top of her. . . . [Even this did not work, and Nero finally had his mother killed with a sword.]

Having disposed of his mother, Nero proceeded to murder his aunt. . . .

After getting rid of [his first wife] Octavia, he took two more wives [whom he later killed].

. . . [Nero] did not take the least trouble to dress as an Emperor should, but always had his hair set in rows of curls and, when he visited Greece, let it grow long and hang down his back. He often gave audiences in an unbelted silk dressing-gown, slippers, and a scarf. . . .

His greatest weaknesses were his thirst for popularity and his jealousy of men who caught the public eye by any means whatsoever. . . .

Nero's unreasonable craving for immortal fame made him change a number of well-known names in his own favor. The month of April, for instance, became Neroneus; and Rome was on the point of being renamed "Neropolis." . . .

Nero's behavior finally became so outrageous that in the year 68 Roman military leaders rose up in revolt. They declared a new emperor, and the Roman Senate ordered that Nero be put to death. Nero fled the capital, but armed guards pursued him. Suetonius says that when the guards tried to arrest him, Nero stabbed himself in the throat and died.

Nero died at the age of thirty-two, on the anniversary of Octavia's murder. In the widespread general rejoicing, citizens ran through the streets wearing caps of liberty, as though they were freed slaves. But a few faithful friends used to lay spring and summer flowers on his grave for some years, and had statues made of him.

Review Questions

1. What were some of the positive accomplishments of Nero's reign?
2. How was Nero's behavior unfitting for an emperor?
3. What was the writer Suetonius's opinion of Nero?
4. How did the Romans react to Nero's death?
5. How does Suetonius's opinion of Nero compare to that of Boudicca (Document 8)?

The Roman Sack of Jerusalem in A.D. 70

The Roman general Pompey annexed Judea in 63 B.C. This act divided the population into those who bitterly resented foreign rule and those who accepted it as long as it did not interfere with their religion. Jewish disunity widened when, some ten years after annexation, a Roman governor separated Judea into five subareas.

In 47 B.C., Julius Caesar reunited the Judean territories. Herod, whose father had converted to Judaism, became king of Judea. Herod worked hard to ensure the survival of Judea. He rebuilt the Jewish Temple in Jerusalem and founded splendid new cities. Nonetheless, his subjects distrusted his closeness to Roman leaders. As Herod grew older, he became suspicious and violent. He horrified the Jews by murdering his wife and two sons. After his death, the Jews tried unsuccessfully to revolt against Rome.

The Romans replaced Herod's successor with a Roman ruler. The question whether foreign influence on their culture endangered the Jews' religious salvation stirred up new conflicts among the Jews. Again they split into opposing factions. A large group felt that as long as they could practice their faith, Roman rule was not a problem. Judea's established religious leaders belonged to this group. More militant Jews considered Roman influence a peril. They joined together in a group that modern historians call the Zealots. These extremists believed themselves to be the only true Jews and felt that their salvation lay in ousting the Romans.

In A.D. 66, the Zealots, believing that Roman influence in the Middle East was weakening, decided it was time to strike. Full war broke out when they captured a Roman fortress and armed themselves with weapons. The priests and their followers tried to prevent open warfare. But their opposition only weakened the rebellion. Although all the Jewish factions united at the end to save their kingdom, the Roman emperor Vespasian and his son Titus, who led the Roman armies, brutally put down the rebellion in A.D. 70. This photograph of a carved stone frieze from the Arch of Titus documents the Roman triumph. It shows soldiers entering Rome with the sacred items they have looted from the Temple of Jerusalem. The arch, built during the reign of Titus, was completed in A.D. 81.

Arch of Titus, Rome (A.D. 81)

Review Questions

1. How did Rome's annexation of Judea divide its people?
2. Why did most Jews distrust Herod?
3. How did the Zealots' religious beliefs differ from those of the established religious leaders?
4. How did the split between the Zealots and the religious leaders affect the outcome of the rebellion against Rome?
5. How does the relief shown here illustrate a result of the failed rebellion of the Jews against Rome?

A Hindu God Speaks to a Warrior

The Hindu religion, which originated in ancient India, emphasizes a belief in *reincarnation*. This is a cycle of rebirths in which a person's soul never dies. The form in which a soul is reborn is determined by the balance of good and bad in that person's actions throughout life. The good and bad actions add up to the person's *karma*. A person with good *karma* may be reborn as someone of a higher rank, while a person with bad *karma* may be reborn as an animal. For a Hindu, a good life involves following one's sacred duty (called *dharma*), developing self-discipline (called yoga), and exhibiting devotion (called bhakti) to a Hindu god.

In the following document, one of the most revered Hindu gods advises a young warrior, Arjuna, who is reluctant to go into battle. He knows that hundreds of soldiers will die and great destruction will take place.

The speaker is the god Krishna. Hindus perceive him as both Creator and Destroyer. (In Hindu thought, creation and destruction are two sides of a single process that comprises both birth and death in never-ending succession.) Krishna has taken the form of a charioteer. This excerpt is from a great Hindu epic known as the *Bhagavad-Gita* ("*The Lord's Song*"). It dates from the period 400 B.C. to A.D. 400. The *Bhagavad-Gita* tells of a feud between two branches—one good, one evil—of a ruling family in northern India. It climaxes in a battle in which Arjuna and the forces of good triumph over the forces of evil.

LORD KRISHNA
Why this cowardice
in time of crisis, Arjuna? . . .
Banish this petty weakness from your heart.
Rise to the fight, Arjuna! . . .

Just as the embodied self [the soul]
enters childhood, youth, and old age,
so does it enter another body;
this does not [confuse] a [determined] man.

Our bodies are known to end,
but the embodied self is enduring,
indestructible, and immeasurable;
therefore, Arjuna, fight the battle!

As a man discards
worn-out clothes
to put on new
and different ones,
so the embodied self
discards
its worn-out bodies
to take on other new ones.

Death is certain for anyone born,
and birth is certain for the dead;
since the cycle is inevitable,
you have no cause to grieve!

Look to your own duty;
do not tremble before it;
nothing is better for a warrior
than a battle of sacred duty.

The doors of heaven open
for warriors who rejoice
to have a battle like this
thrust on them by chance.

If you are killed, you win heaven;
if you triumph, you enjoy the earth;
therefore, Arjuna, stand up
and resolve to fight the battle!

Review Questions

1. What did Krishna say was Arjuna's *dharma*, or sacred duty?
2. How did Krishna view existence?
3. According to Krishna, what happened to the embodied self after a person's death?
4. Why did Krishna say that Arjuna would win no matter what the result of the battle was?
5. How might Krishna's advice have given Arjuna courage to go into battle?

Sayings of the Buddha

The Buddhist religion originated near the border between present-day India and Nepal in the 6th century B.C. Its founder was an Indian prince named Siddhartha Gautama.

Gautama became known as the Buddha—"the Enlightened One." A small band of followers grew into large multitudes of Buddhists in the decades after Gautama died in 483 B.C. Buddhism spread throughout Southeast and East Asia, and into other parts of the world as well. As happened with other religions, followers gathered the founder's teachings and used them as guides in developing a way of life.

The Buddha's teachings are summarized in the Four Noble Truths: (1) All existence is suffering. (2) This suffering has a cause—mainly human desires, which can never be completely satisfied. (3) By suppressing desires or rising above them, one can end one's suffering. (4) The way to do this is to follow eight key rules, known as the Eightfold Path. The Eightfold Path called for (1) knowledge of truth; (2) intention to resist evil; (3) saying nothing to hurt others; (4) respect for life, morality, and property; (5) holding a job that does not injure others; (6) working to free one's mind of evil; (7) controlling one's feelings and thoughts; and (8) practicing proper forms of concentration or meditation. Those who succeed in following the Eightfold Path can escape rebirth and achieve *nirvana*—an end to human desires and an end to individual consciousness.

The document below is a selection of sayings by the Buddha. They are part of a larger collection known as the *Dhammapada*.

1. The Pairs

"I have been insulted! I have been hurt! I have been beaten! I have been robbed!" Anger does not cease in those who harbor this sort of thought. . . .

Occasions of hatred are certainly never settled by hatred. They are settled by freedom from hatred. This is the eternal law. . . .

2. Attention

Those who meditate with perseverance, constantly working hard at it, are the wise who experience nirvana, the ultimate freedom from chains. . . .

3. Thoughts

It is good to restrain one's mind, uncontrollable, fast moving, and following its own desires as it is. A disciplined mind leads to happiness.

4. Flowers

It is not the shortcomings of others, nor what others have done or not done, that one should think about, but what one has done or not done oneself.

Like a fine flower, beautiful to look at but without scent, fine words are fruitless in a man who does not act in accordance with them.

5. The Fool

A fool who recognizes his own ignorance is thereby in fact a wise man, but a fool who considers himself wise—that is what one really calls a fool.

Even if a fool lived with a wise man all his life, he would still not recognize the truth, as a wooden spoon cannot recognize the flavor of the soup.

8. The Thousands

Victory over oneself is better than that over others. When a man has conquered himself and always acts with self-control, neither [gods nor] spirits can reverse the victory of a man like that. . . .

10. Violence

All fear violence, all are afraid of death. Seeing the similarity to oneself, one should not use violence or have it used. . . .

12. Self

One is one's own guardian. What other guardian could one have? With oneself well-disciplined, one obtains a rare guardian indeed. . . .

By oneself one does evil. By oneself one is [corrupted]. By oneself one abstains from evil. By oneself one is purified. Purity and impurity are personal matters. No one can purify someone else. . . .

13. The World

Look on the world as a bubble, look on it as a mirage. The King of Death never finds him who views the world like that. . . .

14. The Buddhas

Long-suffering patience is the supreme ascetic[1] practice. Nirvana is supreme, say the Buddhas. He is certainly not an ascetic who hurts others, and nor is he a man of religion who causes suffering to others.

Not to speak harshly and not to harm others, self-restraint in accordance with the rules of the [Buddhist] Order, moderation in food, a secluded dwelling, and the cultivation of the higher levels of consciousness—this is the teaching of the Buddhas.[2]

17. Anger

Overcome anger with freedom from anger. Overcome evil with good. Overcome meanness with generosity, and overcome a liar with truthfulness.

18. Faults

Other people's faults are easily seen. . . . One hides one's own faults, though, as a dishonest gambler hides an unlucky throw. . . .

22. Hell

He who speaks untruth goes to hell, as does he who, having done something, says, "I didn't do it." Men of ignoble behavior, they both end up the same in the next world. . . .

---

[1]**ascetic**—self-denying, austere
[2]**Buddhas**—Buddhist saints; those who have attained nirvana

24. Craving

The recollection and attraction of pleasures occur to a man, and those who are attached to the agreeable and seeking enjoyment, they are the people subject to birth and aging. . . .

Let go the past, let go the future, and let go what is in between, [rise above] the things of time. With your mind free in every direction, you will not return to birth and aging. . . .

The gift of the Truth beats all other gifts. The flavor of the Truth beats all other tastes. The joy of the Truth beats all other joys, and the cessation of desire conquers all suffering.

26. The Brahmin

One is not a brahmin[3] by virtue of matted hair, lineage or caste. When a man possesses both Truth and truthfulness, then he is pure, then he is a brahmin.

Like water on a lotus leaf, like a mustard seed on the point of a pin, he who is not stuck to the senses—that is what I call a brahmin.

He who has experienced the end of his suffering here in this life, who has set down the burden, freed!—that is what I call a brahmin. . . .

He who has nothing of his own, before, after, or in between, possessionless and without attachment—that is what I call a brahmin. . . .

He who has known his former lives and can see heaven and hell themselves, while he has attained the extinction of rebirth, a seer, master of knowledge, and master of all masteries—that is what I call a brahmin.

Review Questions

1. What is "nirvana"?
2. How did the Buddha define "freedom"?
3. How does a person achieve nirvana?
4. How is evil overcome?
5. a. Who is a brahmin, according to the Buddha?
   b. How can a person attain this state?

---

[3]**brahmin**—a member of the highest caste of Hindu society; also, a person of high moral stature

Confucius on Personal Responsibility

Confucius (Kong Fuzi) was a famous Chinese philosopher who lived from 551 to 479 B.C., during the Zhou Dynasty. He attracted a large group of disciples and followers. After his death, a new generation of followers gathered Confucius's teachings in a work called the *Analects*. The work is a collection of brief sayings attributed to "the Master," as Confucius's followers called him.

The sayings in the *Analects* highlight Confucius's belief that the state, or society, is modeled largely on the family. In this view, the ruler occupies the role of a parent. In a family, says Confucius, children should honor and obey their parents. Likewise in a state, subjects should honor and obey their ruler. Confucius placed great emphasis on respect—respect for traditions, respect for one's elders and other superiors, respect for one's neighbors. He also stressed learning and virtue, urging people to examine their lives, learn what is good, and do good to others. Those rules applied to everyone, rulers included. Respect for such rules would help to ensure harmony in both the family and the nation.

Confucius's teachings reflect the class-conscious society in which he lived. He himself came from the upper class, and he spoke of education as the training of "noblemen." He believed that people should take an active role in public affairs.

The following excerpts are selected from the *Analects*. The questioners (Yu, Jan Yung, Meng I Tzu, Fan Ch'ih, and Tzu-lu) were disciples, or students, of Confucius.

On Education

The Master said, "He who learns but does not think is lost. He who thinks but does not learn is in great danger."

The Master said, "Yu, shall I teach you what knowledge is? When you know a thing, to recognize that you know it, and when you do not know a thing, to recognize that you do not know it. That is knowledge."

The Master said, "I have transmitted what was taught to me without making up anything of my own. I have been faithful to and loved the Ancients. . . ."

On Goodness

Of the [saying] "Only a Good Man knows how to like people, knows how to dislike them," the Master said, "He whose heart is in the smallest degree set upon Goodness will dislike no one."

Jan Yung asked about Goodness. The Master said, "Behave when away from home as though you were in the presence of an important guest. Deal with the common people as though you were [leading] an important [religious ritual]. Do not do to others what you would not like yourself. Then there will be no feelings of opposition to you, whether it is the affairs of a State that you are handling or the affairs of a Family."

On the Gentleman

Tzu-kung asked about the true gentleman. The Master said, "He does not preach what he practices till he has practiced what he preaches."

The Master said, "A gentleman takes as much trouble to discover what is right as lesser men take to discover what will pay."

The Master said, "The gentleman calls attention to the good points in others; he does not call attention to their defects. The small man does just the reverse of this."

The Master said, "The gentleman can influence those who are above him; the small man can only influence those who are below him."

The Master said, "The demands that a gentleman makes are upon himself; those that a small man makes are upon others."

On Respect for Parents (Filial Piety)

Meng I Tzu asked about the treatment of parents. The Master said, "Never disobey!" When Fan Ch'ih was driving his carriage for him, the Master said, "Meng asked me about the treatment of parents and I said, 'Never disobey!'" Fan Ch'ih said, "In what sense did you mean it?" The Master said, "While they are alive, serve them according to ritual. When they die, bury them according to ritual and [make offerings] to them according to ritual."

On Religion

Tzu-lu asked how one should serve ghosts and spirits. The Master said, "Till you have learned to serve men, how can you serve ghosts?" Tzu-lu then ventured upon a question about the dead. The Master said, "Till you know about the living, how are you to know about the dead?"

Review Questions

1. Why did Confucius separate "learning" from "thinking"?
2. What advice did Confucius give for getting along with others?
3. According to Confucius, what qualities did a gentleman possess?
4. According to Confucius, how should a person treat his or her parents?
5. What knowledge did Confucius feel a person needed to be religious?
6. Why was Confucius concerned with tradition?

14 A Sermon From the New Testament

The New Testament is the part of the Christian Bible that relates the life of Jesus and the actions of his disciples. It adds the specifically Christian message to the Old Testament, which is common to both Christians and Jews.

Some of the best-known parts of the New Testament are called the Beatitudes (from the repetition of the Latin words *beati sunt*—in English, "blessed are" or "God blesses"). The Beatitudes are teachings of Jesus about how Christians should live. They are found mainly in the Gospels of Mark and Luke.

In the following passage, taken from Chapter 6 of Luke, Jesus delivers a sermon to a crowd of his followers. He has just chosen twelve of his disciples to become representatives, or apostles, who will spread his teachings.

The Beatitudes

Then Jesus turned to his disciples and said,

"God blesses you who are poor, for the Kingdom of God is given to you.

"God blesses you who are hungry now, for you will be satisfied.

"God blesses you who weep now, for the time will come when you will laugh with joy.

"God blesses you who are hated and excluded and mocked and cursed because you are identified with me, the Son of Man.

"When that happens, rejoice! Yes, leap for joy! For a great reward awaits you in heaven. And remember, the ancient prophets were also treated that way by your ancestors."

Sorrows Foretold

"What sorrows await you who are rich, for you have your only happiness now.

"What sorrows await you who are satisfied and prosperous now, for a time of awful hunger is before you.

"What sorrows await you who laugh carelessly, for your laughing will turn to mourning and sorrow.

"What sorrows await you who are praised by the crowds, for their ancestors also praised false prophets."

Love for Enemies

"But if you are willing to listen, I say, love your enemies. Do good to those who hate you. Pray for the happiness of those who curse you. Pray for those who hurt you. If someone slaps you on one cheek, turn the other cheek. If someone demands your coat, offer your shirt also. Give what you have to anyone who asks you for it; and when things are taken away from you, don't try to get them back. Do for others as you would like them to do for you.

"Do you think you deserve credit merely for loving those who love you? Even the sinners do that! And if you do good only to those who do good to you, is that so wonderful? Even sinners do that much! And if you lend money only to those who can repay you, what good is that? Even sinners will lend to their own kind for a full return.

"Love your enemies! Do good to them! Lend to them! And don't be concerned that they might not repay. Then your reward from heaven will be very great, and you will truly be acting as children of the Most High,[1] for he is kind to the unthankful and to those who are wicked. You must be compassionate, just as your Father[2] is compassionate.

Do Not Condemn Others

"Stop judging others, and you will not be judged. Stop criticizing others, or it will all come back on you. If you forgive others, you will be forgiven. If you give, you will receive. Your gift will return to you in full measure, pressed down, shaken together to make room for more, and running over. Whatever measure you use in giving—large or small—it will be used to measure what is given back to you."

[1]**Most High**—God
[2]**Father**—God

Review Questions

1. What message did Jesus give to the downtrodden?
2. What promise did Jesus make to his followers?
3. How did Jesus view worldly success?
4. How did Jesus define compassion?
5. What did Jesus say would be the consequence of judging others?
6. How do the ideas of Jesus compare to those of Confucius (Document 13)?
7. Why would a person be attracted to Christianity?

15 The Qur'an

The Muslim holy book is called the Qur'an (pronounced kuh-RAN, and often spelled Koran). Muslims believe that it was dictated word for word by Allah (God, in Arabic) to his messenger Muhammad.

Muhammad lived in Arabia and died in A.D. 632. Before Muhammad, most Arabs worshiped many gods. The Qur'an, however, teaches that there is but one God. Drawing on the traditions of the earlier Jewish and Christian scriptures, the Qur'an recognizes as prophets such biblical figures as Abraham, Moses, and Jesus. Muslims believe that Muhammad was God's last and most important prophet.

Muslims believe that only the Arabic version of the Qur'an is truly authentic. When reading other documents that have been translated into English, remember that translations are always approximations of the exact meaning of the original.

In the name of Allah, the Compassionate, the Merciful

Praise be to Allah, Lord of the Creation,
The Compassionate, the Merciful,
King of Judgment-day!
You alone we worship, and to You alone
we pray for help.
Guide us to the straight path
The path of those whom You have favored,
Not of those who have incurred Your wrath,
Nor of those who have gone astray.

[Y]es, . . . there are guardians watching over you, noble recorders who know of all your actions.

The righteous shall surely dwell in bliss. But the wicked shall burn in Hell-fire upon the Judgment-day: They shall not escape.

Would that you knew what the Day of Judgment is! Oh, would that you knew what the Day of Judgment is! It is the day when every soul will stand alone and Allah will reign supreme.

In the name of Allah, the Compassionate, the Merciful

By the declining star, your compatriot [Muhammad] is not in error, nor is he deceived!

He does not speak out of his own fancy. This is an inspired revelation. He is taught by one who is powerful and mighty.[1]

He stood on the uppermost horizon; then, drawing near, he came down within two bows' length or even closer, and revealed to his servant that which he revealed.

His own heart did not deny his vision. How can you, then, question what he sees?

In the name of Allah, the Compassionate, the Merciful

Blessed are the believers, who are humble in their prayers; who avoid profane talk, and give alms[2] to the destitute; . . . who are true to their trusts and promises and never neglect their prayers. These are the heirs of Paradise; they shall abide in it forever.

We first created man from an essence of clay: then placed him, a living germ, in a safe enclosure. The germ We made a clot of blood, and the clot a lump of flesh. This We fashioned into bones, then clothed the bones with flesh, thus bringing forth another creation. Blessed be Allah, the noblest of creators!

You shall surely die hereafter, and be restored to life on the Day of Resurrection. . . .

In the name of Allah, the Compassionate, the Merciful

It was not to distress you that We revealed the Qur'an, but to admonish the God-fearing. It is a revelation from Him who has created the earth and the lofty heavens, the Merciful who sits enthroned on high.

His is what the heavens and the earth contain, and all that lies between them and underneath the soil. You have no need to speak aloud; for He has knowledge of all that is secret and all that is hidden.

He is Allah. There is no god but Him. His are the most gracious names. . . .

---

[1]**one who is powerful and mighty**—the Angel Gabriel
[2]**alms**—gifts to the poor

Muslims set aside one month each year during which the daylight hours are to be devoted to fasting (going without food) and prayer. That month is called Ramadan. It is discussed in the following passage.

In the month of Ramadan the [Qur'an] was revealed, a book of guidance with proofs of guidance distinguishing right from wrong. Therefore whoever of you is present in that month let him fast. But he who is ill or on a journey shall fast a similar number of days later on.

Allah desires your well-being, not your discomfort. He desires you to fast the whole month so that you may magnify Him and render thanks to Him for giving you His guidance. . . .

[O]n the night of the fast[,] . . . [e]at and drink until you can tell a white thread from a black one in the light of the coming dawn. Then resume the fast till nightfall and . . . stay at your prayers in the mosques.

These are the bounds set by Allah: do not come near them. Thus He makes known His revelations to mankind that they may guard themselves against evil.

Review Questions

1. What appeal is made to Allah in the prayer at the beginning of the document?
2. What does the Qur'an say will take place on judgment day?
3. According to the Qur'an, what are the qualities of the "believers"?
4. a. What promise does the Qur'an make to believers for the day of resurrection?
   b. How is this similar to or different from the promise made by Jesus (Document 14)?
5. What instruction does the Qur'an give to Muslims regarding the month of Ramadan?

*Write a well-organized essay that includes an introduction, several paragraphs, and a conclusion. Use evidence from at least **four** documents in this unit in the body of the essay. Support your response with relevant facts, examples, and details. Include additional outside information.*

Historical Context

People in ancient societies struggled to understand their environment and attempted to create order for the purpose of meeting the challenges of day-to-day living.

Task: Using the documents and questions in the unit, and your knowledge of global history, select **three** different societies and write an essay in which you:

- Explain how **each** society attempted to create a sense of order among its people
- Discuss **one** historical example of a consequence that befell a person who did *not* follow the established order of society

Expanding Zones of Exchange and Encounter

(A.D. 500–1200)

Empress Theodora and Her Courtiers

In the centuries following the birth of Christ and the spread of Christianity, the power of the Roman Empire slowly shifted to the eastern Mediterranean. By the 5th century, Rome had been fatally weakened by the invasions of nomadic, uncivilized peoples from northern and eastern Europe. The power of the empire passed to the Byzantine emperors. They ruled from the city of Constantinople, on the shores of the Bosphorus leading into the Black Sea.

The most powerful and successful of the early emperors was Justinian (ruled 527–565). Justinian fought off the invading nomadic armies in Europe and conquered territories around the Mediterranean Sea.

Justinian and his wife, the Empress Theodora, are remembered as the rulers who built great churches in which their powers are celebrated. The illustration on page 54 is part of a mosaic that shows Theodora and some of her courtiers (group of people who helped run the empire). A companion mosaic shows Justinian and his court. Both rulers are making offerings to Christ. These mosaics are the central decoration of the basilica (church) of San Vitale, in Ravenna, Italy.

A mosaic is a picture made of tiny cubes of colored glass set into plaster. In this mosaic, the pieces of glass and their golden background give the figures an otherworldly, spiritual quality. Mosaics in other churches showed holy images of Jesus, Mary, and the Christian saints.

The halo that surrounds Theodora's head symbolizes both spiritual and political power. Byzantine emperors considered themselves the heads of the Church as well as the rulers of the empire. Justinian, like other Byzantine emperors, set Church policy. As empress, Theodora took an active part in religious matters.

Although she did not rule in her own right, Theodora also had considerable political power. Through Justinian, she often determined public policy and the fortunes of his

Empress Theodora and her courtiers, church of San Vitale, Ravenna, Italy (A.D. 526–547)

ministers. During a rebellion, Theodora persuaded Justinian to take a stand against the mob instead of fleeing. He listened to her and kept his throne.

Review Questions

1. Explain how the Empress Theodora might be considered the power behind her husband, the Emperor Justinian.
2. Explain the symbolism of showing Theodora, a worldly ruler, wearing a halo usually reserved for religious persons.
3. Describe a mosaic. How was it made?

China Welcomes Early Christians

Traveling overland from Persia to China in about the year 635, a band of Christians received a warm welcome from an emperor of the Tang dynasty. With the emperor's blessing, the visitors began establishing monasteries in China. For a time, Christianity seemed to be winning converts there. But the emperor's protection was not enough to keep down hostility—especially from Buddhists—against the Christians. By the year 1000, the Christian faith had largely died out in China. Nonetheless, Marco Polo and other later visitors reported finding small Christian communities there in the 13th century.

The Christians who reached China in 635 were known as Nestorians. They belonged to a small branch that broke away from mainstream Christianity because of disagreements about the nature of Jesus. Nestorian communities still exist today, mainly in Syria, Iran (formerly Persia), and Iraq. The missionaries of 635 came from Persia, although the Chinese called them "Syrians" (a category in which they put most of the people of Southwestern Asia).

Below is part of an inscription from a ten-foot-high stone monument erected in China in 781. It celebrates the early history of the Nestorian church in China.

In the time of the accomplished Emperor Tai-tsung, the [famous] and magnificent founder of the [Tang] Dynasty, among the enlightened and holy men who arrived was the most-virtuous Olopun, from the country of Syria. [Bearing] the true sacred books, . . . he braved difficulties and dangers. In the year of our Lord 635 he arrived at [the capital city of] Chang'an. The Emperor sent his Prime Minister, Duke Fang Hiuen-ling; who, carrying the official staff to the west border, conducted his guest into the interior; the sacred books were translated in the imperial library, the [emperor] investigated the subject in his private apartments; when becoming deeply impressed with the [righteousness] and truth of the religion, he gave special orders for its [spread].

In the seventh month of the year A.D. 638, the following imperial proclamation was issued:

> Right principles have no [unchanging] name, holy men have no [unchanging position]; instruction is established in accordance with the locality, with the object of benefiting the people at large. The greatly virtuous Olopun, of the kingdom of Syria, has brought his sacred books and images from that distant part, and has presented them at our chief capital. Having examined the principles of this religion, we find them to be purely excellent and natural; investigating its . . . source, we find it has [risen from] important truths; its ritual is free from [puzzling] expressions, its principles will survive when the framework is forgot; it is beneficial to all creatures; it is advantageous to mankind. Let it be published throughout the Empire, and let the proper authority build a Syrian church in the capital . . . , which shall be governed by twenty-one priests. . . .

. . . According to the Illustrated Memoir of the Western Regions, and the historical books of the Han and Wei dynasties,[1] the kingdom of Syria reaches south to the Coral Sea; on the north it joins the Gem Mountains; on the west it extends toward the borders of the immortals and the flowery forests; on the east it lies open to the violent winds and tideless waters. The country produces fire-proof cloth, life-restoring incense, bright moon-pearls, and night-luster gems. . . . [R]obbers are unknown, . . . the people enjoy happiness and peace. None but [just and famous] laws prevail; none but the virtuous are raised to sovereign power. The land is broad and ample, and its literary productions are . . . clear. . . .

This was erected in the 2nd year of Kien-chung, of the Tang Dynasty [A.D. 781], on the 7th day of the 1st month, being Sunday.

Review Questions

1. Why did the Chinese emperor help the Christians when they arrived in China?
2. How did the emperor's proclamation promote the spread of Christianity in China?
3. Why did the Christian faith fail to succeed in China, despite the emperor's support?
4. What lessons about cultural diffusion can we learn from the example of the Nestorians in Tang China?

---

[1]**Han and Wei dynasties**—ruled China from 206 B.C. to A.D. 265

A Debate Over Buddhism in China

Most of China's people followed one or more of three major religious or philosophical traditions—Confucianism, Taoism, and Buddhism. The founders of these traditions were, respectively, Confucius, Lao-tzu, and Siddhartha Gautama (known as the Buddha, or "enlightened one"). All were born about the 6th century B.C. While Confucius and Lao-tzu were Chinese, the Buddha lived in the Indian subcontinent. Thus, Buddhism was seen by some Chinese as an imported or "foreign" set of ideas.

Our document comes from a Chinese novel, *The Journey to the West*, by Ch'eng-en Wu. Written in 1592, the novel describes events that happened long before. It is based on the actions of a real person, Hsüan-tsang (lived 596–664). He was a Chinese monk who made a remarkable overland journey to India and brought Buddhist scriptures back to China.

The following excerpt from the novel tells of a debate among high Chinese officials over the relative merits of Confucianism and Buddhism. The emperor, Tai-tsung, is the same one referred to in Document 2, and the events take place at about the same time the Nestorian Christians first entered China.

Tai-tsung was exceedingly pleased [at the completion of a Buddhist temple he had ordered built to honor a devout and virtuous couple]. He then gathered many officials together in order that a public notice be issued to invite monks for the celebration of the Grand Mass of Land and Water. . . . The notice went throughout the empire, and officials of all regions were asked to recommend monks [famous] for their holiness to go to Chang-an for the mass. In less than a month's time, the various monks from the empire had arrived. The T'ang emperor ordered the court historian, Fu I, to select an illustrious priest to take charge of the ceremonies. When Fu I received the order, however, he presented a memorial [written statement] to the Throne which attempted to dispute the worth of Buddha. The memorial said:

> The teachings of India deny the relations of ruler and subject, of father and son. [T]hey [deceive] and seduce the foolish. . . . They emphasize the sins of the past in order to ensure the [happiness] of the future. By chanting . . . they seek a way of escape. We submit, however, that birth, death, and the length of one's life are ordered by nature; but the conditions of public disgrace or honor are determined by human [decision]. These phenomena are not . . . [established] by Buddha. The teachings of Buddha did not exist in the time of the Three Kings and the Five Emperors, and yet those [early Chinese] rulers were wise, their subjects loyal, and their reigns long-lasting. It was not until the period of . . . the Han dynasty that the . . . priests of [India] were permitted to [spread] their faith. The event, in fact, represented a foreign intrusion in China, and the teachings are hardly worthy to be believed.

When Tai-tsung saw the memorial, he had it distributed among the various officials for discussion. [T]he prime minister Hsiao Yü came forward to address the Throne, saying, "The teachings of Buddha, which have flourished in several previous dynasties, seek to [glorify] the good and to restrain what is evil. In this way they are an aid to the nation, and there is no reason why they should be rejected. For Buddha after all is also a wise person, and he who spurns this person is lawless. I urge that the dissenter be severely punished."

Taking up the debate with Hsiao Yü, Fu I contended that right conduct had its foundation in service to one's parents and ruler. Yet Buddha left his family; indeed, he defied the ruler all by himself, just as he used an inherited body to rebel against his parents.

Tai-tsung thereupon called on the Lord High Chamberlain, and the President of the Grand Secretariat. . . . The two officials replied, "The emphasis of Buddha is on purity, benevolence, compassion, . . . and the unreality of things. . . . We beseech, therefore, Your Majesty to exercise your clear and [wise] judgment."

Highly pleased, Tai-tsung said, "The words of our worthy subjects are not unreasonable. Anyone who disputes them further will be punished." He thereupon ordered his officials to invite the various Buddhist priests to prepare the site for the grand mass and to select from among them someone of great merit and virtue to preside over the ceremonies. . . . From that time also came the law that any person who denounces a monk or Buddhism will have his arms broken.

Review Questions

1. How did the Chinese emperor decide to celebrate the completion of the Buddhist temple?
2. Describe three protests Fu I made against Buddhism.
3. How did the emperor react to Fu I's protests?
4. How did Hsiao Yu disagree with Fu I?
5. How did the emperor resolve the debate between the critics and the supporters of Buddhism?

Avicenna Tells About His Studies

During the Middle Ages, wars and invasions kept Europe in turmoil. Many writings from Roman, Greek, and earlier times were lost or destroyed. They were no longer available to people in Europe. In the Muslim world, however, learning remained alive. Muslim scholars preserved and studied the ancient texts. These were works on philosophy and politics by Greek writers such as Aristotle and Plato, works on mathematics by Euclid of Alexandria, and plays and histories by many others. Through trade with other countries, Muslims learned of many inventions and ideas. They acquired the compass from China, a system of numbers from India (using what are now called "Arabic" numerals), and methods of astronomy from India and Persia. At the same time, Muslim scholars made their own investigations and added to the sum of human knowledge.

One of the best-known Islamic scholars of this period was a Persian named Ibn Sina, or Avicenna (lived 980–1037). He was philosopher and an astronomer, a student of languages, a mathematician, and a physician. His *Canon of Medicine,* which brought together all the available Greek and Arabic sources on medicine, remained a standard medical textbook for some 600 years.

Our document comes from Avicenna's autobiography. In it, he describes how he became a renowned scholar before he was out of his teens. His self-description may lack modesty but it seems to correspond fairly well with the known facts.

. . . I was . . . born [in a village named Afshana], and after me my brother. Later we moved to Bukhara,[1] where I was put under teachers of the Quran and of letters. By the time I was ten I had mastered the Quran and a great deal of literature, so that I was marveled at for my aptitude.

---

[1]**Bukhara**—capital of the Persian Samanid kingdom, which reached from present-day Baghdad to the Persian Gulf and the borders of India; now in Uzbekistan

. . . My father and my brother would discuss Islamic philosophy together, while I listened and comprehended all that they said; but my spirit would not [agree with] their argument. Presently they began to invite me to join [in supporting an Egyptian-based movement], rolling on their tongues talk about philosophy, geometry, Indian arithmetic; and my father sent me to a certain vegetable-seller who used the Indian arithmetic, so that I might learn it from him. Then there came to Bukhara a man who claimed to be a philosopher; my father invited him to stay in our house, hoping that I would learn from him also. . . . I had already occupied myself with Muslim law, so I was an excellent enquirer. . . . He marveled at me exceedingly, and warned my father that I should not engage in any other occupation but learning; whatever problem he stated to me, I showed a better mental conception of it than he. . . .

From then onward I took to reading texts [by] myself; I studied until I had completely mastered the science of Logic. Similarly with Euclid I read the first five or six figures with . . . [the visiting philosopher], and thereafter undertook on my own account to solve the entire remainder of the book. . . .

I now occupied myself with mastering the various texts and commentaries on natural science and [religious, philosophical] matters until all the gates of knowledge were open to me. Next I desired to study medicine, and proceeded to read all the books that have been written on the subject. Medicine is not a difficult science, and naturally I excelled in it in a very short time, so that qualified physicians began to study medicine with me. I also undertook to treat the sick, and methods of treatment derived from practical experience revealed themselves to me such as baffle description. At the same time I continued between whiles to study and dispute on law, being now sixteen years of age.

The next eighteen months I devoted entirely to reading; I studied Logic once again, and all the parts of philosophy. During all this time I did not sleep one night through, nor devoted my attention to any other matter by day. . . . Whenever I found myself perplexed by a problem . . . I would [go] to the mosque and pray, adoring the All-Creator,[2] until my puzzle was resolved and my difficulty made easy.

---

[2]**All-Creator**—God

At night I would return home, set the lamp before me, and busy myself with reading and writing; whenever sleep overcame me or I was conscious of some weakness, I turned aside to drink a glass of wine until my strength returned to me; then I went back to my reading. If ever the least slumber overtook me, I would dream of the precise problem which I was considering as I fell asleep; in that way many problems revealed themselves to me while sleeping. So I continued until I had made myself master of all the sciences. . . .

. . . [I]t happened that the sultan fell sick of a malady which baffled all the physicians. My name was famous among them because of the breadth of my reading; they therefore mentioned me in his presence, and begged him to summon me. I [worked] with them in treating the royal patient. So I came to be enrolled in his service. One day I asked his leave to enter their library, to examine the contents and read the books on medicine; he granted my request, and I entered a mansion with many chambers, each chamber having chests of books piled one upon another. In one apartment were books on language and poetry, in another law, and so on; each apartment was set apart for books on a single science. I glanced through the catalogue of the works of the ancient Greeks, and asked for those which I required; and I saw books whose very names are as yet unknown to many—works which I had never seen before and have not seen since. I read these books, taking notes of their contents; I came to realize the place each man occupied in his particular science.

So by the time I had reached my eighteenth year I had exhausted all these sciences. . . .

Review Questions

1. a. How was ancient learning kept alive by Muslim scholars during the Middle Ages?
   b. How did these scholars benefit from cultural diffusion?
2. In what subjects did Avicenna become an expert?
3. How did Avicenna become enrolled in the service of the sultan of Bukhara?
4. What do Avicenna's studies and love of knowledge tell us about the Muslim culture in which he lived?
5. How would you describe Avicenna's personality?

The Norman Conquest of England, 1066

During the 5th and 6th centuries, Germanic peoples called Angles, Saxons, and Jutes arrived in Britain from the European continent. Sometimes they came as peaceful settlers, sometimes as invading warriors. Eventually, these people (collectively called Anglo-Saxons) conquered and largely displaced the native Britons, who were of Celtic origin. The newcomers kept their Germanic customs and languages. The land acquired a new name—England, "land of the Angles."

At first, the newcomers organized small states that fought almost constant wars against one another. Over time, certain states swallowed up others, until a handful of middle-sized states remained. Then, in the late 8th century, new invaders arrived—Norsemen, also called Vikings. The Norse invaders were from Scandinavia—present-day Norway, Sweden, and Denmark. Almost two centuries passed before the Anglo-Saxon King Edgar finally drove out the Norse armies in 959. By that time, most Anglo-Saxons had adopted Christianity, in the form of Roman Catholicism.

During the following century, a new wave of Norse invaders arrived, and from 1016 to 1042 Danish kings occupied England's throne. Although the English managed to eject the Danes, they then faced a challenge from another branch of the Norse people. These were the Normans, who came from the area of northwest France known as Normandy. They too were Roman Catholics.

William, duke of Normandy, led the Norman invasion of England in 1066. At the Battle of Hastings, near England's southeastern coast, the Normans defeated the English army and killed England's King Harold. The Normans then took command of the country. They introduced European-style feudal laws to England and displaced the Anglo-Saxon ruling class. This Norman Conquest was an event of the greatest importance in English history.

The following documents give some of the flavor of those momentous times. First is a description of the Battle of

Hastings on October 14, 1066, and of the Anglo-Saxon and Norman people. It is by William of Malmesbury, an English historian writing within a century after the events he describes.

The courageous leaders . . . prepared for battle, each according to his national custom. The English . . . passed the night without sleep, in drinking and singing, and in the morning proceeded without delay against the enemy. All on foot, armed with battle-axes, and covering themselves in front by the [joining] of their shields, they formed an impenetrable body which would assuredly have secured their safety that day had not the Normans, by a [pretended] flight, [caused] them to open their ranks. . . . King Harold himself, on foot, stood with his brothers near the [battle flag] in order that, so long as all shared equal danger, none could think of retreating. . . .

On the other hand, the Normans passed the whole night in confessing their sins, and received the communion of the Lord's body in the morning. Their infantry, with bows and arrows, formed the [front section], while their cavalry, divided into wings, was placed in the rear. The duke, with [a calm expression], declaring aloud that God would favor his as being the righteous side, called for his arms . . . [T]he battle commenced on both sides, and was fought with great [spirit], neither side giving ground during the greater part of the day.

Observing this, William gave a signal to his troops, that, [pretending] flight, they should [leave] the field. By means of this device the [massed troops] of the English opened for the purpose of cutting down the fleeing enemy and thus brought upon itself swift destruction; for the Normans, facing about, attacked them, thus disordered, and compelled them to fly [run away]. . . .

In the battle both leaders distinguished themselves by their bravery. Harold, not content with the [role] of general and with [encouraging] others, eagerly assumed himself the duties of a common soldier. He was constantly striking down the enemy at close quarters, so that no one could approach him [without harm] for straightway both horse and rider would be felled by a single blow. So it was at long range . . . that the enemy's deadly arrow brought him to his death. . . .

William, too, was equally ready to encourage his soldiers by his voice and by his presence, and to be the first to rush forward to attack the thickest of the foe. He was everywhere fierce and furious; he lost three choice horses, which were that day killed under him. . . .

This was a fatal day to England, and [great damage] was [caused] in our dear country during the change of its lords. For it had long before adopted the manners of the Angles, which had indeed altered with the times; for in the first years of their arrival they were barbarians in their look and manner, warlike in their [habits], heathens[1] in their rites.

After embracing the faith of Christ, by degrees and, in process of time, in consequence of the peace which they enjoyed, they [assigned] [war] to a secondary place. . . .

[T]he attention to literature and religion had gradually decreased for several years before the arrival of the Normans. The clergy, contented with a little confused learning, could scarcely stammer out the words of the [religious rites]; and a person who understood grammar was an object of wonder and astonishment. The monks mocked the rule of their order by fine [ceremonial robes] and the use of every kind of food. The nobility, given up to luxury and [self-indulgence], went not to church in the morning after the manner of Christians, but merely, in a careless manner, heard [morning prayers] and masses from a hurrying priest in their chambers, amid the [coaxing] of their wives. The [ordinary people], left unprotected, became a prey to the most powerful, who [built up] fortunes, either by seizing on their property or by selling their persons into foreign countries. . . . The English at that time wore short garments, reaching to the mid-knee; they had their hair cropped, their beards shaven, their arms laden with golden bracelets, their skin adorned with tattooed designs. They were accustomed to [overeat] and to drink till they were sick. These latter qualities they [passed on] to their conquerors; as to the rest, they adopted their manners. . . .

The Normans—that I may speak of them also—were at that time, and are even now, exceedingly [careful] in their dress and delicate in their food, but not so to excess. They are a race [accustomed] to war, and can hardly live without it. . . . [T]hey live in spacious houses,

[1]**heathens**—uncivilized people; people without knowledge of the Bible

envy their superiors, wish to excel their equals, and plunder their subjects, though they defend them from others; they are faithful to their lords, though a slight offense alienates them. They weigh treachery by its chance of success, and change their sentiments for money. The most hospitable, however, of all nations, they [consider] strangers worthy of equal honor with themselves; they also intermarry with their vassals. They revived, by their arrival, the rule of religion which had everywhere grown lifeless in England. You might see churches rise in every village, and monasteries in the towns and cities, built after a style unknown before. . . .

Review Questions

1. How does the author describe the differences between the English and the Normans?
2. How did the Normans' use of trickery help them to win the Battle of Hastings?
3. How do you compare the leadership of King Harold with that of William the Conqueror?
4. Why was the Battle of Hastings a turning point in English history?
5. What changes did the Normans' rule bring to England?

6 The Laws of William the Conqueror

Before 1066, the Anglo-Saxons had developed their own early form of feudalism. This was a system of relations between the powerful and the less powerful, in which the less powerful pledged their loyalty in return for land and protection. William and the Normans introduced a more elaborate form of feudalism. This was the social and political system that dominated European life during the Middle Ages, roughly from 800 to 1400. (Systems of feudalism also existed in China, Japan, the Muslim world, and elsewhere, as we shall see in Unit III.)

Following are some of the rules established for England by William the Conqueror (as he was known after 1066).

Here is set down what William, king of the English, established in consultation with his [nobles] after the conquest of England:

1. First that above all things he wishes one God to be revered throughout his whole realm, one faith in Christ to be kept ever [pure], and peace and security to be preserved between English and Normans.

2. We decree also that every freeman shall affirm by oath and compact that he will be loyal to King William both [inside and outside] England, that he will preserve with him his lands and honor with all fidelity and defend him against his enemies.

3. I [order], moreover, that all the men I have brought with me, or who have come [from Normandy] after me, shall be protected by my peace and shall dwell in quiet. And if any one of them shall be slain, let the lord of his murderer seize him [the murderer] within five days, if he can; but if he cannot, let him [the lord] pay me 46 marks[1] of silver so long as [he has any

[1]**mark**—unit of money, equal to eight ounces of silver or two thirds of an English pound (a large sum in the 11th century)

property]. And when his substance is exhausted, let the whole [township] in which the murder took place pay what remains in common. . . .

6. It was decreed there that if a Frenchman shall charge an Englishman with [lying under oath] or murder or theft or homicide or [plunder] . . . the Englishman may defend himself, as he shall prefer, either by the ordeal of hot iron[2] or by wager of battle. But if the Englishman be [in poor health], let him find another who will take his place. If one of them shall be [defeated], he shall pay a fine of 40 shillings to the king. If an Englishman shall charge a Frenchman and be unwilling to prove his accusation either by ordeal or by wager of battle, I will, nevertheless, that the Frenchman shall [clear] himself by a valid oath.

7. This also I command and will, that all shall have and hold the law of the King Edward in respect of their lands and all their possessions, with the addition of those decrees I have ordained for the welfare of the English people. . . .

9. I prohibit the sale of any man [into slavery] by another outside the country on pain of a fine to be paid in full to me.

10. I also forbid that anyone shall be slain or hanged for any fault, but let his eyes be put out and let him be castrated. And this command shall not be violated under pain of a fine in full to me.

In 1086, twenty years after the Conquest of England, King William ordered a detailed survey of the lands and people. Its purpose was to determine how much income he should be receiving in taxes and other fees. This was England's first official census. Its results were published in a large book called *The Domesday Book*. (The name referred to a public fear that a day of judgment or doomsday lay ahead. On doomsday, it was thought, the facts and figures contained in *The Domesday Book* might help to determine a person's fate for all eternity.)

Under the feudal system, all land was considered to belong to the king. However, the king himself directly used

[2]**ordeal of hot iron**—a "trial by fire," in which people's guilt or innocence was determined by whether or not they could stand to be burned by a hot iron

only 15 percent of the land. Another 25 percent of the land was in the hands of the Christian church. The remaining 60 percent was controlled by a small class of nobles, who had subdivided it into many separate parts. These lands, known as estates, were controlled by people known as lords. Under the feudal system, the lords granted land to peasant farmers known as tenants. The lords had the power to collect rents from the tenants, keep law and order, and set up courts to decide disputes among their tenants. The rents the lords collected were not just payments of money. Tenants might also be required to work a certain number of days each year on a lord's lands and provide him with farm products. (Not all of a lord's lands were rented out. A portion of each estate, known as the *demesne,* was worked by the tenants on behalf of the lord himself.)

Review Questions

1. Why did William list the law proclaiming Christian worship first, before the other laws of the kingdom?
2. How did rule 2 help to promote English unity?
3. How did William's laws promote the loyalty of his subjects?
4. How did William's laws protect the Normans against violence by his English subjects?
5. What methods for resolving disputes were contained in William's laws?
6. What was William's purpose in compiling the information in *The Domesday Book*?
7. How was land controlled under the feudal system?

The Tale of Genji: The World's First Novel

At the eastern edge of Asia, the island nation of Japan established its own form of feudalism under decrees issued by its emperors during the 7th century. Japan was heavily influenced by the more advanced civilization of China. In the following century, Japanese emperors patterned their new capital of Heian (present-day Kyoto) on the Chinese capital of Chang'an. In Heian, a small upper class of wealthy nobles lived lives of leisure in and around the imperial court. Cultivated people held Chinese learning in great respect and sprinkled their conversations with brief poems that they themselves composed in Chinese or Japanese.

Shortly after the year 1000, one of the women of Heian's courtly circles wrote an immense book of more than a thousand pages that is considered to be the world's first novel. *The Tale of Genji*, by Lady Murasaki Shikibu, is still prized today as an outstanding example of Japanese literature. It tells of the life and many loves of a prince named Genji. In the section quoted below, Genji has arranged a special ceremony at which his son Yugiri is initiated into a high academic rank. While the excerpt makes fun of stuffy professors, it shows the importance the Japanese gave to learning. It also reveals a tendency to measure Japanese culture against Chinese standards.

The ceremony . . . took place in the new part of the Nijo-in palace. . . . As such a function seldom takes place in the houses of the great, the occasion was one of great interest, and princes and courtiers of every degree vied with one another for the best seats. The professors who had come to conduct the proceedings were not expecting so large and distinguished an audience, and they were evidently very much put out. "Gentlemen," said Genji, addressing them, "I want you to perform this ceremony in all its [strictness], omitting no detail, and above all not in any way altering the prescribed [customs] either in deference to the company here assembled or out of consideration for the pupil whom you are about to admit into your craft." The professors did their best to look business-like and unconcerned. Many of them were dressed in gowns which they had hired for the occasion; but fortunately they had no idea how absurd they looked in these old-fashioned and ill-fitting clothes. . . . Their grimaces and odd turns of speech [were so strange] that Yugiri's cousins, who had never seen anything of the sort in their lives before, could not refrain from smiling. [When] someone in the audience [giggled], the professors [protested]: "These proceedings cannot continue," they said, "unless absolute silence is preserved. Interruptions are in the highest degree irregular, and if they occur again we shall be obliged to leave our seats." Several more testy speeches followed, and the audience was vastly entertained. . . . It was long indeed since Learning had received . . . [such] encouragement, and for the first time its partisans felt themselves to be people of real weight and consequence. Not a single word might anyone in the audience so much as whisper to his neighbor without calling down upon himself an angry [rebuke], and excited cries of "disgraceful behavior!" were provoked by the mildest signs of restlessness in the crowd. For some time the ceremony had been proceeding in darkness, and now when the torches were suddenly lit, revealing those aged faces contorted with [disapproval] and self-importance. . . . [Genji] thought, looking at the professors, "[T]ruly in more ways than one an extraordinary and unaccountable profession!" "I think it is rather fun," he said, "to see everyone being kept in order by these crabbed old people," and hid himself well behind his curtains-of-state, lest his comments too should be heard and rebuked. . . .

[At the end of the ceremony] Genji . . . made [the professors and doctors] compose poem after poem. He also detained such of the courtiers and princes as he knew to care most for poetry. The professors were called upon to compose complete [eight-line] poems while the company, from Genji downwards, tried their hands at [four-line verses], Teachers of Literature being asked to choose the themes. The summer night was so short that before the time came to read out the poems it was already broad daylight. The reading was done by the Under-secretary to the Council, who, besides being a man of fine appearance, had a remarkably strong and impressive voice, so that his recitations gave everyone great pleasure.

That mere enthusiasm should lead young men of high birth, who might so easily have contented themselves with the life of brilliant [entertainment] to which their position entitled them, to study "by the light of the glow-worm at the window or the glimmer of snow on the bough," was highly [pleasing], and . . . any one of these compositions might well have been carried to the Land Beyond the Sea [China] without fear of bringing our country into contempt. But women are not supposed to know anything about Chinese literature, and I will not shock your sense of propriety by quoting any of the poems—even that by which Genji so deeply moved his hearers.

Review Questions

1. What is the significance of *The Tale of Genji*?
2. a. What was the role of the professors?
   b. Why was there tension between the professors and the audience?
3. What does the ability of the Japanese nobility to write poetry, and appreciate it, tell us about the importance of education in Japan?
4. How does this passage reflect the respect that the Japanese had for Chinese culture and literature?
5. What does the document tell us about the role of women in 11th-century Japan?

Japan, the Divine Country

The Japanese people took great pride in what they believed to be the divine origins of their land and their monarchy. These beliefs were a central part of Japan's Shinto religion. Shinto is an ancient religion, and it is still practiced by the Japanese today. Shinto holds that spirits called kami inhabit objects in the physical world. Shinto shrines are found throughout Japan. Shinto teachings also were the basis for a strong sense of Japanese nationalism (love for one's country and its traditions) that lasted into modern times. The following document was written by a 13th-century Japanese noble who supported the imperial family at a time when various factions in Japanese society were competing for power.

Japan is the divine country. The heavenly ancestor it was who first laid its foundations, and the Sun Goddess left her descendants to reign over it forever and ever. This is true only of our country, and nothing similar may be found in foreign lands. That is why it is called the divine country.

In the Age of the Gods, Japan was known as the "ever-fruitful land of reed-covered plains and luxuriant ricefields." This name has existed since the creation of heaven and earth. . . . [Japan] is also called the country of the great eight islands. This name was given because eight islands were produced when the Male Deity and the Female Deity [gave birth to] Japan. . . .

In writing the name of the country, the Chinese characters Dai-Nippon and Dai-Wa have both been used. The reason is that, when Chinese writing was introduced to this country, the characters for Dai-Nippon were chosen to represent the name of the country, but they were pronounced as "Yamato." This choice may have been guided by the fact that Japan is the Land of the Sun Goddess, or it may have thus been called because it is near the place where the sun rises. . . .

The beginnings of Japan in some ways resemble the Indian descriptions, telling as it does of the world's creation from the seed of the heavenly gods. However, whereas in our country the succession to the throne has followed a single [unchanging] line since the first divine ancestor, nothing of the kind has existed in India. . . . China is also a country of notorious disorders. Even in ancient times, when life was simple and conduct was proper, the throne was offered to wise men, and no single lineage was established. Later, in times of disorder, men fought for control of the country. Thus some of the rulers rose from the ranks of the [common people], and there were even some of barbarian origin who [seized] power. Or, some families after generations of service as ministers surpassed their princes and eventually [replaced] them. There have already been thirty-six changes of dynasty, and unspeakable disorders have occurred.

Only in our country has the succession remained [unbroken], from the beginning of heaven and earth to the present. It has been maintained within a single [line of ancestors], and even when, as inevitably has happened, the succession has been transmitted collaterally,[1] it has returned to the true line. This is due to the ever-renewed Divine Oath, which makes Japan unlike all other countries.

Review Questions

1. a. Why did the Japanese call Japan "the divine country"?
   b. How was the Shinto religion tied into Japanese history?
2. Compare the legends about the origins of Japan with those of India.
3. What comparisons did the author make between the rulers and government of Japan and China?
4. Why did the author believe Japan was "unlike all other countries"?
5. How did the Japanese view themselves?

[1]**collaterally**—through a line other than direct discent

Training of Slaves to Occupy High Rank in a Muslim State

Slavery was a part of most early societies. In some slave-owning societies, enslaved people were harshly treated, overworked, and greatly abused. In some ancient societies, however, slaves had opportunities to attain high positions in government. The following document comes from a Muslim empire. In this society, young men who had been bought as slaves often received education and training. Eventually, the most able and talented rose in rank to take on positions of responsibility in government.

This document comes from a book written late in the 11th century by Nizam al-Mulk. He was a vizier, or chief minister, who served two powerful sultans (rulers) of the Seljuk Dynasty. During the 11th century, the Seljuks, who were descended from Turkish nomads, had conquered a vast area in Southwest Asia. For a time their rule stretched from eastern Iran westward through Iraq, Syria, and much of Turkey (using present-day names). The Seljuk Turks had seized much of that land from the Eastern Roman, or Byzantine, Empire, which had its capital at Constantinople. Nizam's book *Rules for Kings* used historical examples in order to give pointers on wise methods of governing.

This is the system which was still in force [under the Persian dynasty in the 9th and 10th centuries]. Pages were given gradual advancement in rank according to their length of service and general merit. Thus after a page was bought, for one year he was commanded to serve on foot at a rider's stirrup, wearing a [fine] cloak and boots; and this page was not allowed during his first year to ride a horse in private or in public, and if it was found out [that he had ridden] he was punished. When he had done one year's service with boots, the tent-leader spoke to the chamberlain[1] and he informed

[1]**chamberlain**—a high official serving a lord or monarch

the king; then they gave [the page] a small Turkish horse, with a saddle covered in untanned leather and a [plain leather] bridle. . . . After serving for a year with a horse and whip, in his third year he was given a belt [for] his waist. In the fourth year they gave him a [bow with arrows]. In his fifth year he got a better saddle and a bridle with stars on it, together with a cloak and a club. . . . In the sixth year he was made a cup-bearer or water-bearer and he hung a goblet from his waist. In the seventh year he was a robe-bearer. In the eighth year they gave him a tent and put three newly bought pages in his troop; they gave him the title of tent leader and dressed him in a black felt hat decorated with silver wire. . . . Every year they improved his uniform and [decorations] and increased his rank and responsibility until he became a troop-leader, and so on until he became a chamberlain. When his suitability, skill, and bravery became generally recognized and when he had performed some outstanding actions and been found to be considerate to his fellows and loyal to his master, then and only then, when he was thirty-five or forty years of age, did they make him an amir[2] and appoint him to a province.

Review Questions

1. Describe the page system under the Seljuk Turks.
2. What factors determined the promotion of pages?
3. Under what circumstances would a slave be elevated to the rank of amir and given the responsibility for governing an entire province?
4. How do the training and tasks assigned to pages compare with your view of how slaves were treated?

[2]**amir, or emir**—a ruler or commander (in Muslim countries)

A Ruler Helps a Poor Woman

In his book *Rules for Kings,* Nizam al-Mulk tells a story about one of the first Muslim leaders, a man named 'Umar ibn al-Khattab. Nizam wanted to make the point that rulers must assume responsibility for the welfare of their subjects.

The story takes place near the Arabian city of Medina, one of the two holiest cities of Islam (the other is Mecca). Medina became the headquarters of the Prophet Mohammad in 622—the date that marks the start of the Muslim calendar. It was the capital of the first Muslim state. 'Umar led that state as caliph, or ruler, from 634 to 644. During this time, Muslim rule spread across Mesopotamia and Syria and into Persia and Egypt.

[A Muslim writer named Zaid ibn Asham] related the following story:

One night the Commander of the Faithful, 'Umar ibn al-Khattab (may Allah be pleased with him), was on patrol in person in Medina, and I was with him. We went out of the city, and in the fields there was a ruined building in which a fire was burning. 'Umar said to me, "O Zaid, come, let us go there and see who it is who has lit a fire in the middle of the night." So we went, and when we got near we saw a woman with two little children asleep on the ground beside her and a small pot set over a fire; she was saying, "May God Almighty help me to get justice from 'Umar; he has eaten his fill while we are hungry."

When 'Umar heard this he said to me, "O Zaid, this woman is [accusing] me of all people before God. You stay here while I approach her and ask what is the matter." He went up to the woman and said, "What are you cooking at midnight out in the fields?"

She said, "I am a poor woman; I have not got a house of my own in Medina and I am penniless; and I feel so ashamed that these two children of mine are weeping and wailing in hunger and I have nothing to give them, and the neighbors know they are crying because they are hungry and I cannot do anything about it; so I have been out here since yesterday. Every time they cry from hunger and ask for food I put this pot on the fire and say, 'You go to sleep and by the time you wake up the pot will be ready.' By this means I set them at rest and with this hope they go to sleep; when they wake up and find nothing they start howling again. At the moment I have put them to sleep on some pretense; for two days now I have not had anything to eat and neither have they; and there is nothing but plain water in this pot."

'Umar (may Allah be pleased with him) took pity on her and said, "You are justified in cursing 'Umar and appealing to God." The woman did not recognize 'Umar. He said to her, "Wait here for a while until I come back."

'Umar then came back to me and said, "Step out, we are going back to my house." When we reached his house we went in and I sat down at the door. After some time he came out with two leather bags on his back. He said to me, "Come, let us go back to that woman." I said, "O Commander of the Faithful, if we have got to go back there, put those bags on my back and let me carry them." 'Umar said, "O Zaid, if you carry this load, who will take the load of sin off 'Umar's back?"

And he ran all the way to the woman and put the bags down in front of her; one of them was full of flour and the other full of rice, peas and fat. He said to me, "O Zaid, go into the fields, collect all the sticks and wormwood you can find, and bring them quickly." I went to look for firewood. Then 'Umar took a bowl and fetched some water; he washed the rice and peas, put them in the pot and threw in a lump of fat; and with the flour he made a large flat round of bread. I brought the firewood; and with his own hands 'Umar heated the pot and put the bread under the fire.

When the bread and the pot were ready 'Umar filled the bowl with broth and sopped bread, and when it was cooled he told the woman to wake up the children for their food; she awakened the children and 'Umar placed the food in front of them. Then he retired to a distance, spread his prayer-mat and began to pray. After a while he looked; mother and children had eaten their fill and were playing together. 'Umar got up and said, "O woman, you pick up the children, while I take the bags and Zaid carries the pot and bowl, and we will take you home." This they did. The woman took the children into her house; 'Umar put down the bags and as he turned to leave, he said, "Be kind and do not curse 'Umar any more; he cannot withstand God's punishment and rebuke, and he is not [able] to know what everyone's condition is. Use what I have brought and when it is finished let me know and I will bring more."

Review Questions

1. What is the moral of the story about the ruler, 'Umar, and the poor woman?
2. How did the woman seek help?
3. How did 'Umar help the woman?
4. Why did 'Umar refuse to allow Zaid to carry the bags of food?
5. What does this story tell us about the Islamic code of law and justice?

European Christians Launch the Crusades

In 1095, Pope Urban II, leader of the Roman Catholic Church, called on Europe's Christians to take back the Holy Land—the land of the Bible, centered around Jerusalem—from the Muslims. The pope's call led to a series of Crusades, or holy wars. These wars lasted off and on for almost 200 years.

Christian Crusaders who flocked to the Holy Land were usually led by nobles, but the Crusaders included masses of men, women, and children from the middle and lower classes. The Crusades stirred unrest within Europe's feudal societies. Many Crusaders believed they were serving God's will. But others had additional motives—a desire for adventure, hope for a chance to become rich, suspicion of non-Christians, and more.

Ekkehard of Aurach was a German historian who joined a company of Crusaders shortly after finishing a history of the world in 1101. Upon his return, he wrote an account of his experiences. He also revised a history he had written of the First Crusade. Ekkehard was a devout believer in the necessity of the Crusades, although he criticized the way some of the Crusaders behaved. The following document is excerpted from his writings.

After Pope Urban had aroused the spirits of all by the promise of forgiveness of sins to those who undertook the Crusade with single-hearted devotion, [about] one hundred thousand men were appointed to the immediate service of God from Aquitaine and Normandy, England, Scotland, Ireland, Brittany, Galicia, Gascony, France, Flanders, Lorraine, and from other Christian people, . . . It was truly an army of "Crusaders," for they bore the sign of the cross on their garments as a reminder that they should mortify the flesh, and in the hope that they would in this way triumph over the enemies of the cross of Christ. . . . [T]hus, through the marvelous . . . working of [God's will], all these [Christians], so different in speech, origin, and nationality, were suddenly brought together as one body through their love of Christ.

[T]he several peoples were led by their several leaders. . . . Over all of these Pope [Urban} placed Bishop Hademar, a man of venerable holiness and wisdom. To him the pope granted the right to exercise [power] in his stead. . . .

The West Franks were easily induced to leave their fields, since France had, during several years, been terribly visited now by civil war, now by famine, and again by sickness. . . . Among the other nations, the common people, as well as those of higher rank, related that, aside from the [pope's] summons, they had in some instances been called to the land of promise by certain prophets who had appeared among them, or through heavenly signs and revelations. Others confessed that they had been [persuaded] to pledge themselves by some misfortune. A great part of them started forth with wife and child and laden with their entire household equipment.

. . . [T]he signs in the sun and the wonders which appeared, both in the air and on earth, aroused many who had previously been indifferent. It seems to us useful to [include] an account of a few of these signs, although it would carry us too far to [tell] them all. For example, we beheld a comet on the 7th of October to the south, and its brilliancy slanting down seemed like a sword. . . . A few years ago a priest of honorable reputation, by the name of Suigger, about the ninth hour of the day beheld two knights, who met one another in the air and fought long, until one, who carried a great cross with which he struck the other, finally overcame his enemy. . . . Some who were watching horses in the fields reported that they had seen the image of a city in the air and had observed how various troops from different directions, both on horseback and on foot, were hastening [there].

Many, moreover, displayed, either on their clothing or upon their forehead, or elsewhere on their body, the sign of the cross, which had been divinely imprinted, and they believed themselves on this account to have been destined to the service of God. Others likewise were induced, through some sudden change of spirit or some [nighttime] . . . vision, to sell all their property and possessions and to sew the sign of [humility] on their [clothes]. . . . Among all these people who pressed into the churches in incredible numbers, swords were distributed with the priestly [blessing]. . . .

Review Questions

1. How were the Crusades one of the great movements of people in recorded history?
2. What motivated European Christians to leave their homes to join and fight in the Crusades?
3. How did Christianity act as a unifying force for the people of Western Europe?
4. How did a belief in signs and omens show that the European Middle Ages were truly an "age of faith"?

Anna Comnena Describes the Coming of the Crusaders

Between Europe and the Holy Land lay the Byzantine Empire. Its people were mainly Eastern Orthodox Christians with their own traditions that set them apart from the Roman Catholics of western Europe. In the late 11th and early 12th centuries, the Byzantine Emperor, Alexius I Comnenus (ruled 1081–1118), was trying to beat back the advance of the Turks from south and east. He also faced hostile Christians to the north and west. For help, he turned to Pope Urban II—who in response called for the Crusades. But Alexius got more than he bargained for. He quickly saw that the Crusaders might be as much a menace as the Turks. Indeed, a century later, in 1204, Crusaders captured and looted the Byzantine capital of Constantinople.

Emperor Alexis's daughter, Anna Comnena, wrote (in verse) a long history of his reign. The following document is from her history.

[Alexius] heard a report of the approach of [countless] Frankish armies. Now he dreaded their arrival for he knew their irresistible manner of attack, their unstable character, and all the peculiar natural characteristics which the Frank retains throughout. . . .

And indeed the actual facts were far greater and more terrible than rumor made them. For the whole of the West and all the barbarian tribes which dwell [from Italy to Spain] had all migrated in a body and were marching into Asia through the intervening Europe, and were making the journey with all their household. The reason of this upheaval was more or less the following:

A certain Frank, Peter by name [also called "Peter the Hermit"], had gone to worship at the Holy Sepulchre[1] and after suffering

[1]**Holy Sepulchre**—site in Jerusalem revered by Christians as Jesus's tomb

many things at the hands of the Turks and Saracens[2] who were [plundering] Asia, he got back to his own country with difficulty. But he was angry at having failed in his object, and wanted to undertake the same journey again. However, he saw that he ought not to make the journey to the Holy Sepulchre alone again, lest worse things befall him, so he worked out a cunning plan. This was to preach in all the Latin countries that "the voice of God bids me announce to all the Counts in France that they should all leave their homes and set out to worship at the Holy Sepulchre, and to [try] wholeheartedly with hand and mind to deliver Jerusalem from the hand of the [Muslims]." And he really succeeded. For after inspiring the souls of all with this [supposedly] divine command, he contrived to assemble the Franks from all sides, one after the other, with arms, horses, and all the other [equipment] of war. . . .

According to universal rumor, Godfrey[3] was the first to start on the appointed road; this man was very rich and very proud of his bravery, courage, and [ancestry], for every Frank is anxious to outdo the others. And such an upheaval of both men and women took place then as had never occurred within human memory. [T]he simpler-minded were urged on by the real desire of worshipping at our Lord's Sepulchre, and visiting the sacred places; but the [sharper ones] . . . had another secret reason, namely, the hope that while on their travels they might by some means be able to seize [Constantinople] itself. . . . Meanwhile, Peter, after he had delivered his message, [set out] . . . before anybody else with eighty thousand men on foot, and one hundred thousand on horseback, and reached [Constantinople] by way of Hungary. . . .

The emperor, knowing what Peter had suffered before from the Turks, advised him to wait for the arrival of the other Counts, but Peter would not listen, for he trusted to the multitude of his followers. So he crossed [the Bosporus into Asia Minor], and pitched his camp near a small town called Helenopolis. After him followed the Normans numbering ten thousand, who separated themselves from the rest of the army and devastated the country round Nicaea and

[2]**Saracens**—general term used for Muslims in Europe during the Middle Ages
[3]**Godfrey**—Godfrey of Bouillon, duke of Lower Lorraine in what is now eastern France; he sold two of his estates to raise money for the Crusades

behaved most cruelly to all. . . . But when the inhabitants of Nicaea became aware of these doings, they threw open their gates and marched out upon them, and after a violent conflict had taken place they had to dash back inside their citadel as the Normans fought so bravely. And thus the latter recovered all the booty and returned to Helenopolis.

Review Questions

1. Why did Emperor Alexius turn to Pope Urban II for help?
2. Why did Alexius fear the arrival of the Frankish armies?
3. What was the role of Peter the Hermit in promoting the Crusades in Europe?
4. Why did Anna Comnena describe Peter's mission as resulting from a "[supposedly] divine command"?
5. Why did the Byzantine emperor advise Peter to wait for the arrival of the other Crusader leaders?

13 A Crusader Writes to His Wife

One of the first parts of the Holy Land reached by the Crusaders was the Syrian city of Antioch (now part of Turkey). It had been under Byzantine Christian rule for almost 100 years until Turkish Muslims took it over in 1085. Late in 1097, Crusaders laid siege to it. Among those Crusaders was a nobleman named Stephen of Blois. (Blois is a city southwest of Paris.) Stephen was the son-in-law of William the Conqueror.

In the following document, Stephen writes to his wife back home. Soon after he wrote this letter, Stephen decided to leave the Crusade and return home. Crusaders eventually captured Antioch in June 1098 and Jerusalem in 1099. Antioch became one of four Christian-ruled territories in the Holy Land.

[Outside] Antioch, March 29, 1098

Count Stephen to Adele, his sweetest and most amiable wife, to his dear children, and to all his vassals of all ranks—his greetings and blessings.

You may be very sure, dearest, that the messenger whom I sent to you left me before Antioch safe and unharmed and, through God's grace, in the greatest prosperity. And already at that time, together with all the chosen army of Christ, endowed with great valor by Him, we had been continuously advancing for twenty-three weeks toward [Jerusalem]. You may know for certain, my beloved, that of gold, silver, and many other kinds of riches, I now have twice as much as you, my love, supposed me to have when I left you. For all our princes, with the common consent of the entire army, though against my own wishes, have made me, up to the present time, the leader, chief, and director of their whole expedition.

You have assuredly heard that after the capture of the city of Nicaea we fought a great battle with the [faithless] Turks and, by God's aid, conquered them. . .

The bolder of the Turkish soldiers, . . . entering Syria, hastened . . . to occupy the royal city of Antioch before our approach. . . .

Hastening with great joy to Antioch, we besieged it and had many conflicts there with the Turks. Seven times we fought, and in all these seven battles, by the aid of the Lord God, we conquered, and most assuredly killed an innumerable host of them. In those battles, indeed, and in very many attacks made upon the city, many of our followers were killed, and their souls were borne to the joys of paradise.

We found Antioch a very great town, fortified with incredible strength and almost [unconquerable]. In addition, more than five thousand bold Turkish soldiers had entered the city, not counting the Saracens, Publicans, Arabs, Turcopolitans, Syrians, Armenians, and other different races, of whom an infinite multitude had gathered together there. In fighting against these enemies of God and of our own we have, by God's permission, endured may sufferings and innumerable evils up to the present time. Many also have already exhausted all their resources. Very many of our Franks, indeed, would have met death from starvation, if the [mercy] of God and our money had not [helped] them. Moreover, before Antioch we suffered for our Lord Christ, throughout the whole winter, from excessive cold and enormous torrents of rain. What some say about the impossibility of bearing the heat of the sun throughout Syria is untrue, for the winter there is very similar to our winter in the west.

[F]ive [Turkish] amirs, with twelve thousand picked horsemen, suddenly came to aid the inhabitants of Antioch. We, ignorant of all this, had sent many of our soldiers away to the other cities and fortresses;—for there are one hundred and sixty-five cities and fortresses throughout Syria which are in our power. But a little before they reached the city we attacked them with seven hundred soldiers, on a certain plain, near the "Iron Bridge."

God fought for us, his faithful servants, against them; for on that day, fighting in the strength that God gives, we conquered them and killed an innumerable multitude, . . . and we also carried back to the army more than two hundred of their heads, in order that the people might rejoice on that account. The [Muslim] emperor of Babylon also sent Saracen messengers to our army with letters, and through these he established peace with us.

The Crusades continued on and off for over two centuries. At the peak of their success, the Crusaders controlled four territories in the eastern Mediterranean, including the cities of

Jerusalem and Antioch. Several later Crusades lacked good leadership and spiritual motives. And the Crusaders' success did not last. Muslim armies eventually retook the territories from the westerners. In the long run, however, Europe benefited from the Crusades. Europeans came into contact with a large, highly developed Muslim civilization, which was in many ways more advanced than theirs. New ideas, new ways of life, and new goods stimulated and enriched European society as it recovered from centuries of invasions and wars. Emerging economic powers, such as the Italian city-states of Genoa and Venice, grew rich from increased European trade in the Mediterranean. The writings of ancient Greek and Roman authors, which had been preserved in the Muslim world, helped lead to a revival of higher learning in Europe. The small world of the feudal manor and the farm were no longer all that Europeans knew. Now there were newly important ideas to study, places to visit, and people to meet.

Review Questions

1. What evidence does Stephen give in the second paragraph that his motives for going on the Crusade may not have been purely religious?
2. Describe Stephen's attitude toward his Turkish enemies.
3. a. What did Stephen believe happened to the souls of the Crusaders who died fighting the Muslims?
   b. What does this tell us about the nature of the wars fought between the Christians and the Muslims?
4. How does the diversity of the Muslim armies mentioned in this document compare with the diversity of the Crusader armies described in Document 11?
5. What does Stephen's descriptions of the battles against the Turks reveal about the deep religious faith of the Crusaders?
6. How did the Crusades help enrich European life and learning?

Write a well-organized essay that includes an introduction, several paragraphs, and a conclusion. Use evidence from at least ***four*** *documents in this unit in the body of the essay. Support your response with relevant facts, examples, and details. Include additional outside information.*

Historical Context

The clash between competing societies and belief systems has sometimes led to growth, sometimes to conflict, and sometimes to both conflict and growth.

Task: Using the documents and questions in the unit, and your knowledge of global history, select **three** different societies and write an essay in which you:

- Show how **each** society responded to the values and/or beliefs of other, competing societies
- Evaluate, using **one** example, the extent to which contact with a competing society or belief system resulted in conflict, growth, or both for the original society

Global Interactions

(1200–1650)

The Japanese Feudal Code

Japan's feudal period lasted from about 1000 to 1871. In many ways, Japanese feudalism was like European feudalism. As in Europe, high-ranking lords (called *daimyos* in Japan) granted feudal estates (called *fiefs*) to vassals who in return pledged loyalty to the lord and agreed to fight on his behalf. In Japan, such vassal warriors were called *samurai*. The samurai followed a strict code of honor called *Bushido*, or "The Way of the Warrior." This code demanded from the samurai honesty and kindness in everyday dealings, and simplicity of living. This document was written in 1232 to summarize the rules of Japanese feudalism at that time. Because it was drawn up on the orders of a shogun named Hojo, it is sometimes called the Hojo Code.

2. Care of religious buildings. (Buddhist) Temples and pagodas must be kept in repair and the Buddhist services diligently celebrated. Although (Buddhist) temples are different from (Shinto) shrines, both are alike as regards worship and [respect]. Therefore, the merit of maintaining them both in good order and the duty of keeping up the established services . . . is the same in both cases. Let no one bring trouble on himself through negligence [in this matter]. . . .

11. Whether in consequence of a husband's crime the estate of the wife is to be confiscated or not. In cases of serious crime, treason, murder and [crippling], also . . . piracy, night-attacks, robbery, and the like, the guilt of the husband extends to the wife also. In cases of murder and [crippling], cutting and wounding, arising out of a sudden dispute, however, she is not to be held responsible.

12. Of abusive language. Quarrels and murders have their origins in abusive and insulting language. In serious cases the offender shall be sent into banishment;[1] in minor cases, ordered

---

[1]**banishment**—sent out of the country

into confinement. If during the course of a judicial hearing one of the parties uses abusive or insulting language, the matter in dispute shall be decided in favor of the other party. If the other party however has not right on his side, some other fief [or property] of the offender shall be confiscated. If he has no fief, he shall be punished by being sent into banishment.

13. Of the offense of striking (or beating) a person. In such cases the person who receives the beating is sure to want to kill or seriously hurt the other in order to wipe out the insult; so the offense of beating a person is by no means a small one. Accordingly, if the offender be a samurai, his fief shall be confiscated; if he has no fief, he shall be [banished]; persons of lower rank, servants, pages and under, shall be placed in confinement.

41. Of slaves and unclassed persons. (In cases of dispute respecting the ownership of such persons), if more than ten years have elapsed without the former owner having asserted his claim, the possession of the present owner is not to be interfered with.

42. Of inflicting loss and ruin on runaway farmers under the pretext of punishing them. When people living in the provinces run away and escape, the lord of the fief and others, [declaring] that runaways must be [punished], detain their wives and children, and confiscate their property. Such a mode of procedure is quite the reverse of benevolent government. Henceforth, such cases must be referred to [the shogun's government at] Kamakura . . . , and if it is found that the farmer is behind in payment of his taxes, he shall be compelled to pay the amount he owes. If he is found not to be behind, the property seized from him shall be immediately restored to him. And it shall be entirely the choice of the farmer himself whether he shall continue to live in the fief or go elsewhere.

Review Questions

1. How did the Japanese feudal code regard the religions of Buddhism and Shintoism?
2. Under what circumstances was a wife held responsible for crimes committed by her husband?

3. How was property (fiefs) used to settle disputes?
4. How did Japanese feudal society regard slavery?
5. How did the Hojo Code change the way that feudal lords treated the farmers?
6. How were Japanese and European feudalism similar?

"Do Not Place Feet in the Direction of the Master"

Japanese people of all social classes were expected to obey certain rules of behavior or good manners. But the rules were much stricter for those of the samurai class and higher. Some of these rules are described in the following document, which is taken from a book of instructions for samurai.

The Ways of Loyalty and Filial Piety[1] are not limited to the warrior class alone. For the classes of farmers, artisans, and tradesmen as well, these two Ways are to be thoroughly followed in the relations between father and child, master and servant.

However, in the case of farmers, artisans, and tradesmen, manners and etiquette are secondary. For example, when a child or a servant is sitting together with a parent or master, it makes no difference even if he does all sorts of rude things like sitting cross-legged, having his hands in his pockets, or speaking without putting his hands on the floor. All is well as long as his mood is not rough, and his true intentions are in placing importance in the parent or master. This is the loyalty and filial piety of these three classes.

In Bushido, the Ways of Loyalty and Filial Piety cannot be completely fulfilled if etiquette is not kept thoroughly in form, no matter how much they are guarded in the heart. It is, for example, unacceptable for one who would follow the Way of the Warrior to act in a rude or negligent way in front of his parents, much less in front of his lord. The loyalty and filial piety of the warrior are in being [loyal] and not the least bit rude even in places where the master's and parents' eyes do not reach.

For example, no matter where one stops for the night and lays down to sleep, he should not place his feet in the direction of his lord even for a moment. Likewise, when hanging up [weapons] the cutting points should not face in the lord's direction.

---

[1]**filial piety**—a child's respect for its parents

Beyond this, when listening to or speaking about matters concerning one's lord, if lying down, one should sit up; if sitting up normally, one should straighten his posture. It is exactly such [behavior] that is said to be the true intention of the warrior. But to stretch one's feet out in the lord's direction while knowing well where he is, speaking about the lord while lying down, receiving a handwritten letter from one's parents without proper ceremony, reading such a letter while sitting cross-legged or lying down, throwing it into a corner or using it to clean a lantern: all these come from untrustworthy thoughts, and are not in the true mind of loyalty and filial piety of the warrior. A man with such a disposition does not know what duty is, and this because he has not drawn the distinction between himself and others. When meeting men from other places or clans, such a man will relate and explain the bad things about his own lord's dan [order, rank]. If a complete stranger simply acts in an intimate way toward him, he will happily and without reserve relate every one of the bad stories ridiculing his parents and [brothers and sisters], slandering everyone. Thus, sooner or later he will receive punishment from his lord or parents, will meet with some great disaster, or will meet a death belittling a warrior's name. Even if he does live, he will be reduced to a life-style without value, and at any rate will be unable to spend his life without incident. And this is reasonable.

Review Questions

1. How did the rules for the samurai class differ from those for farmers and tradespeople?
2. a. What types of actions by a samurai were considered disrespectful to his parents or his lord?
   b. Explain why one of these acts was considered disrespectful.
3. What were the consequences for the samurai who did not follow the ways of loyalty and respect toward his lord and his parents?

3 Chinese Feudalism: A "Golden Age"

Under the influence of Confucius, Chinese thinkers often looked on the distant past as a "golden age" while seeing the China of their own times as inferior. For many writers, the golden age was the era of Chinese feudalism, which died out around 200 B.C. after flourishing for hundreds of years.

Writers such as Ma Tuan-Lin, who lived in the 13th century A.D., praised the feudal era as a time when China's people had more equal shares of land than in later centuries. Under feudalism, a lord's fief was divided up among peasant families according to the "well-field system." This system got its name from the Chinese symbol for "well." The symbol looked something like a tic-tac-toe grid. Imagine a square plot of land divided into nine equal parts. The eight parts around the outside were farmed by the peasant families for themselves. All eight families worked together on the ninth plot, in the center, with the proceeds going to the lord. As in Europe, the peasants were serfs who were bound to the land and could not move away.

After the feudal system ended, China came under more centralized rule. Emperors had more power than before. People began to buy and sell land privately, and wealthy people built up large estates. Peasants had little if any land on which to grow food for themselves. They were at the mercy of large landowners, upon whom they depended for work.

The following document is from the introduction to a book by Ma that gave a detailed history of Chinese government and society.

The rulers of ancient times did not regard [China's territory] as their own private possession. Therefore, the land of the Son of Heaven [emperor] was a thousand li[1] square, while that of the dukes and marquises was a hundred li square. Earls held seventy li, barons

[1]**li**—1 li = 500 meters or half a kilometer or 0.311 miles; thus, 1,000 li = 311 miles

fifty li, and within the area of the emperor's territory the high ministers and officials were granted lands and villages from which they received [income]. . . . Each of these held possession of his own land, regarded its inhabitants as his personal [responsibilities], and passed it down to his sons and grandsons to possess. He regarded questions of the fertility of the land and the abundance or want of the peasants as of immediate concern to his own family. He took the trouble to examine and supervise things himself so that there was no room for evildoing or deception. Thus at this time all land was under the [authority] of the officials, and the people provided support for the officials. The peasants who received land from the officials lived by their own labor and paid tribute. In their work of supporting their parents and providing for their wives and families they were all treated with equal kindness so that there were no people who were excessively rich nor any who were excessively poor. This was the system of the Three Dynasties.[2]

The rulers of the Ch'in[3] were the first to consider all land as their possession and to exercise all power by themselves. The men who filled the posts of district magistrates [or judges] were shifted about frequently so that they came to regard the land of the district where they were stationed as no more than a temporary lodging. Thus no matter how worthy or wise a magistrate might be, it was impossible for him to know fully the true situation in the villages and hamlets he was supervising. The appointments and terms of office of these local magistrates were subject to time limitations, while evil and [dishonest] practices in connection with the transfer and holding of land multiplied endlessly. Thus from the time of Ch'in and Han[4] on, government officials no longer had the power to grant land, and as a natural result all land came eventually to be the private possession of the common people. Although there were intervals . . . when some effort was made to return to the system of the Three Dynasties, it was not long before [such] . . . reforms became ineffective. This was because without a revival of feudalism it was impossible to restore the well-field system. . . .

[2]**Three Dynasties**—Hsia, Shang, and Western Chou dynasties, 1818–722 B.C.
[3]**Ch'in**—dynasty that ruled 221–207 B.C.
[4]**Han**—dynasty that followed the Ch'in in 202 B.C.

[It has been so long since the time of feudalism] that it would be exceedingly difficult to return to the old ways. If one were to try to revive feudalism, it would mean dividing and parceling out all the land again, and this would be the signal for confusion and strife. If one attempted to restore the well-field system, it would only invite resentment and bitterness. This is why the theories of scholars who recommend such a revival cannot be put into practice.

Review Questions

1. What was the "well-field system"?
2. According to Ma Taun-Lin, how did the well-field system help to maintain an orderly Chinese society?
3. What caused the end of the well-field system?
4. Why did Ma Taun-Lin feel that it would be impossible to restore feudalism and the well-field system to China?

A Muslim Traveler Observes Hindu Customs

Ibn Battuta (1304–1368) was born in Morocco, on the northwest corner of Africa. He began to travel at an early age and spent most of his life on the move. As a devout Muslim, he first made a pilgrimage to Mecca. He went on to visit almost all the Muslim-ruled countries of the world—and others besides. His travels took him as far as China in Asia, as well as to sub-Saharan Africa and parts of Europe. Near the end of his life he returned to Morocco and wrote about his experiences in a book that became a key source of information about this period in history.

Because he was trained in religious and scientific matters, Ibn Battuta gained a high reputation. Sultans and emperors welcomed his arrival. They often granted him high honors and appointments to public office. Ibn Battuta traveled with many companions, including several wives and concubines. He was a keen observer of people and customs, and showed considerable tolerance for people whose ways differed from his own.

In the following excerpt, he describes experiences in northern India, where he arrived about 1333. At the time a Muslim sultan ruled much of India from his capital in Delhi. The custom Ibn Battuta describes—of widows voluntarily being burned with their husband's bodies—is called *suttee.* Muslim rulers later banned the practice, although it continued in parts of India into the mid-1800s.

As I returned to the camp after visiting [a local leader] . . . , I saw the people hurrying out, and some of our party along with them. I asked them what was happening and they told me that one of the Hindu infidels[1] had died, that a fire had been kindled to burn him, and his wife would burn herself along with him. After the burning,

[1]**infidels**—people who are "outside the faith"; for Ibn Battuta, non-Muslims

my companions came back and told me that she had embraced the dead man until she herself was burned with him. Later on I used often to see a Hindu woman, richly dressed, riding on horseback, followed by both Muslims and infidels and preceded by drums and trumpets; she was accompanied by Brahmans, who are the chiefs of the Hindus. In the sultan's [lands] they ask his permission to burn her, which he [grants] them. The burning of the wife after her husband's death is regarded by them as a [praiseworthy] act, but is not compulsory; only when a widow burns herself her family acquire a certain prestige by it and gain a reputation for fidelity. A widow who does not burn herself dresses in coarse garments and lives with her own people in misery, despised for her lack of fidelity, but she is not forced to burn herself.

Once . . . I saw three women whose husbands had been killed in battle and who had agreed to burn themselves. Each one had a horse brought to her and mounted it, richly dressed and perfumed. In her right hand she held a coconut, with which she played, and in her left a mirror, in which she looked at her face. They were surrounded by Brahmans and their own relatives, and were preceded by drums, trumpets, and bugles. Every one of the infidels said to them, "Take greetings from me to my father, or brother or mother, or friend," and they would say, "Yes," and smile at them. I rode out with my companions to see the way in which the burning was carried out. After three miles we came to a dark place with much water and shady trees, among which there were four pavilions [large tents]. . . .

On reaching these pavilions the [women] descended to the pool, plunged into it and [took off] . . . their clothes and ornaments, which they distributed as [gifts to the poor]. Each one was then given an unsewn garment of coarse cotton and tied part of it round her waist and part over her head and shoulders. The fires had been lit near this basin in a low-lying spot, and oil of sesame poured over them so that the flames were increased. . . . The fire was screened off by a blanket held by some men, so that she should not be frightened by the sight of it.

I saw one of them, on coming to the blanket, pull it violently out of the men's hands, saying to them with a smile, "Do you frighten me with the fire? I know that it is a fire, so let me alone." Thereupon she joined her hands above her head in salutation to the fire and cast herself into it. . . . When I saw this I had all but fallen off my horse, if my companions had not quickly brought water to me and [bathed] my face, after which I withdrew.

Review Questions

1. What was suttee?
2. Why did many Hindu widows voluntarily choose suttee?
3. How did Ibn Battuta feel about the practice of suttee?

Europeans Encounter Japanese Eating Habits

The first Europeans to visit Japan were Portuguese traders who arrived in 1542. Soon after came Dutch traders and Roman Catholic missionaries—first Jesuits and later Franciscans.

Europeans and Japanese marveled at each other's strange ways. For example, each group found the other's eating habits to be a source of amazement. The first document is by Alessandro Valignano, an Italian Jesuit. He visited Japan three times between 1579 and 1603.

A. Japanese Food

Their clothes and food are so peculiar that it is impossible to describe them adequately, for although their way of dressing is very neat and clean, in no way does it resemble ours. Even less can one imagine what their food and drink is like and how it is served, for they observe much cleanliness and solemnity at table and are quite unlike us. Each person has his own table, but there are no tablecloths, napkins, knives, forks or spoons. All they have are two small sticks, called hashi, which they manipulate with such cleanliness and skill that they do not touch any of the food with their hands nor let even a crumb fall from their plate on to the table. They eat with such modesty and good manners that they observe just as many rules at table as they do in other things. In addition to rice-wine (which they like very much, although we find it disagreeable), they always drink hot water at the end of every meal, both in summer and winter; the water is so hot, in fact, that it can only be drunk in sips. Their victuals and ways of cooking them are such that they are quite unlike European food, both in substance and taste. Until a man accustoms himself to their food, he is bound to experience much hardship and difficulty.

The second document is by a Portuguese trader named Fernão Mendes Pinto. He reached Japan in the 1540s. After returning to Portugal in 1558, he wrote a book about his adventures. In this excerpt, he describes a meal he and his companions had at the court of a Japanese lord, or *daimyo* (whom he calls a "king").

This translation was done in 1663, which accounts for some of its odd spellings and punctuation.

B. European Table Manners

Then having caused a table to be covered for us, and on it placed store of good meat, . . . [nicely prepared], which was served us by very fair women; we fell to eating after our own manner, of all that was set before us, [while] the [jokes] which the Ladies [made about us] in seeing us feed so with our hands, gave more delight to the King and Queen, than all the Comedies that could have been presented before them: for those people being accustomed to feed with two little sticks, as I have declared elsewhere, they hold it for a great incivilitie [bad manners], to touch the meat with ones hand, as we use to do. Hereupon the Kings Daughter, a marvellous fair Princesse, and not above fourteen or fifteen years of age, [asked] leave of the Queen her Mother, that she and six or seven of her companions might present a certain Play before them concerning the subject in question [that is, the bad table manners of the Europeans]; which the Queen with the Kings assent granted her. That done, they withdrew into another room, where they stayed a pretty while, during the which, they that remained in the place, [passed the time] at our cost, by jeering and gibing at us, who were much ashamed, especially my four companions, which were but [newcomers] in the Country, and understood not the language. . . . [At length,] we saw the young Princesse come out of the other room disguised like a Merchant, wearing a [curved knife] by her side, covered all over with plates of gold; and the rest of her [clothing] answerable to the person [a "typical" European] which she represented.

Review Questions

A. Japanese Food

1. How did the Japanese eat their food?
2. How was the way Europeans ate their food different from that of the Japanese?
3. Why did the Europeans have difficulty eating Japanese meals?

B. European Table Manners

1. How did the Japanese princess respond to the Europeans' manner of eating?
2. a. What does the princess' mocking laughter and "disguise" tell us about the Japanese nobility's opinion of Europeans?
   b. Do you think this opinion was justified? Explain.

6 The Japanese See Their First Firearms

Although the Chinese invented explosive powder in the 9th century, its use spread very slowly. The Chinese used this "black powder" in fireworks and perhaps in cannons and other weapons. Then they seem to have abandoned its use. Not until the 13th century did Europeans learn how to make it, either from Mongols or Arabs who had been in China. Europeans adapted black powder for use in warfare—in cannons, mortars, and small arms such as harquebuses. The harquebus (pronounced "HAR-kuh-buss") was a gun with a long barrel and a mechanical firing mechanism. It was an early version of the musket.

Before firearms reached Japan, the chief weapons of war were swords, spears, knives, and bows and arrows. Samurai often fought one-on-one, although mass battles by foot soldiers were also common. Then in 1543, a Chinese vessel was shipwrecked on one of Japan's many islands. Among its occupants were three Portuguese traders, who had a harquebus. The Portuguese amazed their Japanese rescuers with a demonstration of the gun's operation. Before long, every Japanese daimyo wanted harquebuses for his soldiers. First used in battle in 1549, harquebuses brought about a revolution in Japanese warfare. They increased the firepower of the strongest daimyos, who seized many small territories. This resulted in a greater centralization of power under a few daimyos.

In our document, a Japanese observer of 1543 describes his reaction to the new weapons.

There were two chiefs among the [Portuguese] merchants, . . . In their hands they carried an object two or three feet long, straight on the outside with an inside tube, and made with some kind of heavy material. The inner tube ran the whole length of it, but was closed at one end. On one side there was a hole, which was the opening for firing. I have never seen anything remotely like it in shape. To use it, fill it with powder and little balls of lead, fix a small white target on to a [barrel], stand firm and closing one eye, apply the fire to the hole. Then the bullet hits the target right in the middle. The explosion is like lightning and the report like thunder. The onlookers have to stop their ears. . . . [The daimyo] Tokitaka was so interested in this weapon that he asked several smiths to inspect and study it for some months to enable them to make some. Outwardly, the result of their experiments looked like the foreign weapon, but the smiths did not know how to seal the inner tube. Foreign merchants came again the following year to the Bay of Kumano, one of our islands. Fortunately, one of them was a smith whom Tokitaka regarded as a messenger from the gods. He ordered the commanding-officer, Kimbei Kiyosada, to learn from this smith how to seal the end of the gun. He learned that there was a spring in the gun, and this discovery led to the production of several dozen firearms (*teppô*) in little more than a year. Then all his vassals from far and near trained with the new weapons and soon, out of every hundred shots they fired, many of them could hit the target as many times. Later on, a man called Tachibana-ya Matasaburô, a merchant who stayed in our island for a year or two, learnt the art of making firearms. He became skillful at it and, on his return home, everyone called him, not by his real name, but Teppômata. Soon the provinces of the inner circuit mastered this art, and very quickly . . . the western and the eastern provinces learned it too.

Review Questions

1. How did the Japanese react when introduced to a European gun?
2. What did the Japanese lord Tokitaka ask his smiths to do?
3. Why did the Japanese smiths have trouble copying a gun?
4. How did the introduction of firearms change Japan?

7 The Magna Carta

In Europe, the feudal system underwent changes as time went on. Kings became more powerful. Lesser lords lost some of their powers and privileges. But kings too sometimes had to accept limits on their power.

In England, a "revolt of the barons" that began in 1214 succeeded in placing limits on what a king could do. The barons forced King John to agree to a document later called the Magna Carta, or "Great Charter." This charter guaranteed the rights of English nobles and placed both the king and the nobles under the rule of law. While the Magna Carta applied mainly to England's nobles, it marked an important milestone in the development of English freedoms. Later, some of the rights that applied originally to nobles were extended to all English people. Eventually, they became a basic part of the justice system in the United States.

The first document tells of events that led up to the signing of the Magna Carta. After taking the throne in 1199, King John had imposed heavy taxes and other fees on the nobles in order to pay for a series of foreign wars. His actions became so burdensome that his nobles rebelled.

A. The Barons Rebel

About this time [November 1214] the earls and barons of England assembled at St. Edmunds, as if for religious duties, although it was for another reason; for after they had [talked] together secretly for a time, there was placed before them the charter of King Henry the First [ruled 1100–1135]. . . . This charter contained certain liberties [rights] and laws granted to the holy Church as well as to the nobles of the kingdom, besides some liberties which the king added of his own accord. All therefore assembled in the church of St. Edmund, . . . and, commencing with those of the highest rank, they all swore on the great altar that, if the king refused to grant these liberties and laws, they themselves would withdraw from their allegiance to him, and make war on him until he should, by a charter under his own seal, confirm to them everything that they required. And finally it was unanimously agreed that, after Christmas, they should all go together to the king and demand the confirmation of the [previously mentioned] liberties to them, and that they should in the meantime provide themselves with horses and arms, so that if the king should endeavor to depart from his oath they might, by taking his castles, compel him to satisfy their demands; and having arranged this, each man returned home. . . .

In Easter week of [1215] . . . , the above-mentioned nobles assembled at Stamford, with horses and arms. They had now [persuaded] almost all the nobility of the whole kingdom to join them, and constituted a very large army; for in their army there were computed to be two thousand knights, besides horse-soldiers, attendants, and foot-soldiers, who were variously equipped. . . . The king . . . sent the archbishop of Canterbury and William Marshal, earl of Pembroke, with some other prudent men, to them to inquire what the laws and liberties were which they demanded. . . . The king, when he heard, said [scornfully], with the greatest indignation, "Why, among these unjust demands, did not the barons ask for my kingdom also? Their demands are vain and visionary, and are unsupported by any plea of reason whatever." And at length he angrily declared with an oath that he would never grant them such liberties as would render him their slave. . . .

[W]hen the nobles heard what John said, they appointed Robert Fitz-Walter commander of their soldiers, giving him the title of "Marshal of the Army of God and the Holy Church." . . .

> [After unsuccessfully laying siege to a castle at Northampton, in central England, the barons' army headed for London.]

[T]hey marched the whole night and arrived early in the morning at the city of London, and, finding the gates open, on the 24th of May [a Sunday] . . . they entered the city without any tumult while the inhabitants were [at church] . . . ; for the rich citizens were favorable to the barons, and the poor ones were afraid to murmur against them. The barons, having thus got into the city, placed their own guards in charge of each of the gates, and then arranged all matters in the city at will. They then . . . sent letters through England to those earls, barons, and knights who appeared to be still faithful to the king (though they only pretended to be so) and advised them with threats . . . to abandon [the king]. . . . The greatest part of these, on receiving the message of the barons, set out to London and joined them, abandoning the king entirely. . . .

King John, when he saw that he was deserted by almost all, so that . . . he retained scarcely seven knights, was much alarmed lest the barons should attack his castles and [conquer] them without difficulty, as they would find no obstacle in their so doing. . . . He sent . . . a request to the barons . . . that they appoint a suitable day and place to meet. . . . They in their great joy appointed the fifteenth of June for the king to meet them, at a field lying between Staines and Windsor. Accordingly, at the time and place agreed upon the king and nobles came to the appointed conference, and when each party had stationed itself some distance from the other, they began a long discussion about terms of peace and the aforesaid liberties. . . . At length, after various points on both sides had been discussed, King John, seeing that he was inferior in strength to the barons, without raising any difficulty, granted the [following] . . . laws and liberties.

The document to which King John attached his seal (he did not actually sign) was in part a restatement of rights granted by previous kings. Much of it concerns aspects of feudal law that have no relevance to modern life. But the Magna Carta quickly became a symbol of English freedoms. In later centuries, people who sought greater freedoms for themselves looked back to its main ideas for inspiration.

B. The Magna Carta ("The Great Charter")

What It Says	What It Means
John, by the grace of God, king of England, lord of Ireland, duke of Normandy, Aquitaine, and count of	*John's promises will be binding on his successors (his heirs).*

Anjou, to his . . . faithful subjects, greeting. Know ye, that we, in the presence of God, and for the salvation of our soul, and the souls of all our ancestors and heirs, and unto the honor of God and the advancement of Holy Church, . . . have, in the first place, granted to God, and by this our present Charter confirmed, for us and our heirs forever:

1. That the Church of England shall be free, and have her whole rights, and her liberties inviolable. . . .

John gives extensive rights to the Church of England. In the rest of this article, John repeats a promise he had made to let the church choose its own bishops.

2. We also have granted to all the freemen of our kingdom, for us and our heirs forever, all the [following] liberties, to be [held] by them and their heirs, of us and our heirs forever. If any of our earls, or barons, or others who hold of us in chief[1] by military service, shall die, and at the time of his death his heir shall be of full age, and owe a relief, he shall have his inheritance by the ancient relief—that is to say, the heir or heirs of an earl, for a whole earldom, by a hundred pounds; the heir or heirs of a knight, for a whole knight's fee, by a hundred shillings at most; and whoever oweth less shall give less, according to the ancient custom of fees. . . .

This article applies only to freemen—not to serfs. It limits the reliefs (inheritance taxes) that earls, barons, and others who are direct vassals of the king can be forced to pay to the king. John had charged vastly higher amounts than his predecessors in order to finance expensive foreign wars.

12. No scutage or aid shall be imposed in our kingdom, unless by the general council of our king-

This article restricts the king's right to charge scutage *(a payment made in place of military service) or* aid *(a*

[1]**hold of us in chief**—hold fiefs directly from us

dom; except for ransoming our person, making our eldest son a knight, and once for marrying our eldest daughter; and for these there shall be paid no more than a reasonable aid. In like manner it shall be concerning the aids of the City of London. . . .

special fee or tax). Only in the three circumstances named can the king impose these charges. At all other times, the general council (a feudal body made up of lords who were the king's direct vassals) would have to approve.

14. And for holding the general council of the kingdom concerning the assessment of aids, except in the three cases aforesaid, and for the assessing of scutage, we shall cause to be summoned the archbishop, bishops, abbots, earls, and greater barons of the realm, singly by our letters. And furthermore, we shall cause to be summoned generally, by our sheriffs and bailiffs, all others who hold of us in chief, for a certain day, that is to say, forty days before their meeting at least, and to a certain place. And in all letters of such summons we will declare the cause of such summons. And summons being thus made, the business shall proceed on the day appointed, according to the advice of such as shall be present, although all that were summoned come not.

The general council included greater lords and clergy (as named) and lesser lords (others who held fiefs directly from the king). They were to receive due notice of coming meetings. There was no quorum *(minimum number of people in attendance) required.*

15. We will not in the future grant to any one that he may take aid of his own free tenants, except to ransom his body, and to make his eldest son a knight, and once to marry his eldest daughter; and for this there shall be paid only a reasonable aid. . . .

The same rules about special taxes that applied to the king applied to other lords. They too were restricted in the amounts of fees they could charge their free tenants.

36. Nothing from henceforth shall be given or taken for a writ of inquisition of life or limb, but it shall be granted freely, and not denied. . . .

A writ of inquisition *was a document that required a public official to conduct an investigation. Someone who was in prison awaiting trial for murder, for example, might seek such a writ to speed up the legal process or to be allowed free on bail. This provision stopped King John's practice of charging high fees to people who wanted such writs.*

39. No freeman shall be taken or imprisoned, . . . or outlawed, or banished, or in any way destroyed, nor will we [use force against]. . . him, unless by the lawful judgment of his peers, or by the law of the land.

This article hints at the later right of trial by jury—a jury of one's peers (people of equal rank). In feudal times, a baron's peers were other barons. All this article did was to assure nobles that they would be tried by other nobles.

40. We will sell to no man, we will not deny to any man, either justice or right.

This article means that people would not have to pay bribes to obtain justice in the courts.

41. All merchants shall have safe and secure conduct to go out of, and to come into, England, and to stay there and to pass as well by land as by water, for buying and selling by the ancient and allowed customs, without any unjust tolls, except in time of war, or when they are of any nation at war with us. . . .

This provision marked a step toward freer commerce and trade. However, it did not prevent cities from charging their own fees or tolls.

42. It shall be lawful, for the time to come, for any one to go out of our kingdom and return safely and securely by land or by water, saving his allegiance to us (unless in time of war, by some short space, for the common benefit of the realm), except prisoners and outlaws, according to the law of the land, and people in war with us. . . .

Anyone who was loyal to the king would be allowed to leave or enter England. This right could only be suspended in time of war, and then for a limited period. Later, in 1382, this right was restricted to lords, merchants, and soldiers.

60. All the aforesaid customs and liberties, which we have granted to be holden in our kingdom, as much as it belongs to us, all people of our kingdom, as well clergy as laity, shall observe, as far as they are concerned, toward their dependents.

The same rules that applied to the king would apply to the barons, clergy, and others who had feudal rights over people under them.

61. . . . Willing to render [all these pledges] . . . firm and lasting, we do give and grant our subjects the [following] . . . , namely, that the barons may choose five and twenty barons of the kingdom, whom they think convenient, who shall take care, with all their might, to hold and observe, and cause to be observed, the peace and liberties we have granted them. . . .

This article sets up a commission of 25 barons to make sure the king keeps his word.

63. . . . It is also sworn, as well on our part as on the part of the barons, that all the things aforesaid shall be observed in good faith, and without evil duplicity. Given under our hand, in the presence of the witnesses above named, and many others, in the meadow called Runnymede, between Windsor and Staines, the 15th day of June, in the 17th year of our reign.

In effect, the king and the barons said: "We mean what we say. Really."

Review Questions

A. The Barons Rebel

1. What did the barons demand of King John?
2 a. How did King John react to the barons' demands?
  b. Why did the king react in this manner?
3. How were the barons able to force King John to agree to their demands?

B. The Magna Carta (Great Charter)

1. What effect did signing the Magna Carta have on the king's powers?
2. Explain three ways in which the Magna Carta affected the king's powers.
3. How did the Magna Carta benefit all English freemen?

Thomas Aquinas on Human Law

The 13th century was a time of intellectual excitement and discovery in Europe. At the new universities, such as the one founded in Paris in the previous century, thinkers debated such matters as the relation between God and nature, or between religion and science.

One of the most influential thinkers of the time was Italian-born Thomas Aquinas (1224–1274). He joined the Dominican order of monks and taught at the University of Paris. Aquinas's lectures and writings sought to bring together two ways of thinking—one based on faith, or religion, the other on reason, or science. Aquinas argued that the truth of the Church teachings did not depend on reason. At the same time, he said that reason (or what would later be called scientific inquiry) should be used to learn about the natural world. Faith and reason could coexist, he believed, as people sought a deeper understanding of the world about them.

Aquinas's ideas became a central part of Catholic teachings. Half a century after Aquinas's death in 1274, the Roman Catholic Church declared him a saint—Saint Thomas.

The following passage is from Aquinas's most famous work, *Summa theologiae,* or *Compendium of Theology*. (Theology is the study of God and of religious theory.) In the passage, Aquinas distinguishes between God's law and human law, and discusses whether laws can ever be changed or broken. Aquinas treated topics very precisely. He broke them down into distinct parts and then commented on those parts.

Whether human law binds a man's conscience. Human laws are either just or unjust. If they are just, they have the power to bind our conscience because of the eternal law from which they are derived. As Proverbs says, "Through me kings reign and lawmakers decree just laws" (*Proverbs 8:15*).

Laws are said to be just either because of their end [goal], when they are [dedicated] to the common good; or because of their author, when the law does not exceed the power of the lawmaker; or because of their form, when burdens are distributed [fairly] among subjects for the common good. . . .

Laws are unjust in two ways: First, they may be such because they oppose human good by denying the three [points] just mentioned. This can occur because of their [goal], when a ruler imposes burdens with an eye, not to the common good, but to his own enrichment or glory; because of their author, when someone imposes laws beyond the scope of his authority; or because of their form, when burdens are [unfairly] distributed, even if they are [intended for] . . . the common good.

Second, laws may be unjust because they are opposed to the divine good, as when the laws of tyrants lead men to idolatry[1] or to something else contrary to divine law. Such laws must never be observed, because "one must obey God rather than men" (*Acts 5:29*).

Whether someone subject to the law can act outside the letter of the law. All law is [designed to bring about] the common well-being of men and gains the force of law from precisely that fact. To the degree that it fails in accomplishing this end, it loses its binding force. . . .

It often happens that a law aimed at the general welfare is useful in most cases and yet on occasion is very harmful. Because a legislator cannot foresee all possible individual cases, he [makes] . . . a law which fits the majority of cases, having the common good in mind. If a case emerges in which the law is harmful to the common good, it should not be observed. For example, if a law says that the gates of a certain besieged city should remain closed, such a law is beneficial to the city in most cases. Yet if the enemy is pursuing some of the very citizens by whom the city is defended, refusal to open the gates and let them in would be harmful to the city. In such cases, the gates should be opened despite the letter of the law, in order to attain the common good intended by the legislator.

Note, though, that if obedience to the letter of the law involves no immediate danger calling for instant remedy, not everyone is competent to decide what is good or bad for the city, but only the leaders, who have authority to [reverse] the law in such cases. If it is

---

[1]**idolatry**—worship of physical objects as gods

indeed a matter of immediate danger, allowing no time to consult a superior, such necessity carries its own [approval], for necessity knows no law.

Whether human law should be changed in any way. Human law is a [ruling principle] of reason by which human actions are directed. Thus change in law has a twofold source: One on the part of reason, the other on the part of the men whose actions are regulated by law.

On the part of reason, [law] can be changed because it seems natural for human reason to advance gradually from the imperfect to the perfect. Thus we see in the [theoretical] sciences that the early philosophers produced imperfect teachings which were later improved by their successors. So also in the practical realm, those who first tried to discover what was beneficial for human community, being unable to think everything through by themselves, created imperfect situations which were lacking in many ways. These institutions were then altered by subsequent lawmakers, producing institutions which departed from the common good in fewer instances.

On the part of the men whose activities are regulated by law, a law is rightly changed when there is a change in the conditions of men, for different things are [suitable] to different conditions. Augustine[2] offers the following example: "If the people are moderate, responsible, and careful guardians of the common good, it is proper to enact a law allowing them to choose [leaders] through whom the commonwealth can be administered. If, however, in time the people become corrupted and sell their votes, entrusting the government to scoundrels and criminals, they [lose] their power to elect public officials and the right [passes to] a few good men."

Whether human law should always be changed when something better is possible. It is right to change human law if such a change is [helpful] to the common good. Nevertheless, the very act of changing a law damages the common good to some extent, because custom encourages people to observe the law. . . . Thus when a law is changed its binding force is [weakened because] . . . custom is [overthrown]. For this reason, human law should never be changed unless the

[2]**Augustine**—early Catholic theologian and church father (A.D. 354–430)

advantage to the common good resulting from its alteration outweighs the damage done by the change itself.

Such may be the case if some great and evident benefit is derived from the new law, or if some extreme emergency [results from] . . . the fact that the existing law is clearly unjust or its observance extremely harmful. . . .

Review Questions

1. How did Aquinas determine whether a law was just or unjust?
2. Under what circumstances did Aquinas feel that a law might be broken?
3. a. What did Aquinas mean when he wrote "necessity knows no law"?
   b. Under what circumstances might this rule apply?
4. When did Aquinas feel that a law should be changed?
5. Why did Aquinas feel that rulers should avoid making frequent changes in the laws?

Dante's Vision of Hell

One of the most famous literary works of western civilization is *The Divine Comedy.* It is a book-length epic poem on religious and historical themes that was written early in the 14th century by the Italian poet Dante Alighieri. The poem is also an allegory—that is, it uses fictional happenings to stand for general truths about the world. Dante, a Roman Catholic, based his work on Catholic doctrines about life and afterlife. He aims to persuade his readers to reform themselves and Italian society, which he considered to be sinful and corrupt.

The Divine Comedy describes Dante's imagined trip through three regions lying beyond the grave—hell, purgatory, and paradise. (In Roman Catholic doctrine, purgatory is where most souls go immediately after the person's death. There they can purge themselves of sin and prepare to enter heaven.) Dante has two ghostly guides—first, the classical Roman poet Virgil; second, a woman named Beatrice, who represented for Dante the ideal of spiritual love and goodness.

Dante was a native of Florence in north central Italy. Unlike most major European poets and scholars of the Middle Ages before him, Dante did not write in Latin. Rather, he wrote in the local language or *vernacular*, of his native land, which for him was Florentine Italian. Similarly, later writers, such as Geoffrey Chaucer in England, wrote in the languages spoken at the time.

Our excerpt is from the early part of the poem, in which Dante enters hell. The narrator depicts the terrors he believed awaited the souls of sinners and slackers. The excerpt opens with an inscription over the gateway of hell.

Through me the way into the suffering city,
Through me the way to the eternal pain,
Through me the way that runs among the lost.

Justice urged on my high artificer; [1]
my maker was divine authority,
The highest wisdom, and the primal[2] love.
Before me nothing but eternal things
were made, and I endure eternally.
Abandon every hope, who enter here.

These words—their [appearance] was obscure—I read
inscribed above a gateway, and I said:
"Master, their meaning is difficult for me."
And he to me, as one who comprehends:
"Here one must leave behind all hesitation;
here every cowardice must meet its death.
For we have reached the place of which I spoke,
where you will see the miserable people,
those who have lost the good of the intellect."
And when, with gladness in his face, he placed
his hand upon my own, to comfort me,
he drew me in among the hidden things.

Here sighs and lamentations and loud cries
were echoing across the starless air,
so that, as soon as I set out, I wept.
Strange utterances, horrible pronouncements,
accents of anger, words of suffering,
and voices shrill and faint, and beating hands—
all went to make a tumult that will whirl
forever through that [thick] timeless air,
like sand that eddies when a whirlwind swirls.

And I—my head oppressed by horror—said:
"Master, what is it that I hear? Who are
those people so defeated by their pain?"
And he to me: "This miserable way
is taken by the sorry souls of those
who lived without disgrace and without praise.

---

[1]**artificer**—creator
[2]**primal**—original

They now commingle [mix] with the coward angels,
the company of those who were not rebels
nor faithful to their God, but stood apart.
The heavens, that their beauty not be lessened,
have cast them out, nor will deep Hell receive them—
even the wicked cannot glory in them."
And I: "What is it, master, that oppresses
these souls, compelling them to wail so loud?"
He answered: "I shall tell you in few words.
Those who are here can place no hope in death,
and their blind life is so [spiritless] that they
are envious of every other fate.
The world will let no fame of theirs endure;
both justice and compassion must disdain them;
let us not talk of them, but look and pass."

Dante goes on to describe in great detail the inhabitants of hell and the punishments they receive. His depiction of hell still has dramatic force today.

Review Questions

1. According to Dante, who was condemned to the first part of hell?
2. a. How did the souls occupying the first part of hell act?
   b. Why do you think these souls acted in the manner Dante described?
3. What do you think Dante meant by the following lines?
   a. "Abandon every hope, who enter here."
   b. "This miserable way is taken by the sorry souls of those who lived without disgrace and without praise."
4. What do you think Dante's purpose was when he wrote about the first part of hell?
5. How does the poem show the religious beliefs of Dante's time?

10 The Black Death

Beginning in 1347, a devastating disease swept through Europe. The disease, bubonic plague, or the Black Death, was carried by fleas living on rats. Flea bites quickly spread the disease to humans. The manner in which the disease spread was unknown at the time, and many people blamed it on witchcraft. Millions died of the plague, for which there was no known cure.

The following document is an excerpt from Giovanni Boccaccio's book *The Decameron*. Boccaccio, an Italian writer, was 34 years old when the plague reached Europe. His book tells a series of stories–some comic, some tragic–supposedly told by a group of men and women who had gone to the countryside to escape the Black Death in the city of Florence. This excerpt is from Boccaccio's opening pages. Boccaccio wrote in his native Italian.

[I]n men and women alike [bubonic plague] first betrayed itself by the emergence of certain tumors in the groin or the armpits, some of which grew as large as a common apple, others as an egg, some more, some less. . . . From the two said parts of the body this deadly [tumor] . . . soon began to . . . spread itself in all directions . . . ; after which the form of the [sickness] began to change, black spots . . . making their appearance in many cases on the arm or the thigh or elsewhere, now few and large, now [tiny] and numerous. And as the [tumor] . . . had been and still was [a sure sign] of approaching death, such also were these spots on whomsoever they showed themselves. . . . [Doctors could do nothing against the disease.] [I]ndeed, whether it was of a nature to defy such treatment, or that the physicians were at fault—besides the qualified [doctors] there was now a multitude both of men and of women who practiced without having received the slightest [trace] of medical science—and, being in ignorance of its source, failed to apply the proper remedies. . . . [n]ot merely were those that recovered few, but almost all within three days from the appearance of the said symptoms died, and in most cases without any fever or other attendant malady.

Moreover, the [severity] of the [plague] was the greater [because any contact] was apt to [spread] it from the sick to the[healthy], just as fire devours things dry or greasy when they are brought close to it. [T]he evil went yet further, for not merely by speech or association with the sick was the malady [communicated] to the healthy with consequent peril of common death; but any that touched the clothes of the sick or [anything] else that had been touched or used by them, seemed thereby to [catch] the disease. . . .

[It is] [t]edious to recount how citizen avoided citizen, how among neighbors was scarce found any that showed fellow-feeling for another, how kinsfolk held aloof, and never met, or but rarely. . . . [I]n the horror [of this disease], brother was forsaken by brother, nephew by uncle, brother by sister, and oftentimes husband by wife; what is more, and scarcely to be believed, fathers and mothers were found to abandon their own children, untended, unvisited, to their fate, as if they had been strangers. Wherefore the sick of both sexes, whose number could not be estimated, were left without resource but in the charity of friends (and few such there were), or the interest of servants. . . .

It was the common practice of most of the neighbors, moved no less by fear of contamination by the [decaying] bodies than by charity toward the deceased, to drag the corpses out of the houses with their own hands, aided, perhaps, by a porter, if a porter was to be had, and to lay them in front of the doors, where any one who made the round might have seen, especially in the morning, more of them than he could count; afterwards they would have biers[1] brought up or [else] . . . planks, whereon they laid them. [Often] . . . one and the same bier carried two or three corpses at once . . . , one bier [carrying] . . . husband and wife, two or three brothers, father and son, and so forth. And times without number it happened, that, as two priests, bearing the cross, were on their way to perform the last [rites] for someone, three or four biers were brought up by the porters in rear of them, so that, whereas the priests supposed that they had but one corpse to bury, they discovered that there were six

[1]**bier**—a stand on which a body is placed

or eight, or sometimes more. Nor, for all their number, were their [funerals] . . . honored by either tears or lights or crowds of mourners; rather, it was come to this, that a dead man was then of no more account than a dead goat would be today.

Review Questions

1. What were the symptoms of bubonic plague?
2. Why did the plague lead a greater number of persons to act as doctors?
3. a. What did Boccaccio say that people thought caused the plague?
   b. How was the plague actually spread?
4. What effect did the plague have on European society?
5. Why did Boccaccio state that "a dead man was then of no more account than a dead goat"?

The Trial of Joan of Arc

One of the French nation's most popular historical persons is a young woman known as Joan of Arc. During the Hundred Years' War between France and England (1337–1453), Joan led French soldiers in several victorious battles, beginning in 1429 when she was 16 or 17 years old.

Joan was a devout Roman Catholic. Religious faith played a central role in her life and death. Beginning when she was 13 years old, Joan said, a voice from God spoke directly to her. She said such a voice told her to go into battle on behalf of Charles, the dauphin, or heir, to the throne of France. (England's King Henry VI also claimed the French throne.) Dressed as a man, Joan passed through enemy territory to find Charles and offer her services. He was doubtful at first, and had important church officials question her about her motives and religious experiences. After three weeks of questioning, they said they were satisfied with her story. Charles gave his approval, and Joan led French soldiers to a major victory at Orleans in May 1429.

Although other victorious battles followed, the war was far from over. This conflict was not just between the French and English. It was also a civil war between rival French factions. A French lord, the duke of Burgundy, was allied with the English, and in May 1430 one of his commanders captured Joan. Church officials in Paris (who had sided with the Duke of Burgundy and the English) insisted that she be tried for heresy—that is, for violating church teachings. For one thing, they were alarmed at her claim to have direct contact with God, since that undermined the authority of the church. They also held against her the fact that she dressed in man's clothing. The following document is from a church official's record of Joan's trial in 1431.

. . . [W]hen Joan was thirteen years old she had [heard] a voice from God to aid her in self-discipline. And the first time she was greatly afraid. And this voice came about noon in summer in her father's garden, and she had fasted the day before. And she heard the voice on her right hand toward the church, and she seldom heard it without a light. Which light comes from the same side as the voice, but is usually great. And when she came to France [at the time, France did not include Burgundy and Lorraine] she often heard this voice. . . . [T]he voice seemed to her worthy, and she believes that it was sent by God; and after she had heard it three times she knew that it was the voice of an angel. She also said that it always guarded her well, and that she knew it well.

Asked about the teaching which her voice gave her respecting the salvation of her soul, she said that it taught her to govern herself well, to go often to church, and that it said she must go to France. . . . The voice told her that she should raise [put an end to] the [English] siege of Orleans. [H]er voice told her that she should go to Robert de Baudricourt, captain of the fortress of Vaucouleurs, and he would give her attendants and she then answered that she was a poor girl who knew not how to ride a horse nor head a campaign. . . .

She also said that when she came to Vaucouleurs she recognized Robert de Baudricourt, although she had never seen him before; and she recognized him by the aid of her voice, for the voice told her that it was he; and she told Robert that she must go into France. Twice he denied and withstood her, and the third time he took her [to France] and gave her attendants; and so it happened even as her voice had said. . . . [I]n leaving Vaucouleurs she put on men's clothing, wearing a sword which Robert de Baudricourt had given her. . . . Accompanied by a knight, a shield-bearer and four servants, she reached the town of St. Urbain, and there passed a night in the abbey. . . .

She said that she sent letters to the English [at] Orleans telling them to raise the siege. . . .

Joan went to [the dauphin Charles] . . . without hindrance. . . . She reached [Chinon]. . . about noon and lodged in an inn; and after dinner she went to the king. . . . When she entered his chamber she knew him from the rest by the revelation of her voice. And she told her king that she wished to go making war against the English. . . .

She moreover said that there was no day when she did not hear this voice, and that she stood in great need of it. She said that she had never asked from her voice any other final reward except the salvation of her soul. . . .

After these things had been thus transacted, because it seemed quite enough for one day, we, the said bishop, postponed the trial until Saturday next following, at eight o'clock in the morning.

The trial found Joan guilty of heresy. Upon conviction, she was immediately turned over to civil authorities (the English and their French allies) and burned at the stake. In 1456, the church reversed its verdict of heresy, and in 1920 Pope Benedict XV declared Joan to be a saint.

Review Questions

1. How did Joan know that God had sent the voice she heard?
2. Why did Joan offer to lead the dauphin's soldiers into battle?
3. How often did Joan hear her voice?
4. Why was Joan declared a heretic and burned at the stake?
5. Why do you think the Catholic Church reversed its decision in 1456 and declared Joan a saint in 1920?

St. Francis of Assisi

St. Francis was born in Assisi, Italy, in about 1182. His father was a wealthy merchant. As a young man, St. Francis led a wild and worldly life. Repenting of his ways, he gave up his wealth in 1206, and began to practice piety and charity. Becoming more and more religious, he became a hermit. He preached to others, many of whom began to follow his example. Pope Innocent III was so impressed with St. Francis that he had him ordained a deacon. St. Francis eventually founded the order of monks called the Franciscans.

Francis preferred a simple life of prayer to one of administration. He took little part in the governing of his order. He was said to have received the *stigmata*—that is, temporary marks on the palms of his hands that resembled the wounds made on Christ's hands when he was nailed to the cross. St. Francis was canonized (declared a saint) by the Catholic Church two years after his death in 1228. In spite of his asceticism (lack of interest in material things), St. Francis loved nature and animals. He felt that they expressed God's glory.

Giovanni Bellini's painting *St. Francis in the Desert* (1485) combines the ascetic principles of the Middle Ages with the life-embracing attitude of the Renaissance. Art scholars tell us that the landscape outside St. Francis' hermit cave (which is not literally in a "desert") symbolizes the Heavenly Jerusalem and that the mountain in the background stands for Mount Zion. The donkey is a symbol for the stubborn human body, whose demands must be subdued by ascetic living. They point out that St. Francis referred to himself as "Brother Ass." The rocky landscape behind the saint suggests the life that he led as a hermit.

For all its otherworldly associations, however, the landscape in this painting is full of an innocent but sensuous beauty. The stony ground beneath St. Francis' bare feet seems to swirl and drape like a rich fabric. Vines, grasses, and delicate trees spring from the rocky cliff behind him. Although St. Francis has stretched out his hands to receive the stigmata, the wounds can scarcely be seen. He and his surroundings are bathed in a soft, warm light. It is almost as though the beauty of nature has caused this miracle. Indeed, Bellini may have intended such an interpretation. He painted this picture to illustrate St. Francis' "Hymn of the Sun," in which he praises the sun and the natural world it reveals as symbols of God and his creation.

Review Questions

1. How did St. Francis change his life?
2. What is happening to St. Francis in the picture?
3. Why does the artist show St. Francis's hermit cave in a setting of fields, buildings, and mountains?

St. Francis in the Desert, by Giovanni Bellini (1485)

13 Leonardo da Vinci, Renaissance Man

Leonardo da Vinci (1452–1519) was one of the leading figures of the Italian Renaissance. Unable to confine himself to working in a single field, Leonardo worked at many things. He was a supreme artist whose paintings include *The Last Supper* and *Mona Lisa*. He was also a sculptor, an engineer, an architect, a scientist, and an adviser to kings and princes. In fact, Leonardo became the model of the "Renaissance man"—a person who was capable of doing many things, and doing them all extremely well.

The excerpt that follows is from a life of Leonardo written by Giorgio Vasari, an Italian painter who was born a few years before Leonardo died. Vasari describes some of Leonardo's quirks and gives insight into his painting techniques.

This marvellous and divinely inspired Leonardo was the son of Piero da Vinci. He would have been very [skilled] at his early lessons if he had not been so [changeable] and unstable; for he was always setting himself to learn many things only to abandon them almost immediately. Thus he began to learn arithmetic, and after a few months he had made so much progress that he used to baffle his master with the questions and problems that he raised. For a little while he attended to music, and then he very soon resolved to learn to play the lyre, for he was naturally of an elevated and refined disposition; and with this instrument he accompanied his own charming improvised singing. All the same, . . . Leonardo never ceased drawing and [sculpting] . . . , pursuits which best suited his temperament. . . .

Clearly, it was because of his profound knowledge of painting that Leonardo started so many things without finishing them; for he was convinced that his hands, for all their skill, could never perfectly express the subtle and wonderful ideas of his imagination. . . .

[*The Last Supper*] Leonardo also executed in Milan, for the Dominicans of [the convent] Santa Maria delle Grazie, a marvellous and beautiful painting of the Last Supper.[1] Having depicted the heads of the apostles full of splendor and majesty, he deliberately left the head of Christ unfinished, convinced he would fail to give it the divine spirituality it demands. This all but finished work has ever since been held in the greatest [awe] by the Milanese and others. In it, Leonardo brilliantly succeeded in [imagining] and reproducing the tormented anxiety of the apostles to know who had betrayed their master; so in their faces one can read the emotions of love, dismay, and anger, or rather sorrow, at their failure to grasp the meaning of Christ. And this excites no less admiration than the contrasted spectacle of the obstinacy, hatred, and treachery in the face of Judas or, indeed, than the incredible [care] with which every detail of the work was executed. The texture of the very cloth on the table is [reproduced] so cunningly that the linen itself could not look more realistic.

It is said that the prior [person in charge of the convent where Leonardo was painting] used to keep [urging] Leonardo . . . to hurry up and finish the work, because he was puzzled by Leonardo's habit of sometimes spending half a day at a time contemplating what he had done so far. [I]f the prior had had his way, Leonardo would have toiled like one of the laborers hoeing in the garden and never put his brush down for a moment. Not satisfied with this, the prior then complained to the duke [of Milan], making such a fuss that the duke was [forced] to send for Leonardo and, very tactfully, question him about the painting, although he showed perfectly well that he was only doing so because of the prior's insistence. Leonardo, knowing he was dealing with a prince of [great] . . . intelligence, was willing (as he never had been with the prior) to explain his mind at length; and so he talked to the duke for a long time about the art of painting. He explained that men of genius sometimes accomplish most when they work the least; for, he added, they are thinking out inventions and forming in their minds the perfect ideas which they subsequently express and reproduce with their hands.

Leonardo then said that he still had two heads to paint. The head of Christ was one, and for this he was unwilling to look for any human model, nor did he dare suppose that his imagination could conceive

---

[1]**Last Supper**—according to the Christian Bible, the meal Jesus ate with his 12 disciples (apostles), just before he was betrayed by one of them named Judas

the beauty and divine grace that properly belonged to the incarnate[2] Deity. Then, he said, he had yet to do the head of Judas. . . . However, . . . he would try to find a model for Judas; and if he did not succeed in doing so, why then he [could use] the head of that tactless and [bothersome] prior. The duke roared with laughter at this and said that Leonardo had every reason in the world for saying so. The unfortunate prior retired in confusion. . . . Leonardo skillfully finished the head of Judas and made it seem the very [model] of treachery and inhumanity. The head of Christ remained, as was said, unfinished. . . .

[*Mona Lisa*] For Francesco del Giocondo, Leonardo undertook to execute the portrait of his wife, Mona Lisa. He worked on this painting for four years, and then left it still unfinished; and today it is in the possession of King Francis of France, at Fontainebleau. If one wanted to see how faithfully art can imitate nature, one could readily perceive it from this head; for here Leonardo subtly reproduced every living detail. The eyes had their natural [shine] and moistness, and around them were the lashes and all those rosy and pearly tints that demand the greatest delicacy of execution. . . . Leonardo also made use of this device: while he was painting Mona Lisa, who was a very beautiful woman, he employed singers and musicians or jesters to keep her full of merriment and so chase away the melancholy that painters usually give to portraits. As a result, in this painting of Leonardo's there was a smile so pleasing that it seemed divine rather than human; and those who saw it were amazed to find that it was as alive as the original.

Review Questions

1. What kind of student was young Leonardo da Vinci?
2. a. In his painting *The Last Supper*, why did Leonardo leave the head of Christ unfinished?
   b. Why have so many people admired *The Last Supper*?
3. Why did Leonardo tell the duke of Milan that "men of genius sometimes accomplish most when they work the least"?
4. In what ways was the *Mona Lisa* a realistic painting?
5. Why has Leonardo da Vinci been considered the primary example of the "ideal" or "Renaissance man"?

---

[2]**incarnate**—in the flesh; in human form

French King Orders Feudal Castles Demolished

During the Middle Ages, there had been dozens of powerful lords, each relatively equal to the others. But rarely was there a strong central government. From the 14th through the 16th centuries, the rulers of Europe fought many wars. Sometimes they fought one another. Sometimes they fought feudal lords who were supposed to be their loyal vassals. Gradually, the monarchs gained more land and more power. Governments became increasingly centralized, or concentrated.

By the 17th century, modern Europe was beginning to take shape. In England and France, especially, central governments ruled large areas with definite boundaries and a unified population. These areas became nation-states. But several centuries passed before feudal rule gave way completely to nation-states throughout Europe. Eventually, nation-states became the standard political unit, and they remain so today.

In both England and France, civil wars accompanied the growth of the nation-state. Eventually, one side in each country won out. Power settled into the hands of new royal families. In England, the rule of the Tudors began in 1485 with Henry VII and continued until the death of Elizabeth I in 1603. Then came the Stuarts, who ruled until 1649. France was ruled by the House of Bourbon, beginning with Henry IV in 1589. The document that follows was issued in the name of another Bourbon king, Louis XIII. By issuing the following edict (official order), in 1626, Louis XIII showed that the balance of power had swung away from feudal lords to his own central government.

Whereas formerly the assemblies of the estates of this realm . . . have repeatedly requested and very humbly [begged] our . . . father and ourselves to [order] the demolition of many strongholds in [various] places of this realm, which, being neither on hostile frontiers nor in important passes or places, only serve to [increase] our expenses by the maintenance of useless [military] garrisons, and also serve as retreats for [various] persons who on the least provocation disturb the provinces where they are located; . . .

For these reasons, we announce, declare, ordain, and will that all the strongholds, either towns or castles, which are in the interior of our realm or provinces of the same, not situated in places of importance either for frontier defense or other [important] considerations . . . , shall be razed and demolished. . . . [E]ven ancient walls shall be destroyed so far as it shall be deemed necessary for the well-being and repose of our subjects and the security of this state, so that our said subjects henceforth need not fear that the said places will cause them any inconvenience, and so that we shall be freed from the expense of supporting [military] garrisons in them.

Review Questions

1. a. What is the meaning of the word "strongholds"?
   b. Why did the French kings oppose such places?
2. Why did King Louis XIII order that feudal castles and walls be demolished?
3. What effect would the demolition of feudal castles have on the power of the king and the central government of France?

Creating the French Academy

In the following document, issued in 1635, King Louis XIII authorizes the creation of a special public group to make rules about the French language. This group is called the French Academy. To this day, the academy makes decisions about what is and is not "proper French."

The wording of the document reflects the king's claim (also made by other monarchs of the time) to have been chosen by God and to rule in God's name. In other words, these monarchs claimed to rule by divine right. Cardinal Richelieu (pronounced reesh-uh-LYOO) served as regent (temporary ruler) until Louis XIII reached maturity. The cardinal continued to make important government decisions throughout the king's rule.

When God called us to the head of the state, we cherished the purpose not only of putting an end to the disorders caused by the civil wars which had so long distracted the realm [country], but we also aimed to adorn the state with all the ornaments appropriate to the oldest and most illustrious of existing monarchies. Although we have labored without intermission to realize this purpose, it has been impossible [up to now] fully to accomplish it. . . . [But now] the confusion has at last given way to good order, which we have reestablished by the best of all means, namely, by reviving commerce, enforcing military discipline in our armies, adjusting taxes, and checking luxury. Everyone is aware of the part that our very dear and beloved cousin, the cardinal, duke of Richelieu, has had in the accomplishment of all these things.

Consequently, when we communicated our intention to him, he [told] us that one of the most glorious proofs of the happiness of a realm is that the sciences and arts flourish within it. . . . [L]earning as well as warfare are both held in esteem, since these constitute one of the chief ornaments of a powerful state. . . . After so many memorable exploits, we had now only to add the agreeable to the essential, and to adorn the useful. He believed that we could not do better than to commence with the most noble of all arts, namely, eloquence. The French language . . . is now more capable than ever of taking its high place, owing to the great number of persons who possess a special knowledge of the advantages which it enjoys and who can [increase] these advantages. The cardinal informed us that, with a view of establishing fixed rules for the language, he had arranged meetings of scholars whose decisions in these matters had met with his hearty approval. In order to put these decisions into execution and render the French language not only elegant but capable of treating all the arts and sciences, it would only be necessary to [continue] these [meetings]. This could be done with great advantage should it please us to [authorize] them, to permit rules and regulations to be drawn up for the order of procedure to be observed, and to reward those who compose the association by some honorable marks of our favor.

For these reasons, and in view of the advantages which our subjects may derive from the said meetings, [agreeing to] the desires of our said cousin:

We do permit, by our special favor, power, and royal authority, and do authorize and approve by [this document], signed by our hand, the said assemblies and conferences. We will that they continue hereafter in our good city of Paris, under the name of the French Academy; that our said cousin shall be . . . its head and protector; that the number of members be limited to forty persons.

Review Questions

1. How does this document show that King Louis XIII claimed to rule by divine right?
2. To whom do the words “we” and “us” in the document refer?
3. What had previously been done in France to eliminate “confusion” and reestablish “good order”?
4. Why did Cardinal Richelieu have such great power?
5. Why was the French Academy created? Why do you think the number of members was limited to forty?
6. In what way is the document an example of the increasing power of the French nation state?

Unit III Document-Based Question

Write a well-organized essay that includes an introduction, several paragraphs, and a conclusion. Use evidence from at least ***four*** *documents in this unit in the body of the essay. Support your response with relevant facts, examples, and details. Include additional outside information.*

Historical Context

The period 1200–1650 saw societies gradually developing and increasingly interacting with one another, which resulted in an ever-growing demand for change.

Task: Using the documents and questions in the unit, along with your knowledge of global history, write an essay in which you:

- Describe **three** situations in which the development of a society or its interaction with another society caused change
- Evaluate the historical significance of the impact of **one** of the changes you described

The First Global Age

(1450–1770)

A Maya Creation Story

The Mayas, who built one of the early civilizations of Middle America, thrived from about 600 B.C. to A.D. 1400. They worshiped many gods. Like the Aztecs, the Mayas sometimes sacrificed human beings as part of their religious ceremonies. An important ritual in Maya religion was a ball game played in a large rectangular court with a hard rubber ball. Players used sticks, or yokes, to propel the ball. This game was played very seriously. Sometimes, the losing side was killed as part of a religious sacrifice.

A ritual ball game of this sort occurs in a Maya story about the creation of the world. That story was told by the Maya living in the highlands of what are now southern Mexico and Guatemala. It was written down soon after the Spanish conquest in a book called *Popol Vuh* ("Council Book"). A section of that book tells the story of heroic twin brothers, Xbalanque (shbahl-ahn-KAY) and Hunahpu (hoo-nah-POO), who descended into the underworld to avenge the death of their father. The father had been killed there by the lords of the underworld (whose names were One Death and Seven Death) and their helpers. In the underworld (called Place of Fear, or Xibalba, pronounced shee-bahl-BAH), the twins were subjected to a series of tests—ones that their father had failed. The boys passed all the tests and defeated the lords of the underworld in a ritual ball game. The excerpt that follows picks up the story at their final test. They spend a night in a house filled with immense and deadly bats. As you will see, the story contains elements of magic, and the twins are able to call upon members of the animal kingdom for help.

Now they [the twins] were put inside Bat House, a house of snatch-bats, monstrous beasts, their snouts like knives, the instruments of death. To come before these is to be finished off at once.

When they were inside they just slept in their blowgun; they were not bitten by the [bats]. . . .

And all night the bats are making noise:

"Squeak! Squeak!"

they say, and they say it all night.

Then it let up a little. The bats were no longer moving around. So there, one of the boys crawled to the end of the blowgun. Xbalanque said:

"Hunahpu? Can you see how long it is till dawn?"

"Well, perhaps I should look to see how long it is," he replied. So he kept trying to look out the muzzle of the blowgun, . . . to see the dawn.

And then his head was taken off by a snatch-bat, leaving Hunahpu's body still stuffed inside.

"What's going on? Hasn't it dawned?" said Xbalanque. No longer is there any movement from Hunahpu. "What's this? Hunahpu hasn't left, has he? What have you done?" He no longer moves. . . .

After that, Xbalanque despaired:

"Alas! We've given it all up!" he said. And elsewhere, the head meanwhile went rolling onto the [ball] court, in accordance with the word of One and Seven Death, and all the Xibalbans were happy over the head of Hunahpu.

After that, Xbalanque summoned all the animals; coati,[1] peccary,[2] all the animals, small and great. It was at night . . . when he asked them for their food.

"Whatever your foods are, each one of you: that's what I summoned you for, to bring your food here," Xbalanque told them.

"Very well," they replied, then they went to get what's theirs . . .

There's the one who only brought his rotten wood.

There's the one who only brought leaves.

There's the one who only brought stones.

There's the one who only brought earth, on through the varied foods of the animals, small and great, until the very last one remained: the coati. He brought a squash, bumping it along with his snout as he came.

---

[1]**coati**—tropical American mammal related to the raccoon

[2]**peccary**—American mammal related to the pig

And this became [an artificial] head for Hunahpu. His eyes were carved right away, then brains came from the thinker, from the sky. This was the Heart of Sky, Hurricane[3] who came down, came on down into Bat House. The face . . . came out well. His strength was just the same, he looked handsome, he spoke just the same. . . .

"Isn't it good?" Hunahpu was asked.

"Good indeed," he replied. His head was as if it had every bone; it had become like his real head.

After that, they . . . made arrangements with each other:

"How about not playing ball yourself? You should just make lots of threats, while I should be the one to take all the action," Xbalanque told [Hunahpu]. . . . After that, he gave instructions to a rabbit:

"Your place is there above the court, on top. Stay there in the oaks," the rabbit was told by Xbalanque, "until the ball comes to you, then take off while I get to work." . . .

After that, when it dawned, both of them were just as well as ever.

And when the ball was dropped in again, it was the head of Hunahpu that rolled over the court:

"We've won! You're done! Give up! You lost!" [the Xibalbans cried]. . . .

But even so Hunahpu was shouting: "Punt the head as a ball!" he told them.

"Well, we're not going to do them any more harm with threats," and with this the lords of Xibalba sent off the ball and Xbalanque received it, the ball was stopped by his yoke, then he hit it hard and it took off, the ball passed straight out of the court, bouncing just once, just twice, and stopping among the oaks. Then the rabbit took off hopping, then they went off in pursuit, then all the Xibalbans went off, shouting, shrieking, they went after the rabbit, off went the whole of Xibalba.

After that, the boys got Hunahpu's head back. Then Xbalanque . . . set the squash above the court.

So the head of Hunahpu was really a head again, and the two of them were happy again. And the others, those Xibalbans, were still going on in search of the ball.

---

[3]**Hurricane**—Mayan god of the skies and of lightning (spelled "Hurakan"; source of the English word "hurricane")

After that, having recovered the ball [that is, the squash] from among the oaks, the boys cried out to them:

"Come back! Here's the ball! We've found it!" they said, so they stopped. When the Xibalbans got back:

"Have we been seeing things?" they said. Then they began their ball game again, and they made equal plays on both sides again.

After that, the squash was punted by Xbalanque. The squash was wearing out; it fell on the court, bringing to light its light-colored seeds, as plain as day right in front of them.

"How did you get hold of that? Where did it come from?" said Xibalba.

With this, the masters of Xibalba were defeated by Hunahpu and Xbalanque. There was great danger there [in the tests they had faced], but [the twins] did not die from all the things that were done to them.

Having defeated the lords of the underworld, the twins were ready to face their own inevitable death. But they arranged to have their bones ground fine, like cornmeal, and sprinkled in a river. Five days later, the twins secretly sprang back to life. Appearing in the underworld as two vagabonds, they exhibited such magical powers that the lords of the underworld (who did not recognize them as Xbalanque and Hunahpu) summoned them to show off their tricks. One of those tricks was to kill someone and then bring him back to life. As a demonstration, Xbalanque cut off Hunahpu's head, and then restored him to life and wholeness. Excitedly, One Death and Seven Death asked to have the trick performed on them. And it was—only the twins did not restore them to life. They were dead forever. "Such was the defeat of the rulers of Xibalba," *Popol Vuh* says. "The boys accomplished it only through wonders, only through self-transformation." Eventually, the heroic twins became the sun and the moon.

Before descending into the underworld, the twins had told their grandmother to plant corn in their memory. "When the corn dries up," they said, "this will be a sign of our death. 'Perhaps they died,' you'll say, when it dries up. And when the sprouting comes: 'Perhaps they live,' you'll say." For the Maya people, the story of the twins gives a special meaning to the annual cycles of wet and dry weather. The meaning is this: There is a season for death, and a season for life, and they go on and on, first the one, then the other, forever.

Review Questions

1. Why did Xbalanque and Hunahpu descend into the underworld?
2. How did Xbalanque bring Hunahpu back to life?
3. How does this story illustrate the Mayan belief that animals possessed magical powers?
4. How did the twins win the ritual ball game?
5. How were the twins able to come back to life after they died?
6. How did the twins use trickery to kill the lords of Xibalba and avenge their father?
7. According to the Maya, what was the special meaning of the twins' story?

The Great Binding Law: The "Constitution" of the Iroquois League

Sometime before A.D. 1600, five Iroquois nations living in what is now New York State formed a confederation, or union. Called the Iroquois League, the confederation lasted for nearly two centuries. By uniting the five (later six) nations and providing ways for them to make joint decisions and take joint actions, the confederation helped the Iroquois to build a powerful empire and dominate their Native American neighbors. Some of the early leaders of the United States were impressed with the Iroquois system. Those leaders proposed borrowing some of the league's features for the U.S. Constitution. These included having parallel systems of laws, with each member state or nation possessing its own laws separate from those of the league.

The founding nations of the Iroquois League were the Mohawk, Onondaga, Seneca, Oneida, and Cayuga nations. In 1715 the Tuscarora nation joined the league as its sixth nation.

When the American Revolution began in 1775, the Iroquois League could not agree on what action to take. Most members wanted to support the British against the American colonists. But the league could not go to war without the consent of all six nations, and the Oneidas refused their consent. In the end, Mohawks, Onondagas, Cayugas, and Senecas fought on the British side. The lack of agreement weakened the Iroquois League. So did the ultimate victory of the colonists and the establishment of an independent United States. The league went into a decline from which it never recovered.

Not having a system of writing, the founders of the Iroquois League did not create a written constitution. But oral records of the founding agreement were carefully passed down from generation to generation. During the 19th century, the document that includes the following excerpt was compiled. It is one version (there are others) of the Iroquois "constitution." All versions agree that an imposing chief named Dekanawidah was the driving force in the league's creation. He had helped to end a period of destructive warfare in which Iroquois nations fought one another.

This excerpt describes the Confederate Council, at which the Five Nations' political decisions were made. You will note that the document mentions a number of individuals by name. Later, successors from the five nations were named to replace them in their official positions.

1. I am Dekanawidah and with the Five Nations Confederate Lords I plant the Tree of Great Peace. I plant it in your territory, Adodarhoh, and the Onondaga Nation, in the territory of you who are Fire Keepers.

I name the tree the Tree of the Great Long Leaves. Under the shade of this Tree of the Great Peace we spread the soft white feathery down of the globe thistle as seats for you, Adodarhoh, and your cousin Lords. . . .

3. To you Adodarhoh, the Onondaga cousin Lords, I and the other Confederate Lords have entrusted the caretaking and the watching of the Five Nations Council Fire.

When there is any business to be transacted and the Confederate Council is not in session, a messenger shall be [sent] either to Adodarhoh, Hononwirehtonh or Skanawatih, Fire Keepers, or to their War Chiefs with a full statement of the case desired to be considered. . . .

When the Lords are assembled the Council Fire shall be kindled . . . and Adodarhoh shall formally open the Council. . . .

5. The Council of the Mohawk shall be divided into three parties. . . . The third party is to listen only to the discussion of the first and second parties and if an error is made or the proceeding is irregular they are to call attention to it, and when the case is right and properly decided by the two parties they shall confirm the decision of the two parties and refer the case to the Seneca Lords for their decision.

When the Seneca Lords have decided in accord with the Mohawk Lords, the case or question shall be referred to the Cayuga and Oneida Lords on the opposite side of the house.

6. I, Dekanawidah, appoint the Mohawk Lords the heads and the leaders of the Five Nations Confederacy. The Mohawk Lords are the foundation of the Great Peace and it shall, therefore, be against the Great Binding Law to pass measures in the Confederate Council after the Mohawk Lords have protested against them.

No council of the Confederate Lords shall be legal unless all the Mohawk Lords are present.

7. Whenever the Confederate Lords shall assemble for the purpose of holding a council, the Onondaga Lords shall open it by expressing their gratitude to their cousin Lords and greeting them, and they shall make an address and offer thanks to the earth where men dwell, to the streams of water, the pools, the springs, and the lakes, to the maize and the fruits, to the medicinal herbs and trees, to the forest trees for their usefulness, to the animals that serve as food and give their pelts for clothing, to the great winds and the lesser winds, to the Thunderers, to the Sun, the mighty warrior, to the moon, to the messengers of the Creator who reveal his wishes and to the Great Creator who dwells in the heavens above, who gives all the things useful to men, and who is the source and the ruler of health and life.

Then shall the Onondaga Lords declare the council open. . . .

8. The Fire Keepers shall formally open and close all councils of the Confederate Lords, and they shall pass upon all matters deliberated upon by the two sides and render their decision. . . .

9. All the business of the Five Nations Confederate Council shall be conducted by the two combined bodies of Confederate Lords. First the question shall be passed upon by the Mohawk and Seneca Lords, then it shall be discussed and passed by the Oneida and Cayuga Lords. Their decisions shall then be referred to the Onondaga Lords (Fire Keepers) for final judgment.

The same process shall obtain when a question is brought before the council by an individual or a War Chief.

10. In all cases the procedure must be as follows: when the Mohawk and Seneca Lords have unanimously agreed upon a question, they shall report their decision to the Cayuga and Oneida Lords who shall deliberate upon the question and report a unanimous decision to the Mohawk Lords. The Mohawk Lords will then report the standing of the case to the Fire Keepers, who shall render a decision as they see fit in case of a disagreement by the two bodies, or confirm the decisions of the two bodies if they are identical. The Fire Keepers shall then report their decision to the Mohawk Lords, who shall announce it to the open council.

11. If through any misunderstanding or obstinacy on the part of the Fire Keepers, they render a decision at variance with that of the Two Sides, the Two Sides shall reconsider the matter and if their decisions are jointly the same as before they shall report to the Fire Keepers who are then compelled to confirm their joint decision.

12. When a case comes before the Onondaga Lords (Fire Keepers) for discussion and decision, Adodarhoh shall introduce the matter to his comrade Lords who shall then discuss it in their two bodies. Every Onondaga Lord except Hononwiretonh shall deliberate and he shall listen only. When a unanimous decision shall have been reached by the two bodies of Fire Keepers, Adodarhoh shall notify Hononwiretonh of the fact when he shall confirm it. He shall refuse to confirm a decision if it is not unanimously agreed upon by both sides of the Fire Keepers. . . .

14. When the Council of the Five Nation Lords convene, they shall appoint a speaker for the day. He shall be a Lord of either the Mohawk, Onondaga, or Seneca Nation.

The next day the Council shall appoint another speaker, but the first speaker may be reappointed if there is no objection, but a speaker's term shall not be regarded more than for the day.

15. No individual or foreign nation interested in a case, question, or proposition shall have any voice in the Confederate Council except to answer a question put to him or them by the speaker for the Lords.

16. If the conditions which shall arise at any future time call for an addition to or change of this law, the case shall be carefully considered and if [it] seems necessary or beneficial, the proposed change shall be voted upon. . . .

Review Questions

1. How was the creation of the league beneficial to the Iroquois nation?
2. How did the Iroquois' "constitution" provide for a system of checks and balances?
3. How does this document show the Native Americans' deep respect for the earth and its creatures?
4. How might the clear-cut procedures for lawmaking have helped to avoid conflict among the Iroquois nations?
5. a. Why was it an advantage that all decisions of the league had to be unanimous?
   b. How might the requirement for unanimity also have proved to be a disadvantage?
6. What provisions were made for changing or amending the laws of the Iroquois?

3 An Arab Traveler in Mali

The empire of Mali flourished in West Africa during the 13th and 14th centuries. Rulers like Sundiata (who founded the Mali empire in 1235) and Mansa Musa (in power about 1312–1337) made Mali a powerful state. Its rulers and many of its leaders were Muslims. Mansa Musa, for example, was widely admired for taking an immense caravan on a pilgrimage to Mecca in 1324.

As a powerful trading nation, Mali was home to many Arab and Berber traders. They arranged for the transport of gold, slaves, and salt between Mali and other Muslim nations. In June 1352, the famous Muslim traveler Ibn Battuta (see Unit III) arrived in Mali on one of his journeys. He remained until the following February to observe the customs of the people and enjoy the hospitality of Arabs and blacks alike.

In the following document, Ibn Battuta comments on his experiences. He makes some unflattering remarks about the ruler, Mansa Sulaiman (a brother of Mansa Musa), whose gifts did not come up to the traveler's expectations. Often, on his journeys, Ibn Battuta would receive free lodging and have his other expenses paid for. At first, he received no such gifts from Mali's ruler—only a single offering of bread, fried meat, and curdled milk. Finally, after four months, Ibn Battuta complained directly to Mansa Sulaiman, who then offered him a place to stay and money for expenses. (The italicized words and sentences are in the translated document.)

Account of the sultan of Mali. He is the Sultan Mansa Sulaiman; *Mansa* means *sultan* and Sulaiman is his personal name. He is a miserly king and a big gift is not to be expected from him. . . .

Account of [the sultan's] audience in his cupola. He has a raised cupola[1] . . . in his house and where he sits most of the time. On the

[1]**cupola**—structure with a raised and rounded roof

side of the audience hall are three arches of wood covered with silver plates, below which are three more, covered with plates of gold, or silver gilt.[2] They have curtains of blanket cloth. On a day when there is an audience in the cupola, the curtains are raised and it is known that there is a session. When he takes his seat a silk tassel is put through the grill of one of the arches, to which is tied a striped Egyptian handkerchief. When people see the handkerchief, drums are beaten and trumpets sounded. Then some three hundred slaves come out from the door of the palace, some with bows in their hands and some with short spears and leather shields. The spearmen stand on the right and left; the archers sit in the same way. Then two saddled and bridled horses are brought and with them two rams. They say that they are useful against the evil eye. When he takes his seat three of his slaves run and call his deputy, Qanja Musa. The [military commanders, or amirs] come, and the preacher and the jurists who all sit in front of the armed men on the right and left of the audience hall. . . . The soldiers, the governors, the pages . . . and the rest sit outside the audience hall in a wide thoroughfare with trees. Each [military commander] has in front of him his men with spears, bows, drums, trumpets made from elephants' tusks, and musical instruments made from reeds and gourds, which are struck with sticks and make a pleasant sound. Each [military commander] has his quiver [arrow case] hung between his shoulders and his bow in his hand. He is on a horse; some of his men are on horseback, some on foot. . . .

Account of the session in the audience hall. On some days [the sultan] also sits in the audience hall. There is a bench under a tree, which has three steps and which is called *banbi.* It is covered with silk and cushions are placed on it. A parasol, that is to say, something like a silken cupola, is raised over it. On top of it is a gold bird the size of a falcon. The sultan comes out of a door in a corner of the palace with his bow in his hand, his quiver between his shoulders, a gold skull-cap on his head held in place by a gold headband with points like thin knives . . . . He is mostly dressed in a red tunic of . . . European cloth. . . . He comes out preceded by

---

[2]**gilt**—thin covering made of a precious metal

singers with gold and silver [musical instruments]. He is followed by about three hundred armed slaves. He walks slowly and often pauses, and sometimes stands still. When he reaches the *banbi* he stops and looks at the people. Then he climbs up it slowly as the preacher climbs the pulpit. When he takes his seat the drums are beaten and the trumpets and bugles sounded. Three slaves come out running and summon the sultan's deputy and the [military commanders], who enter and sit down. Two horses and rams are brought. . . . [T]he rest of the people are in the street under the trees.

Account of the comical way poetry is recited to the sultan. On the Feast Day . . . , the poets come in. . . . Each of them is inside a costume made of feathers resembling the *shaqshaq* [a green woodpecker] on which is a wooden head with a red beak like the head of the *shaqshaq*. They stand before the sultan in this laughable get-up and recite their poems. . . .

[T]he chief poet climbs the steps of the *banbi* and puts his head in the sultan's lap; then he climbs to the top of the *banbi* and puts his head on the sultan's right shoulder, then on his left shoulder, talking all the time in their language. Then he comes down. I have been told that this custom has continued among them since ancient times before Islam, and that they have [continued] in it. . . .

Account of what I found good and what I found bad in the conduct of the Blacks. Among their good practices are their avoidance of injustice; there are no people more [opposed] to it, and their sultan does not allow anyone to practice it in any measure; the universal security in their country, for neither the traveler nor the resident there has to fear thieves or bandits: they do not interfere with the property of white men who die in their country, even if it amounts to vast sums; they just leave it in the hands of a trustworthy white man until whoever is entitled to it takes possession of it: their [care] in praying, their perseverance in joining the congregation, and in compelling their children to do so; if a man does not come early to the mosque he will not find a place to pray because of the dense crowd; it is customary for each man to send his servant with his prayer-mat to spread it out in a place reserved for him until he goes to the mosque himself; their prayer-mats are made of the leaves of a tree like the date-palm, but which has no fruit. They dress in clean white clothes on Fridays; if one of them has only a threadbare shirt he washes it and cleans it and wears it for prayer on Friday. They pay great attention to memorizing the Holy Qur'an. If their children appear to be backward in learning it they put shackles[3] on them and do not remove them till they learn it. I called on the qadi[4] on the Feast Day. His children were in shackles. I said to him: "Are you not going to free them?" He said: "Not till they learn the Qur'an by heart." One day I passed by a handsome youth, who was very well dressed, with a heavy shackle on his foot. I said to the person with me: "What has he done? Has he killed someone?" The youth understood what I said and laughed. I was told: "He has been shackled to make him memorize the Qur'an."

Among their bad practices are that the women servants, slave-girls and young daughters appear naked before people. . . . I used to see many like this in Ramadan, for it is customary for the [military commanders] . . . to break the fast in the sultan's palace, where their food is brought to them by twenty or more slave-girls, who are naked. Women who come before the sultan are naked and unveiled, and so are his daughters. . . . They put dust and ashes on their heads as a matter of good manners. There is the clowning we have described when poets recite their works. Many of them eat carrion,[5] dogs and donkeys [in violation of Muslim religious laws].

Review Questions

1. Why might someone visiting Mansa Sulaiman be impressed by his palace and by the sultan himself?
2. What practices and customs appear to have preceded the arrival of Islam in Mali?
3. Describe three observations Ibn Battuta made about the people of Mali.

---

[3]**shackles**—iron rings and chains
[4]**qadi or cadi**—Muslim judge who handles religous cases
[5]**carrion**—dead and rotting flesh; "road kill"

4. How did the people of Mali make their children learn the Qur'an?
5. a. What did Ibn Battuta find favorable about the people and practices of Mali?
   b. What did Ibn Battuta find unfavorable about the customs of Mali?
6. How might Ibn Battuta's own religious convictions have influenced his opinion of the people of Mali?

Columbus Finds "Indians" in the Americas

The first recorded meeting between Europeans and Native Americans took place on a Caribbean island on October 12, 1492. That is when three sailing ships under the command of Christopher Columbus reached land after an ocean voyage of more than a month. The people who met them were Arawaks (sometimes called Tainos). The exact island where Columbus landed is uncertain, because once he had sailed off for further exploration he never returned. Columbus gave the natives' name for the island as Guaraní.

The following document contains extracts from Columbus's diary that were later copied out by a Spanish historian, Bartolomé de las Casas. (The original diary was lost.) The document contains Columbus's first observations about the people he called "Indians."(He believed that he had reached the Indies, in Asia.) Can you find any hints in this document of the enslavement, brutality, and genocide that the Spanish later practiced on the Native Americans?

[Friday, October 12] In order that we might win good friendship, because I knew that they were a people who could better be freed and converted to our Holy Faith by love than by force, I gave to some of them red caps and to some glass beads, which they hung on their necks, and many other things of slight value, in which they took much pleasure; they remained so much our friends that it was a marvel; and later they came swimming to the ships' boats in which we were, and brought us parrots and cotton threads in skeins and darts and many other things, and we swopped them for other things that we gave them, such as little glass beads and hawks' bells. Finally they swopped and gave everything they had, with good will, but it appeared to us that these people were very poor in everything. They go quite naked as their mothers bore them; and also the women,

although I didn't see more than one really young girl. All that I saw were young men, none of them more than 30 years old, very well made, of very handsome bodies and very good faces; the hair coarse almost as the hair of a horse's tail and short; the hair they wear over their eyebrows, except for a hank behind that they wear long and never cut. Some of them paint themselves black (and they are of the color of the Canary Islanders, neither black nor white), and some paint themselves white, and others red, and others with what they have. Some paint their faces, others the whole body, others the eyes only, others only the nose. They bear no arms, nor know thereof; for I showed them swords and they grasped them by the blade and cut themselves through ignorance; they have no iron. Their darts are a kind of rod without iron, and some have at the end a fish's tooth and others, other things. . . I saw some who had marks of wounds on their bodies, and made signs to them to ask what it was, and they showed me how people of other islands which are near came there and wished to capture them, and they defended themselves. And I believed and now believe that people do come here from the mainland to take them as slaves. They ought to be good servants and of good skill, for I see that they repeat very quickly all that is said to them; and I believe that they would easily be made Christians, because it seemed to me that they belonged to no religion. I, please Our Lord, will carry off six of them at my departure to Your Highnesses, so that they may learn to speak [Spanish]. I saw no beast of any kind except parrots in this island.

Saturday, October 13. At daybreak there came to the beach many of these men, all young men as I have said. . . . They came to the ship in dugouts which are fashioned like a long boat from the [trunk] of a tree, and all in one piece, and wonderfully made (considering the country), and so big that in some came 40 or 45 men, and others smaller, down to the size that held but a single man. They row with a thing like a baker's [paddle] and go wonderfully [fast], and if they capsize all begin to swim and right it and bail out with [the shells of gourds] that they carry. They brought skeins of spun cotton, and parrots and darts and other trifles that would be tedious to describe, and gave all for whatever was given to them.

Review Questions

1. Why did Columbus think it would be wise not to use force against the Native Americans?
2. What observations did Columbus make about the islanders' wealth?
3. How might those interested in conquest have used Columbus's observations against the people?
4. Why did Columbus believe that some islanders had been taken as slaves in the past?
5. Why did Columbus want to teach some of the people Spanish?
6. Describe the trading that took place between the Spaniards and the islanders.

Montezuma and Cortés: Two Views

In the years after Christopher Columbus reached the Caribbean in 1492, Spanish soldiers explored the region from bases on the islands of Hispaniola and Cuba. They were intrigued by reports of the Aztec culture of Middle America and its wealth in gold and silver. In 1519, Captain General Hernan Cortés landed in eastern Mexico with 600 Spanish soldiers, 16 horses, and a few cannons.

Word of Cortés's arrival alarmed the Aztecs. From the Aztec capital of Tenochtitlán (present-day Mexico City), the king sent messengers to meet the strangers and report back. The messengers told of men whose skin was light and whose beards were long. These men rode on the backs of "deer." Their clothing was made of iron and so were their swords. They possessed strange devices (cannons), out of whose insides came sparks and fire and a "ball of stone" that could split a tree. "This is a most unnatural sight," the messengers reported, "as if the tree had exploded from within."

The Aztec king, Montezuma II (or Motecuhzoma, in the Aztec language), believed he knew who the strangers were. According to Aztec legend, a light-skinned god named Quetzalcoatl had founded the Aztec nation long ago. Then he sailed away to the east, promising one day to return. Now that day had arrived. The god was back—or perhaps just his representatives. Not wanting to anger the god, Montezuma sent gifts to the strangers. But he also tried using magic to keep them away from Tenochtitlán. When that did not work, he finally resigned himself to their coming.

Cortés intended to conquer the Aztecs—but not by a direct attack. On his way to Tenochtitlán, he made alliances with Indian groups like the Tlaxcalans (the people of the Tlaxcala nation), who had suffered under Aztec domination. Thus, Cortés's strength was more than the 600 soldiers in his own group. Cortés was aided in his negotiations by a captive woman named La Malinche (Doña Marina to the Spanish), who served as a translator. Cortés, his men, and about a thousand Tlaxcalan allies entered the Aztec capital peacefully, and the Aztecs treated them as if they were gods.

Tenochtitlán was built on an island in the middle of a lake and was reached by causeways and bridges. It had a very large population and impressive buildings. (See document 6.)

The documents that follow present two accounts of the encounter between the Spanish and the Aztecs. The Aztec report was written down by a Spanish priest who gathered oral accounts from Aztec priests and nobles. The Spanish account is from a letter Cortés wrote to the Holy Roman Emperor, Charles V.

The Welcome: An Aztec Account

The Spaniards arrived in Xoloco, near the entrance to Tenochtitlán. That was the end of the march, for they had reached their goal.

Motecuhzoma now arrayed himself in his finery, preparing to go out to meet them. The other great princes also adorned their persons, as did the nobles and their chieftains and knights. They all went out together to meet the strangers.

They brought trays heaped with the finest flowers. . . . They also brought garlands of flowers, and ornaments for the breast, and necklaces of gold, necklaces hung with rich stones, necklaces fashioned in the petatillo style.[1]

Thus Motecuhzoma went out to meet them, there in Huitzillan. He presented many gifts to the Captain and his commanders, those who

The Welcome: Cortés's Account

[W]e were received by that lord, Montezuma, with about two hundred chiefs, all barefooted, and dressed in a kind of [uniform], very rich. . . . They approached in two processions near the walls of the street, which is very broad, and straight, and beautiful, . . . and having, on both sides, very large houses . . . and . . . [temples]. Montezuma came in the middle of the street, with two lords. . . . [A]s we approached each other, I descended from my horse, and was about to embrace him, but the two lords in attendance prevented me, . . . and they, and he also, made the ceremony of kissing the ground. . . .

When I approached to speak to Montezuma, I took off a collar of pearls and glass diamonds, . . . and put it on his neck, and, after we

[1]**petatillo style**—cross-hatched or closely woven, like a sleeping mat

had come to make war. He showered gifts upon them and hung flowers around their necks. . . . Then he hung the gold necklaces around their necks and gave them presents of every sort as gifts of welcome.

had gone through some of the streets, one of his servants came with two collars, . . . which were made of colored shells. . . . [F]rom each of the collars hung eight golden shrimps. . . . When he received them, he . . . put them on my neck, and again went on . . . until we came to a large and handsome house, which he had prepared for our reception. There he took me by the hand, and led me into a spacious room, in front of the court where we had entered, where he made me sit on a very rich platform, . . . and told me to wait there; and then he went away.

After a little while, . . . he returned with many valuables of gold and silver work, and five or six thousand pieces of rich cotton stuffs, woven, and embroidered in diverse ways. After he had given them to me, he sat down on another platform . . . near the one where I was seated, and . . . spoke in the following manner:

When Motecuhzoma had given necklaces to each one, Cortes asked him: "Is it true that you are the king Motecuhzoma?"

And the king said: "Yes, I am Motecuhzoma." Then he stood up to welcome Cortes; he came forward, bowed his head low and addressed him in these words: "Our lord, you are weary. The journey has tired you, but now you have arrived on the earth. You have

"We have known for a long time, from the [accounts] of our forefathers, that neither I, nor those who inhabit this country, are descendants from the [original inhabitants] of it, but from strangers who came to it from very distant parts; and we also hold that our race was brought to these parts by a lord, whose vassals they all were, and who returned to his native country. After a long time he come to your city, Mexico. You have come here to sit on your throne, to sit under its canopy.

"The kings who have gone before, your representatives, guarded it and preserved it for your coming. The kings . . . ruled for you in the City of Mexico. The people were protected by their swords and sheltered by their shields.

"Do the kings know the destiny of those they left behind, their [descendents]? If only they are watching! If only they can see what I see!

"No, . . . I am not seeing you in my dreams. . . . I have met you face to face! I was in agony for five days, for ten days, with my eyes fixed on the Region of the Mystery. And now you have come out of the clouds and mists to sit on your throne again.

"This was foretold by the kings who governed your city, and now it has taken place. You have come back to us; you have come down from the sky. Rest now, and take possession of your royal houses. Welcome to your land, my lords!"

came back, but it was so long, that those who remained here were married with the native women of the country, and had many descendants, . . when, therefore, he wished to take them away with him, they would not go, nor still less receive him as their ruler, so he departed. And we have always held that those who descended from him would come to [take over] this country and us, as his vassals; and according to the direction from which you say you come, which is where the sun rises, and from what you tell us of your great lord, or king, who has sent you here, we believe. . . that he is our rightful sovereign, especially as you tell us that since many days he has had news of us. Hence you may be sure that we shall obey you, and hold you as the representative of this great lord of whom you speak, . . . and throughout the whole country you may command at your will . . . , because you will be obeyed, and recognized, and all we possess is at your disposal. . . .

"I shall now go to other houses where I live; but you will be provided here with everything necessary for you and your people, and you shall suffer no annoyance, for you are in your own house and country."

When Motecuhzoma had finished, La Malinche translated his address into Spanish so that the

I answered to all he said, certifying that which seemed to be suitable, especially in confirming his

Captain could understand it. Cortés replied in his strange and savage tongue, speaking first to La Malinche. "Tell Motecuhzoma that we are his friends. There is nothing to fear. We have wanted to see him for a long time, and now we have seen his face and heard his words. Tell him that we love him well and that our hearts are contented."

La Malinche translated this speech and the Spaniards grasped Motecuhzoma's hands and patted his back to show their affection for him.

belief that it was Your Majesty whom they were expecting. After this, he took his leave, and, when he had gone, we were well provided with chickens, and bread, and fruits, and other necessities. . . . Thus I passed six days well provided with everything necessary, and visited by many of the lords. . . .

The Gold: An Aztec Account

[*Once in Tenochtitlán, the Spaniards seized Motecuhzoma and held him prisoner.*]

When Motecuhzoma was imprisoned, [his princely attendants] . . . ran away to hide and treacherously abandoned him! . . .

When the Spaniards entered the Royal House, they placed Motecuhzoma under guard. . . . [All but one of] . . . the other lords were permitted to depart.

Then the Spaniards fired one of their cannons . . . . The people scattered in every direction; they fled without rhyme or reason. . . . It was as if they had eaten the mushrooms that confuse the mind, or had seen some dreadful apparition. . . . And when night fell, the panic spread through the city and their fears would not let them sleep.

The Gold: Cortés's Account

In the morning the Spaniards told Motecuhzoma what they needed in the way of supplies. . . . Motecuhzoma ordered that it be sent to them. The chiefs who received this order were angry with the king and no longer revered or respected him. But they furnished the Spaniards with all the provisions they needed—food, beverages, and water, and fodder for the horses.

When the Spaniards were installed in the palace, they asked Motecuhzoma about the city's resources and reserves and about the warriors' [badges] and shields. They questioned him closely and then demanded gold.

Motecuhzoma guided them to it. They surrounded him and crowded close with their weapons. . . .

When they arrived at the treasure house called Teucalco, the riches of gold and feathers were brought out to them: . . .

The Spaniards immediately stripped the feathers from the gold shields and [badges]. They gathered all the gold into a great mound and set fire to everything else, regardless of its value. Then they melted down the gold into [bars]. As for the precious green stones, they took only the best of them; the rest were snatched up by the Tlaxcalans. The Spaniards searched through the whole treasure house, questioning and quarreling, and seized every object they thought was beautiful.

I spoke to Montezuma one day, and told him that Your Highness was in need of gold, on account of certain works ordered to be made. . . . [Montezuma collected much gold from his lords in many cities.] [A]ll those lords to whom he sent gave very compliantly, as had been asked, not only in valuables, but also in bars and sheets of gold, besides all the jewels of gold, and silver, and the featherwork, and the stones, and the many other things of value which I [set aside for] Your Sacred Majesty, amounting to the sum of one hundred thousand ducats [gold coins], and more. These, besides their value, are . . . so marvellous, that for the sake of their novelty and strangeness they have no price, nor is it probable that all the princes ever heard of in the world possess such treasures. Let not what I say appear fabulous to Your Majesty, because, in truth, all the things created on land, as well as in the sea, of which Montezuma had ever heard, were imitated in gold, most naturally, as

Next they went to Motecuhzoma's storehouse, in the place called [Place of the Palace of the Birds], where his personal treasures were kept. The Spaniards grinned like little beasts and patted each other with delight.

When they entered the hall of treasures, it was as if they had arrived in Paradise. They searched everywhere and coveted everything; they were slaves to their own greed. All of Motecuhzoma's possessions were brought out: fine bracelets, necklaces with large stones, ankle rings with little gold bells, the royal crowns and all the royal finery—everything that belonged to the king and was reserved to him only. They seized these treasures as if they were their own, as if this plunder were merely a stroke of good luck. . . .

well as in silver, and in precious stones, and featherwork, with such perfection that they seemed almost real. He gave me a large number of these for Your Highness, besides others, he ordered to be made in gold, for which I furnished him the designs, such as images, crucifixes, medals, jewelry of small value, and many other of our things which I made them copy. In the same manner, Your Highness obtained, as the one-fifth of the silver which was received, . . . which I made the natives cast in large and small plates, [bowls], cups, and spoons, which they executed as perfectly as we could make them [understand]. . . .

Relations between the Spanish and the Aztecs deteriorated over a period of months. In the spring of 1520, Spanish soldiers massacred many Aztec warriors as they took part in a religious ceremony. In response, the Aztecs drove the Spanish and their Indian allies out of the capital. The Spanish eventually reentered and destroyed Tenochtitlán in 1521. On its ruins, they built Mexico City, which became the capital for the Spanish empire in North America.

Review Questions

1. Why were Native American groups like the Tlaxcalans willing to help the Spaniards?

2. Was La Malinche a traitor to her people, an agent of change, or both? Explain.
3. Why did Montezuma welcome the Spaniards as rulers rather than oppose them with armed force?
4. How did the Aztecs' version of their welcome differ from Cortés's account?
5. How did the Aztecs' version of the Spanish seizure of their gold and treasures differ from Cortés's account?
6. What factors contributed to the Spanish conquest of the Aztecs?

The City of Tenochtitlán

Tenochtitlán, the capital of the Aztec Empire, amazed the 16th-century conquistadors. Not only was it bigger than European cities of the time—its 1519 population numbered about 250,000—it was also more advanced in design than most of them.

Tenochtitlán had developed from two early Aztec settlements built on a marshy lake island. As their villages grew into a great city, the Aztecs built causeways (raised highways) to connect it to the shores of the lake. They drained the marsh and planted gardens in the fertile soil. They built a dike to protect the city from flooding. Since the lake was too muddy to supply drinking water, they constructed an aqueduct to bring pure water from faraway springs. This water also supplied fountains that ornamented the city parks.

The people who planned the city gave Tenochtitlán a convenient and logical layout. Its streets and canals formed a grid pattern. They ran past public squares, marketplaces, and residential areas, which contained small houses. At the center of the city was a walled area containing temples, schools, and priests' houses.

The picture on page 170 shows a reconstruction of the walled central plaza as it probably looked to the conquistadors. The great pyramid at the left of the picture was the temple of the god of war. At the center of the plaza is a platform where prisoners of war were sacrificed. A wall of thousands of their skulls is seen in the background. The flat-roofed buildings on either side of the temple were royal palaces. The structures in the central plaza included the stadium where the ritual Aztec ball game was played. Sometimes, the losers of the game were sacrificed to the gods.

The Spaniards' admiration of Tenochtitlán did not prevent them from tearing it down once they had conquered the Aztecs. They built a new capital, Mexico City, on its ruins. Once it was thought that the Spanish had completely erased the ancient city. Recently, however, archaeologists have uncovered the remains of a great Aztec temple.

View of 16th-century Tenochtitlán (based on historical documents)

Review Questions

1. Why did Tenochtitlán amaze the Spanish conquistadors?
2. How did the plaza shown in the illustration play a key role in the political and religious life of the Aztec Empire?
3. What civilization used architectural designs similar to those of the Aztecs?

Pizarro Takes the Inca King Captive

Thousands of miles south of Mexico lay the Inca Empire, which sprawled across the Andes Mountains of South America. A Spanish expedition led by Francisco Pizarro reached Inca lands in 1532. The Incas had just experienced a brutal civil war. The war ended with the capture (and later execution) of the Inca king Huascar. His half-brother, Atahuallpa, was now ruler.

When Pizarro and his men arrived, Atahuallpa and his soldiers were resting in the small city of Cajamarca, preparing a triumphal entry into the nearby capital, Cuzco. Pizarro offered a feast in the new ruler's honor. Outnumbered by more than ten to one, the 180 Spanish soldiers laid plans to attack the Incas without warning during the feast. The attack was a success. Pizarro captured Atahuallpa, held him for a large ransom in gold and silver, and then had him killed after the Incas had paid the ransom.

The following account is by a Spanish official who gathered firsthand reports from Pizarro's companions several years later.

[Atahuallpa's Incas] thought so little of the Christian army that they expected to capture it with their bare hands. . . . [A]n Indian governor had sent to inform Atahuallpa that the Spaniards were very few and so . . . lazy that they could not walk without getting tired, for which reason they rode on a sort of large sheep that they called horses.

When Atahuallpa entered the square in . . . Cajamarca and saw so few Spaniards, all of them on foot since the horsemen were concealed, he thought that they were afraid to appear before him and would not resist an attack. Rising on his litter [a couch carried by servants], therefore, he said to his people: "They are our prisoner," and they all answered, "Yes."

Then the bishop, Fray Vicente de Valverde, came forward . . . and [told] how One God in three persons had created heaven and earth and all that was in it, . . . and how the popes had divided the whole world between the Christian princes and kings, entrusting each with a task of conquest; and that this province of Atahuallpa's had been assigned to His Majesty the Emperor and King Don Carlos, our master; and that he had sent Don Francisco Pizarro to represent him as governor and inform Atahuallpa on behalf of God and the Emperor of all that he had just said; that if Atahuallpa chose to believe and receive the waters of baptism and obey him, as did the greater part of Christendom, the Emperor would defend and protect him, maintaining peace and justice in the land and preserving his liberties as he did those of other kings and lords who accepted his rule without risk of war; but if Atahuallpa were to refuse, the Governor would make cruel war on him with fire and sword, and lance in hand. . . .

After listening to all this, Atahuallpa replied that these lands and all that was in them had been won by his father, and his ancestors, who had left them to his brother Huascar Inca, and that, since he had conquered him and now held him prisoner, they were his possessions, and he did not know how [the pope] . . . could give them to anyone; and that even if he had given them, he Atahuallpa did not [consider them a] gift and would give the Emperor nothing. . . . He had never heard of anything being created except by the sun, whom they worshipped as they did the earth their mother . . . ; and that Pachacamac had created everything in that country. . . . He asked the bishop how he could know that all he said was the truth and how he could prove such statements.

The bishop said that it was written in this book, which was God's scripture. And Atahuallpa asked him for the Bible. . . . The bishop gave it to him, and Atahuallpa turned over the leaves from end to end, saying that it said nothing to him. In fact it did not speak at all. And he threw it on the ground.

Then the bishop turned toward the Spaniards and cried "At them! At them!"

. . . [T]he Governor [Francisco Pizarro] . . . immediately ordered a gun to be fired, and the horsemen attacked the Indians from three sides. The Governor himself advanced with his infantry in the direction from which Atahuallpa was coming, and on reaching his litter they began to kill the bearers. But as fast as one fell several more came with great resolution to take his place.

The Governor realized that if the defense were to be at all prolonged his men would be defeated. For though they might kill many Indians a single Christian death would count for more. So he attacked the litter with great fury, seizing Atahuallpa by the hair (which he wore very long) and dragging him roughly toward him till he fell out. Meanwhile the Christians were slashing the litter—which was of gold—so fiercely with their swords that they wounded the Governor in the hand. But in the end Francisco Pizarro threw Atahuallpa to the ground and, though many Indians rushed forward to rescue him, took him prisoner.

When the Indians saw their lord lying on the ground a prisoner, and themselves attacked from so many sides and so furiously by the horses they so feared, they turned round and began to flee in panic, making no use of their arms but running away so fast that they bowled one another over. So many of them were driven into one corner of the enclosure in which the battle had taken place that they knocked down a piece of the wall through which to escape.

The horsemen continued to chase the Indians till night turned them back.

Review Questions

1. How did events occurring within the Inca Empire aid the Spanish conquest?
2. Why did the Incas underestimate the Spaniards?
3. What message did the bishop bring to the Incas
   a. From the pope?
   b. From the Spanish king, Don Carlos?
4. What was Atahuallpa's reaction to
   a. Christianity?
   b. Spanish rule?
5. Why did the Incas panic when they were attacked by Pizarro's men?
6. What factors contributed to the Spanish conquest of the Incas?

A Portrait for a New Age

Hans Holbein, the Younger, was born in Augsberg, Germany, in 1497. Holbein started his career as a portrait painter in his native Germany. But he soon became so successful that King Henry VIII of England hired him as his court painter. Holbein painted several portraits of Henry, and he traveled abroad to paint portraits of various noblewomen whom Henry was interested in marrying.

Holbein did not always paint rulers or the nobility, however. His first portraits were of members of the upper middle class, such as the Swiss burgomaster (magistrate; the equivalent of today's city mayor) Jacob Meyer, and of the important thinkers and writers of the day, such as Erasmus and Sir Thomas More. These people, pleased with the artist's work, arranged commissions for him from their friends and associates.

Holbein's range of subjects and patrons reveals much about the social changes that were taking place in the 1500s, during the Renaissance. Members of the European middle class now had the leisure and education to appreciate excellent painting and the wealth to support the artist who produced it. The wealthy middle classes were beginning to rival the aristocracy and royalty in power.

The painting shown here—the portrait of a merchant named Georg Gisze—illustrates the new status of business people. Gisze sits in an office cluttered with workaday objects. His surroundings are rather shabby, but he is richly dressed and physically imposing. The viewer is led to assume that the merchant obtained his fine clothes and self-confidence by hard work rather than by inherited wealth. The work was obviously mental rather than physical, however. In the first place, Gisze is literate. A book sits prominently on the shelf behind him. He is handling a letter, which he has just finished writing or is opening to read. The hands that hold the letter show no trace of heavy labor. More importantly, his facial expression shows a shrewd intelligence and a realistic assessment of his own high rank. The crystal vase holding a pink flower suggests a love of finer things.

Portrait of merchant Georg Gisze, by Hans Holbein (1532)

Review Questions

1. What does this portrait reveal about the growing status of Europe's merchant class?
2. How did the rise of a new social class illustrate the important changes of the Renaissance period?
3. What is the profession of the man in the portrait?

A Reformed Slave Trader's Regrets

For hundreds of years, European slave ships (called "slavers") shuttled back and forth between Africa and the Americas. It was a brutal business, and it left its mark on the crews of the ships as well as on their captives.

John Newton was a British slave ship captain who finally left the business and spoke against its inhumanity. Born in 1725, he first went to sea at the age of 11, on a merchant ship commanded by his father. When he was 19, he was impressed (forcibly enlisted) by the British navy. While serving on a warship, he deserted but was caught and beaten. Later he joined the crew of a slave ship and began a series of adventures and misadventures.

After a few years in the slave trade, Newton returned to England, where he eventually became a Protestant minister. His main claim to fame is as the author of a popular hymn, "Amazing Grace." The hymn's opening lines had a very personal meaning for Newton:

> Amazing grace! (how sweet the sound)
> That sav'd a wretch like me!
> I once was lost, but now am found,
> Was blind, but now I see.

In 1788 Newton wrote a book, *Thoughts Upon the African Slave Trade*, from which the following excerpts are taken.

[I]n the year 1750, I was appointed commander; in which capacity I made three voyages to the [west coast of Africa] for slaves.

Disagreeable I had long found [the slave trade] . . . ; but I think I should have quitted it sooner, had I considered it as I do now, to be unlawful and wrong. But I never had a [moral doubt] upon this [topic] at the time; nor was such a thought once suggested to me by any friend. What I did I did ignorantly; considering it as the line of life which Divine Providence had allotted me, and having no concern, in point of conscience, but to treat the slaves, while under my care, with as much humanity as a regard to my own safety would admit. . . .

[I]n general, I know of no method of getting money, not even that of robbing for it upon the highway, which has so direct a tendency to [wear away] the moral sense, to rob the heart of every gentle and humane [feeling], and to harden it, like steel, against all [softer feelings].

Usually, about two-thirds of a cargo of slaves are males. When a hundred and fifty or two hundred [healthy] men, torn from their native land, many of whom never saw the sea, much less a ship, till a short space before they had [to board one]; . . . it is not to be expected that they will tamely resign themselves to their situation. It is always taken for granted that they will attempt to gain their liberty if possible. Accordingly, as we dare not trust them, we receive them on board, from the first as enemies; and, before their number exceeds, perhaps, ten or fifteen, they are all put in irons; in most ships, two and two together. And frequently, they are not thus confined, as they might most conveniently stand or move, the right hand and foot of one to the left of the other, but across; that is, the hand and foot of each on the same side, whether right or left, are [bound] together [with iron bracelets]: so that they cannot move either hand or foot, but with great caution, and with perfect consent. Thus they must sit, walk, and lie, for many months (sometimes for nine or ten), without any . . . relief, unless they are sick.

In the night, they are confined below; in the daytime (if the weather be fine) they are upon deck; and as they are brought by pairs, a chain is put through a ring upon their irons, and this likewise locked down to the ringbolts, which are fastened, at certain intervals, upon the deck. These, and other precautions are no more than necessary; especially, as while the number of slaves increases, that of the people who are to guard them, is [lessened], by sickness, or death, or by being absent in the boats: so that, sometimes, not ten men can be mustered, to watch, night and day, over two hundred, besides having all the other business of the ship to attend.

That these precautions are so often effective is much more to be wondered at, than that they sometimes fail. One unguarded hour, or minute, is sufficient to give the slaves the opportunity they are always waiting for. An attempt to [rebel against] . . . the ship's company brings on instantaneous and horrid war: for, when they are once in motion, they are desperate; and where they do not conquer, they are seldom quelled without much mischief and bloodshed on both sides.

Sometimes, when the slaves are ripe for an insurrection, one of them will [inform on the others] . . .; and then necessity, and the state policy, of these small but most absolute governments [meaning the rule of a ship's captain over a ship], enforce [rules] directly contrary to the nature of things. The traitor to the cause of liberty [that is, the informer] is caressed, rewarded, and deemed an honest fellow. The patriots [those planning a rebellion] who formed and animated the plan, if they can be found out, must be treated as villains, and punished, to intimidate the rest. These punishments, in their nature and degree, depend upon the [absolute] will of the captain. Some are content with inflicting such moderate punishment as may suffice for an example. But unlimited power, instigated by revenge, . . . is terrible!

I have seen them [the rebellious captives] sentenced to unmerciful whippings, continued till the poor creatures have not had power to groan under their misery, and hardly a sign of life has remained. I have seen them agonizing for hours, I believe for days together, under the torture of the thumbscrews; . . . Surely, it must be allowed, that [crew members] who are long [familiar] with such scenes as these, are liable to [develop] a spirit of ferociousness, and savage insensibility, of which human nature, depraved as it is, is not, ordinarily, capable.

[W]e have heard and read a melancholy story, too notoriously true to admit of contradiction, of more than a hundred grown slaves thrown into the sea, at one time, from on board a ship, when fresh water was scarce; to fix the loss upon the [insurers], which otherwise, had they died on board, must have fallen upon the owners of the vessel. [In other words, if the slaves had died on board, their loss would have been at the ship owners' expense, but if they were "lost at sea," insurers would cover the loss.] These incidents are specimens of the spirit produced by the African trade in men who once were no more [lacking in] the milk of human kindness than ourselves.

Review Questions

1. Why did Captain Newton believe the slave trade had a negative moral influence on the slave ships' English crews?
2. a. How were the slaves confined in an inhumane manner?
   b. Why did the English believe it was necessary to treat the slaves so cruelly?
3. Why did Newton believe that the rules of a slave ship were "contrary to the nature of things"?
4. a. How were informers treated on the slave ships?
   b. How were rebels treated on the slave ships?
5. How does Newton demonstrate that the slave trade was strictly a business venture?
6. Why did the opening lines of the hymn "Amazing Grace" have personal meaning for Captain Newton?

Eyewitness: Olaudah Equiano, an African Boy

One of the millions who experienced the Atlantic crossing as a captive was an African boy of about the age of 12 who came to be known as Olaudah Equiano. (He also went by another name, Gustavas Vassa.) In later years, having grown to manhood and obtained an education, Equiano wrote a book about his experiences. These passages are from that book, which was published in 1789.

. . . I was born, in the year 1745, in a charming fruitful [valley] named Essaka. The distance of this province from the capital of Benin and the sea coast must be very considerable; for I had never heard of white men or Europeans, nor of the sea: and our subjection to the king of Benin was [insignificant]; for every transaction of the government, as far as [I could tell], was conducted by the chiefs or elders of the place. . . .

Our [farming] is [carried out] in a large plain or common, some hours walk from our dwellings, and all the neighbors resort thither in a body. They use no [farm animals] and their only instruments are hoes, axes, shovels, and beaks, or pointed iron to dig with. . . . This common is often the theater of war; and therefore when our people go out to till their land, they not only go in a body, but generally take their arms with them for fear of a surprise; and when they apprehend an invasion they guard the avenues to their dwellings, by driving sticks into the ground, which are so sharp at one end as to pierce the foot, and are generally dipped in poison. From what I can recollect of these battles, they appear to have been [invasions] of one little state or district on the other, to obtain prisoners or booty. Perhaps they were [urged] to this by those traders who brought . . . European goods . . . amongst us. Such a mode of obtaining slaves in Africa is common; and I believe more are [gotten] this way and by kidnapping, than any other. When a trader wants slaves, he applies to a chief for them, and tempts him with his wares. . . . Accordingly [the chief] . . . falls on his neighbors, and a desperate battle ensues. . . .

We have fire-arms, bows and arrows, broad two-edged swords and [light spears]: we have shields also which cover a man from head to foot. All are taught the use of these weapons; even our women are warriors, and march boldly out to fight along with the men. Our whole district is a kind of militia: on a certain signal given, such as the firing of a gun at night, they all rise in arms and rush upon their enemy. It is perhaps something remarkable, that when our people march to the field a red flag or banner is borne before them. I was once a witness to a battle in our common. We had been all at work in it one day as usual, when our people were suddenly attacked. I climbed a tree at some distance, from which I beheld the fight. There were many women as well as men on both sides; among others my mother was there, and armed with a broad sword. After fighting for a considerable time with great fury, and after many had been killed our people obtained the victory. . . . Those prisoners which were not sold or [bought back] we kept as slaves: but how different was their condition from that of the slaves in the West Indies! With us they do no more work than other members of the community, even their masters; their food, clothing and lodging were nearly the same as theirs (except that they were not permitted to eat with those who were free-born); and there was scarce any other difference between them, than a superior degree of importance which the head of a family possesses in our state, and that authority which, as such, he exercises over every part of his household. Some of these slaves have even slaves under them as their own property, and for their own use. . . .

My father, besides many slaves, had a numerous family, of which seven lived to grow up, including myself and a sister, who was the only daughter. . . . In this way I grew up till I was turned the age of eleven, when an end was put to my happiness in the following manner:— One day, when all our people were gone out to their works as usual, and only I and my dear sister were left to mind the house, two men and a woman got over our walls, and in a moment seized us both, and, without giving us time to cry out, or make resistance, they stopped our mouths, and ran off with us into the nearest wood. Here they tied our hands, and continued to carry us as far as they could. . . . [On the third day] my sister and I were . . . separated. . . . I cried and grieved continually; and for several days I did not eat anything but what they forced into my mouth. . . .

From the time I left my own nation I always found somebody that understood me till I came to the sea coast. The languages of different nations [in Africa] did not totally differ, nor [had they so many words] as those of the Europeans, particularly the English. They were therefore easily learned. . . .

I was [several times] . . . sold, and carried through a number of places, till, after traveling a considerable time, I came to a town called Tinmah, in the most beautiful country I had yet seen in Africa. . . . Here I first saw and tasted cocoa-nuts. . . . Here I also saw and tasted for the first time sugar-cane. . . .

[Olaudah was bought by a wealthy widow who lived in Tinmah.] Her house and premises . . . were the finest I ever saw in Africa: they were very [large], and she had a number of slaves to attend her. The next day I was washed and perfumed, and when meal-time came I was led into the presence of my mistress, and ate and drank before her with her son, a young gentleman about my own age and size. . . . [H]e would not at any time either eat or drink till I had taken first, because I was the eldest, which was agreeable to our custom. Indeed every thing here, and all their treatment of me, made me forget that I was a slave. . . . In this resemblance to my former happy state I passed about two months; and I now began to think I was to be adopted into the family, . . . when all at once the delusion vanished; for, without the least previous knowledge, one morning early, while my dear master and companion was still asleep, I was wakened out of my [dream] to fresh sorrow, and hurried away. . . .

[A]t the end of six or seven months after I had been kidnapped, I arrived at the sea coast. . . .

The first object which [greeted] my eyes when I arrived on the coast was the sea, and a slave ship, which was then riding at anchor, and waiting for its cargo. These filled me with astonishment, which was soon [changed] into terror when I was carried on board. I was immediately [physically examined], and tossed up to see if I were sound, by some of the crew. . . .

[Olaudah describes the horrors of the Middle Passage from Africa to the Caribbean.]

At last we came in sight of the island of Barbados, at which the whites on board gave a great shout, and made many signs of joy to us. . . . Many merchants and planters now came on board . . . . They put us in separate parcels, and examined us attentively. They also made us jump, and pointed to the land, signifying we were to go there. We thought by this we should be eaten by these ugly men. . . . [T]here was much dread and trembling among us, and nothing but bitter cries to be heard all the night from these [fears]. . . . [T]he white people got some old slaves from the land to pacify us. They told us we were not to be eaten, but to work, and were soon to go on land, where we should see many of our country people. This report eased us much; and sure enough, soon after we were landed, there came to us Africans of all languages.

We were conducted immediately to the merchant's yard, where we were all [shut up] together like so many sheep in a fold, without regard to sex or age. . . .

We were not many days in the merchant's custody before we were sold after their usual manner, which is this: On a signal given (as the beat of a drum) the buyers rush at once into the yard where the slaves are confined, and make choice of that parcel they like best. . . . In this manner, are relations and friends separated, most of them never to see each other again. I remember in the vessel in which I was brought over, in the men's apartment, there were several brothers, who, in the sale, were sold in different lots; and it was very moving on this occasion to see and hear their cries at parting. . . . [T]his [separation of families] . . . , while it has no advantage to atone for it, . . . adds fresh horrors even to the wretchedness of slavery.

Bought by a kindly ship's captain, who taught him to read and write, Equiano traveled widely and was eventually freed. He joined the abolitionist movement (campaign to abolish slavery) in England and lectured there about the evils of slavery. His autobiography was widely read by abolitionists. It went through many editions between its first appearance in 1789 and Equiano's death in 1797.

Review Questions

1. How did European traders encourage African rulers to participate in the slave trade?
2. How were the slaves owned by Africans treated differently from the slaves owned by Europeans?
3. How was Olaudah captured and taken into slavery?
4. How was Olaudah able to use his education to fight against the evils of slavery?

Unit IV Document-Based Question

*Write a well-organized essay that includes an introduction, several paragraphs, and a conclusion. Use evidence from at least **four** documents in this unit in the body of the essay. Support your response with relevant facts, examples, and details. Include additional outside information.*

Historical Context

By the eve of the first global age, the peoples of West Africa and the Americas had already developed complex societies. Contact with European civilization brought many dramatic changes for these societies.

Task: Using the documents and questions in the unit, along with your knowledge of global history, write an essay in which you:

- Show how **three** groups, from Africa and the Americas, had developed complex societies complete with sophisticated governments and/or belief systems
- Evaluate the effect of European contact on **one** African or Native American society

An Age of Revolutions

(1750–1914)

Copernicus Writes "On the Revolutions of the Heavenly Bodies"

When Nicolaus Copernicus was born in Poland in 1473, most astronomers believed (as the Greek philosopher Aristotle had concluded some 1,900 years before) that the sun, planets, and stars revolved around the earth. By the time he died 70 years later, Copernicus had adopted a competing theory—that the earth and the five other known planets revolved around the sun. This theory was called *heliocentric*, meaning centered on the sun. (*Helios* is the Greek word for sun.)

Like other astronomers of his time, Copernicus took careful notes based on his direct observations of the movements of stars and planets. (The telescope was not invented until the early 1600s.) He arrived at his overall theory largely by mathematical reasoning. Earlier mathematicians had worked out theories about how the sun and planets moved—not in simple circles, but in circles within circles and in various other ways. All this was extremely complicated. To Copernicus, a major argument for the heliocentric theory was that it was simpler and more straightforward.

The idea that the earth moved around the sun was highly controversial because it seemed to go against the word of the Bible. For example, the 93rd Psalm says that God "fixed the earth upon its foundation, not to be moved forever." As a devout Roman Catholic, Copernicus took care to point out that he had no desire to challenge religious authority. Challenging church doctrine could be risky, since there were severe penalties for heresy (holding positions contrary to religious doctrines). Cautiously, Copernicus delayed publishing his conclusions until late in life. He was on his deathbed in 1543 when he finally saw a copy of his book (*On the Revolutions of the Heavenly Bodies*) in print.

This document is from a preface that Copernicus wrote, dedicating his book to Pope Paul III, the leader of the Roman Catholic Church. The pope received the book cordially.

To Pope Paul III

I can easily conceive, most Holy Father, that as soon as some people learn that, in this book which I have written concerning the revolutions of the heavenly bodies, I [attribute] certain motions to the Earth, they will cry out at once that I and my theory should be rejected. For I am not so much in love with my conclusions as not to weigh what others will think about them. . . . [W]hen I consider . . . how absurd a performance it must seem to those who know that the judgment of many centuries has approved the view that the Earth remains fixed as center in the midst of the heavens, if I should on the contrary, assert that the Earth moves; I was for a long time at a loss to know whether I should publish the commentaries which I have written in proof of its motion. . . .

I began to consider the mobility of the Earth. . . . [B]ecause I knew that the liberty had been granted to others before me to postulate all sorts of little circles for explaining the phenomena of the stars, I thought I also might be permitted to try whether, by postulating some motions of the Earth, more reliable conclusions could be reached regarding the revolution of the heavenly bodies, than those of my predecessors.

. . . I have found by many and long observations that if the movements of the other planets are assumed for the circular motion of the Earth and are substituted for the revolution of each star, not only do their phenomena follow logically therefrom, but the relative positions and magnitudes both of the stars and all their orbits, and of the heavens themselves, become so closely related that in none of its parts can anything be changed without causing confusion in the other parts and in the whole universe.

. . . Nor do I doubt that ingenious and learned mathematicians will . . . [support] me, if they are willing to recognize and weigh . . . those matters which have been [offered as proof] by me in this work to demonstrate these theories.

. . . If perchance there shall be idle talkers, who, though they are ignorant of all mathematical sciences, . . . should dare to criticize and attack this . . . theory of mine because of some passage of scripture which they have falsely distorted for their own purpose, I care not at all; I will even despise their judgment as foolish. . . .

Copernicus's book was so full of mathematics that it was hard for most people to follow his argument. Mathematicians and astronomers, however, quickly applied the book's path-breaking advances in their studies of the stars and planets. Yet many of those scientists still did not accept the idea that the Earth moves. For example, Thomas Blundeville, an English astronomer, praised Copernicus for his mathematics while rejecting his heliocentrism.

Christian leaders—Protestants and Catholics alike—greeted the theory of heliocentrism with hostility. Martin Luther, the founder of Protestantism, criticized Copernicus for contradicting the Bible.

Review Questions

1. Why did Copernicus publish his theory late in his life?
2. a. What was the tone of Copernicus's dedication to Pope Paul III?
   b. Why did Copernicus write to the pope in this manner?
3. What was Copernicus's theory about the movement of the planets?
4. Why were many Christians hostile to Copernicus's conclusions?

The Inquisition Convicts Galileo of Heresy

Some 66 years after Copernicus's death, advances in the science of optics allowed the Italian scientist Galileo Galilei (1564–1642) to gather evidence that supported Copernicus' heliocentric theory. Galileo built a telescope in 1609, which improved upon a recent Dutch invention. This new invention allowed him to observe things that no one had seen before. For example, he discovered four moons circling the planet Jupiter. This proved that at least some heavenly bodies do not revolve around the earth. He also saw that the planet Venus had bright and dark phases, just like the moon. The timing of those phases indicated that Venus revolved around the sun rather than the Earth.

Galileo began to publish his findings and to draw conclusions from them, as others were also doing. Roman Catholic authorities became alarmed at the attention the heliocentric theory was attracting. In 1615, the Inquisition—a body set up by the Church to root out errors—declared the heliocentric theory to be a heresy. A Church official warned Galileo not to "hold or defend" Copernicus's theory.

Galileo thought he saw a way to get his ideas across and stay within the rules of the Church. In 1632, with the approval of Church censors in Florence, he published *Dialogue Concerning the Two Chief World Systems*. This book described an imaginary conversation among three people—a supporter of the earth-centered universe, a supporter of the heliocentric universe, and a third person who wanted to know how the theories worked. This format allowed Galileo to state the arguments for the heliocentric theory without actually advancing it as his own belief. But Church authorities suspected that Galileo's purpose was to defend the theory that the Earth moved, in violation of earlier warnings not to. In 1633, the Inquisition put Galileo on trial and convicted him.

The following document contains the inquisitors' findings.

We say, pronounce, sentence and declare that you, Galileo, by reason of these things which have been detailed in the trial and which you have confessed already, have rendered yourself according to this Holy Office vehemently suspect of heresy[1] namely, of having held and believed a doctrine that is false and contrary to the divine and Holy Scripture: namely, that the Sun is the center of the world and does not move from east to west, and that one may hold and defend as probable an opinion after it has been declared and defined contrary to Holy Scripture. Consequently, you have [brought upon yourself] all the censures and penalties [specified in] . . . the sacred [doctrines] and all particular and general laws against such delinquents. We are willing to [set] you [free] from [the consequences of your guilt] provided that first, with a sincere heart and [sincere] faith, in our presence you [reject], curse, and detest the said errors and heresies, and every other error and heresy contrary to the Catholic and Apostolic[2] Church in the manner and form we will prescribe to you.

Furthermore, so that this grievous and [destructive] error and [sin] of yours may not go altogether unpunished, and so that you will be more cautious in future, and an example for others to abstain from delinquencies of this sort, we order that the book *Dialogue* of Galileo Galilei be prohibited by public edict. We condemn you to formal imprisonment in this Holy Office at our pleasure. . . . [W]e impose on you to recite the seven penitential[3] psalms once a week for the next three years. And we reserve to ourselves the power of moderating, commuting, or taking off the whole or part of the said penalties and penances. This we say, pronounce, sentence, declare, order and reserve by this or any other better manner or form that we reasonably can or shall think of. So we the undersigned Cardinals pronounce:

F. Cardinal of Ascoli
B. Cardinal Gessi
G. Cardinal Bentivoglio
F. Cardinal Verospi
Fr. D. Cardinal of Cremona
M. Cardinal Ginetti
Fr. Ant. s Cardinal of S. Onofrio.

[1]**vehemently suspect of heresy**—"vehement suspicion of heresy" was one of three possible grades of heresy; it was in the middle between "formal heresy" (the most serious finding) and "slight suspicion of heresy"

[2]**Apostolic**—based on the apostles, or original disciples of Jesus

[3]**penitential**—having to do with penance, an act by which one shows regret for wrongdoing

Despite the seriousness of the charge of heresy, Galileo was treated with relative leniency. The Inquisition forced him to make a public statement renouncing the theory of heliocentrism. Then he was placed under house arrest. He was required to remain at home and could not freely travel. Galileo lived under these restrictions for eight years, until he died in 1642. During that time, he completed and published an important book on the science of motion. He was also able to continue to use his telescope to observe the heavens.

Review Questions

1. How did the telescope help Galileo prove the accuracy of Copernicus's heliocentric theory?
2. Why did the inquisitors declare Galileo guilty of heresy?
3. How was Galileo punished?
4. Why do you think Galileo was treated leniently?

John Locke on the Origins of Human Society and Government

One of Western history's most influential statements of people's rights to live in a society that is run by just and rational laws was made by the English philosopher John Locke (lived 1632–1704). In the introduction to his *Two Treatises of Government* (1689), Locke describes his purpose as "to justify to the world the people of England, whose love of their just and natural rights, with their resolution to preserve them, saved the nation when it was on the very brink of slavery and ruin." A year earlier, England had undergone a revolution. A monarch who believed in absolute rule, King James II, had been overthrown. In his place, the English Parliament installed James' daughter, Mary, and her husband, the Dutch Prince William of Orange. This Glorious Revolution (1688) affirmed the supremacy of the legislature, or Parliament, over the monarchy. The English Parliament at the time was not truly representative of all English people, because only certain property holders and land-owning aristocrats could be members. Not until the late 1880s were most Englishmen able to vote, and women first received the right to vote in 1918.

John Locke was one of a new breed of writer-philosopher. He was deeply influenced by the work of scientists like Isaac Newton, who stated the fundamental laws of gravity, and by others who made discoveries in biology and chemistry. He was also influenced by philosophers like René Descartes of France, whose major concern was how people acquired knowledge. Locke's *Essay Concerning Human Understanding* stands in the tradition of independent thought and inquiry that gave his era the name the Age of Enlightenment.

Locke's political writings had great influence on the thinkers of the 18th century. The Baron Montesquieu in France, in *The Spirit of the Laws* (1748), extended Locke's argument that power in government rests with the citizens of a state and on their choice of leaders (what Locke calls the "legislative"). Montesquieu described the functions of the three separate branches of government—executive, legislative, and judicial—that are needed for good government. This division of powers would be the basic organization of the government of the new United States and other democratic nations that arose in the next century.

Excerpts from Locke's *Second Treatise of Government*, in which he describes the reasons why people form societies, why only the people may choose their rulers and decide how they are to be governed, are given below.

Men being, as has been said, by nature all free, equal, and independent, no one can be put out of this estate and subjected to the political power of another without his own consent. The only way whereby any one divests himself of his natural liberty and puts on the bonds of civil society is by agreeing with other men to join and unite into a community for their comfortable, safe, and peaceable living one amongst another, in a secure enjoyment of their properties and a greater security against any that are not of it. This any number of men may do, because it injures not the freedom of the rest; they are left as they were in the liberty of the state of nature. When any number of men have so consented to make one community or government, they are thereby presently incorporated and make one body politic wherein the majority have the right to act and conclude [bind] the rest.

For when any number of men have, by the consent of every individual, made a community, they have thereby made that community one body, with a power to act as one body, which is only by the will and determination of the majority. . . .

And thus every man, by consenting with others to make one body politic under one government, puts himself under an obligation to every one of that society to submit to the determination of the majority and to be concluded [bound] by it; or else this original compact . . . would otherwise signify nothing, and be no compact. . . .

The great and chief end, therefore, of men's uniting into commonwealths and putting themselves under government is the preservation of their property. . . .

But though men when they enter into society give up the equality, liberty, and executive power they had in the state of nature into the hands of the society, to be so far disposed of the legislative as the good of the society shall require, yet it being only with an intention in every one the better to preserve himself, his liberty and property . . . the power of the society, or legislative constituted by them, can never be supposed to extend farther than the common good, but is obliged to secure every one's property by providing against those . . . defects that made the state of nature so unsafe and uneasy.

> Locke described three defects of the state of nature: (1) lack of established, settled, known law, by common consent to be the standard of right and wrong; (2) lack of a known and indifferent (impartial) judge with authority to determine (settle) all differences according to the established law; (3) lack of power to back and support the sentence (of judges) when right, and to give it due execution (carry it out).

And all this is to be directed to no other end but the peace, safety, and public good of the people.

By commonwealth, I must be understood all along to mean, not a democracy or any form of government, but any independent community which the Latins [ancient Romans] signified by the word *civitas*, to which the word which best answers in our language is "commonwealth," and most properly expresses such a society of men, which "community" or "city" in English does not, . . .

. . . [T]he first and fundamental positive law of all commonwealths is the establishing of the legislative power; as the first and fundamental natural law which is to govern even the legislative [power] itself is the preservation of the society and, as far as will consist [be consistent] with the public good, of every person in it. This legislative [power] is not only the supreme power of the commonwealth, but sacred and unalterable in the hands where the community have once placed it; not can any edict of anybody else, in what form soever conceived or by what power soever backed, have the force and obligation of a law which has not its sanction from that legislative which the public has chosen and appointed; for without this the law could not have that which is absolutely necessary to its being a law: the consent of the society over whom nobody can have a power to make laws, but by their own consent and by authority received from them.

The end of government is the good of mankind.

Review Questions

1. What event or action prompted Locke to publish his treatises of government?
2. Why did human beings enter into civil society, according to Locke?
3. a. What did Locke mean by a "commonwealth"?
   b. What end or purpose did Locke see for people uniting in a commonwealth?
4. What was the purpose of the legislature?
5. What was the end or ultimate purpose of government?

Madame du Châtelet: "Inferior to No One"

One of the outstanding women of 18th-century Europe was Émilie du Châtelet (1706-1749), whose translation into French of the English scientist Isaac Newton's famous *Principia* helped to spread his ideas on the European continent. A brilliant thinker in her own right, Madame du Châtelet also performed scientific experiments and wrote a highly regarded physics textbook. She is often remembered, however, not for such accomplishments but for her romantic attachment to the leading French writer of the time, Voltaire.

Voltaire fully appreciated Madame du Châtelet's intellectual powers. Voltaire and Madame du Châtelet collected a vast array of scientific devices, and the two often worked together on experimental projects. They invited many of the leading scientific and literary figures of France to visit them.

All her life, Madame du Châtelet had to struggle for acceptance as an equal to men. Proud of her own accomplishments, she argued forcefully with those she saw as undervaluing her. The following paragraphs are from a letter she wrote to the man later who later became known as King Frederick the Great of Prussia. In his twenties, before assuming the Prussian throne, Frederick befriended Voltaire and spent time discussing science and philosophy with him. Feeling that Frederick was snubbing her, Madame du Châtelet made a fervent plea that might have been seconded by women of any era.

Hate me if you must. I would not deny you the pleasure that this primitive feeling would give you. But be not indifferent to me, I beg you, as I could not tolerate it. Ridicule my scientific studies and my translations from the classics of antiquity, if it gives you pleasure to treat me with contempt, but do not ignore me.

Judge me for my own merits, or my lack of them, but do not look upon me as a mere appendage[1] to this great general or that renowned scholar, this star that shines at the court of France or that famed author. I am in my own right a whole person, responsible to myself alone for all that I am, all that I say, all that I do. It may be that there are metaphysicians[2] and philosophers whose learning is greater than mine, although I have not met them. Yet, they are but frail humans, too, and have their faults; so, when I add the sum total of my graces, I confess that I am inferior to no one.

Review Questions

1. Why did Madame du Châtelet write to Frederick the Great?
2. How did Madame du Châtelet wish Frederick to treat her?
3. Why did Madame du Châtelet ask not to be treated as an "appendage"?
4. What do you think Madame du Châtelet would say about the treatment of women today?

[1]**appendage**— a person who is dependent on another; a body part of limited importance
[2]**metaphysicians**—those who study the fundamental nature of reality

France: A Prison Falls and a Revolution Begins

In the year 1789, France was suffering from a severe economic crisis. King Louis XVI decided he had to raise taxes in order to finance the operation of the government. To do this, he called a meeting of the Estates General, the French parliament. The organization of the parliament revealed the basic inequality of French government. The parliament was divided into three sections, or estates. The First and Second Estates consisted of high-ranking clergy and nobles. Together, these two estates stood for what has been called the Old Regime—the system of injustice and privilege that led to revolution. These classes, although rich and influential, were a small minority of the population, and they paid few taxes. The Third Estate consisted of professional people, peasants, laborers, and minor clergy. They represented 98 percent of the population. But they had little voice in political decisions, and most of them paid high taxes.

The First and Second Estates each had 300 representatives in the Estates General. The Third Estate had 600. Yet each estate had only one vote when it came time to vote on a resolution. This meant that the First and Second Estates could override the Third Estate by a margin of two to one. Determined to end the oppression under which the majority of the French people lived, the representatives of the Third Estate proposed that all three estates meet together and decide matters as one group. This would give those seeking reforms an edge in passing needed legislation. When the king denied their request, the members of the Third Estate left the Estates General and set up a new government. They called this body the National Assembly. The king then threatened to arrest the leaders of the assembly, and riots broke out all over France.

On July 14, 1789, a city mob joined by members of the Parisian militia seized the Bastille. The Bastille was the notorious prison where French kings kept political enemies. People were imprisoned in the Bastille for long periods of time without any legal process having taken place. The July 14 revolutionaries freed the Bastille's prisoners and armed themselves with the weapons stored there. This was the beginning of the revolution that eventually overthrew the Old Regime.

The artist who created this picture lived at the time, and perhaps witnessed the event. The illustration shows citizens fighting in the streets to bring down the imposing fortress.

Every July 14, the French people celebrate Bastille Day as a national holiday. For them, it has the historic and emotional importance that July 4 has for United States citizens.

Fall of the Bastille, July 14, 1789

Review Questions

1. How did the Estates General illustrate the inequality of the French government?
2. Why was the National Assembly created?
3. How does the illustration show the significance of the attack on the Bastille?

Declaration of the Rights of Man and of the Citizen

The National Assembly of the new French Republic wanted to make radical changes in French government. The revolutionary leaders meant the following document to be the basis of a government that worked for the general good and treated all people in the same fair manner. Like the leaders of the earlier American Revolution, French leaders had adopted the ideas of such political writers as John Locke (1632–1704). They were especially influenced by Locke's *Two Treatises of Government*. (See Document 3 in this unit.) Locke discusses what he called the natural rights of man, or humankind. These are the rights to life, liberty, and property. It is the government's role to act as protector of those rights, and the people's right to replace a government that does not guarantee or safeguard their rights. Locke's ideas formed the cornerstone of the American Declaration of Independence and the French Declaration of the Rights of Man and of the Citizen.

Preamble

The representatives of the French people, formed into a National Assembly, considering ignorance, forgetfulness, or contempt of the rights of man to be the only causes of public misfortunes and the corruption of Governments, have resolved to set forth, in a solemn Declaration, the natural, unalienable [incapable of being taken away], and sacred rights of man, to the end that this Declaration, constantly present to all members of the body politic [a group of people politically organized under one government], may remind them unceasingly of their rights and their duties; to the end that the acts of the legislative power and those of the executive power, since they may be continually compared with the aim of every political institution, may thereby be the more respected; to the end that the demands of citizens, founded henceforth on simple and [certain] principles, may always be directed toward the [support] of the Constitution and the happiness of all.

In consequence whereof, the National Assembly recognizes and declares, in the presence and under the [power] of the Supreme Being, the following Rights of Man and of the Citizen.

Article 1. Men are born and remain free and equal in rights. Social distinctions may be based only on considerations of the common good.

Article 2. The aim of every political association is the preservation of the natural . . . rights of man. These rights are Liberty, Property, Safety, and Resistance to Oppression.

Article 3. The source of all sovereignty lies essentially in the Nation. No corporate body, no individual may exercise any authority that does not expressly [arise] from it.

Article 4. Liberty consists in being able to do anything that does not harm others: thus, the exercise of the natural rights of every man has no bounds other than those that ensure to the other members of society the enjoyment of these same rights. These bounds may be determined only by Law.

Article 5. The Law has the right to forbid only those actions that are injurious to society. Nothing that is not forbidden by Law may be hindered, and no one may be compelled to do what the Law does not [establish].

Article 6. The Law is the expression of the general will. All citizens have the right to take part, personally or through their representatives, in its making. It must be the same for all, whether it protects or punishes. All citizens, being equal in its eyes, shall be equally eligible to all high offices, public positions, and employments, according to their ability, and without other distinction than that of their virtues and talents.

Article 7. No man may be accused, arrested, or detained except in the cases determined by the Law, and following the procedure that it has prescribed. Those who solicit, expedite, carry out, or cause to be carried out [dictatorial] orders must be punished; but any citizen summoned or [arrested] by virtue of the Law, must give instant obedience; resistance makes him guilty.

Article 8. The Law must [order] only the punishments that are strictly and evidently necessary; and no one may be punished except by virtue of a Law drawn up and [made public] before the offense is committed, and legally applied.

Article 9. As every man is presumed innocent until he has been declared guilty, if it should be considered necessary to arrest him, any undue harshness that is not required to secure his person must be severely curbed by Law.

Article 10. No one may be disturbed on account of his opinions, even religious ones, as long as the [display] of such opinions does not interfere with the established Law and Order.

Article 11. The free communication of ideas and of opinions is one of the most precious rights of man. Any citizen may therefore speak, write, and publish freely, except what is [equivalent] to the abuse of this liberty in the cases determined by Law. . . .

Article 16. Any society in which no provision is made for guaranteeing rights or for the separation of powers, has no Constitution.

Article 17. Since the right to Property is inviolable and sacred, no one may be deprived thereof, unless public necessity, legally [identified] obviously requires it, and just and prior [compensation] has been paid.

Review Questions

1. How did the English writer John Locke influence the writers of the French Declaration of the Rights of Man and of the Citizen?
2. What is the stated purpose of the Declaration of the Rights of Man and of the Citizen?
3. How is "liberty" defined?
4. According to the declaration, what is the purpose of lawmaking?
5. According to the declaration, who should make the laws?
6. Why does the declaration state "any society in which no provision is made for guaranteeing rights or the separation of powers, has no constitution"?

Adam Smith on the "Invisible Hand"

One of the earliest and most influential theorists of free-enterprise capitalism was a Scottish economist named Adam Smith. In *The Wealth of Nations,* published in 1776, Smith argued powerfully against the prevailing policy of mercantilism. Under mercantilism, governments imposed strong guidance over a nation's economic activities, heavily restricting foreign trade and protecting various kinds of domestic monopolies (businesses that have almost exclusive control over a product or industry). Smith was a fervent opponent of monopolies, and a strong supporter of free trade.

In the following excerpt, Smith argues that government interference in business is almost always a mistake. However, he does allow for a few exceptions.

Every individual is continually exerting himself to find out the most advantageous employment [use] for whatever capital [money] he can command. It is his own advantage, indeed, and not that of the society, which he has in view. But the study of his own advantage naturally, or rather necessarily, leads him to prefer that employment which is most advantageous to the society. . . .

[E]very individual . . . endeavors as much as he can both to employ his capital in the support of domestic industry [the business of his native country] and so to direct that industry that its produce may be of the greatest value; [thus,] every individual necessarily labors to render the annual [earnings] of the society as great as he can. He generally, indeed, neither intends to promote the public interest, nor knows how much he is promoting it. By preferring the support of domestic to that of foreign industry, he intends only his own security; and by directing that industry in such a manner as its produce may be of the greatest value, he intends only his own gain, and he is in this, as in many other cases, led by an invisible hand to promote an end which was no part of his intention. . . . By pursuing his own interest he frequently promotes that of the society more effectually than when he really intends to promote it. I have never known much good done by those who affected [pretended] to trade for the public good.

[Individuals can judge better than political leaders in which industry or product it would be profitable to invest their money.] The statesman [political leader], who should attempt to direct private people in what manner they ought to employ their capitals, would . . . [take on] an authority which could safely be trusted, not only to no single person, but to no council or senate whatever, and which would nowhere be so dangerous as in the hands of a man who [was foolish and conceited] enough to [imagine] himself fit to exercise it.

To give the monopoly of the home market to the produce of domestic industry, in any particular art or manufacture, is in some measure to direct private people in what manner they ought to employ their capitals, and must, in almost all cases, be either a useless or a hurtful regulation. If the produce of domestic [industry] can be brought there as cheaply as that of foreign industry, the regulation is evidently useless. If it cannot, it must generally be hurtful. It is the [rule] of every prudent master of a family, never to attempt to make at home what it will cost him more to make than to buy. The tailor does not attempt to make his own shoes, but buys them from the shoemaker. The shoemaker does not attempt to make his own clothes, but employs a tailor. The farmer attempts to make neither the one nor the other, but employs those different [craftspeople]. All of them find it for their interest to employ their whole industry in a way in which they have some advantage over their neighbors and to purchase with a part of its produce, or what is the same thing, with the price of a part of it, whatever else they have occasion for.

What is prudence in the conduct of every private family can scarcely be folly in that of a great kingdom. If a foreign country can supply us with a [product] cheaper than we ourselves can make it, better buy it from them with some part of the produce of our own industry, employed in a way in which we have some advantage. . . .

There seem, however, to be two cases in which it will generally be advantageous to lay some burden upon [or tax] foreign, for the encouragement of domestic, industry.

The first is, when some particular sort of industry is necessary for the defense of the country. . . .

The second case is when some tax is imposed at home upon the produce of [domestic industry]. In this case, it seems reasonable that an equal tax should be imposed upon the like produce of [foreign industry]. . . .

Review Questions

1. What did Adam Smith believe was the relationship between an individual's economic decisions and the economic interests of a nation?
2. What did Smith mean by the term "invisible hand"?
3. What was Smith's attitude regarding government regulation of a nation's economy?
4. In what situations did Smith feel that government could interfere with free trade?

The Steam Engine: Power for a New Revolution

Fuel crises in the 20th and 21st centuries have affected the world's economy and the balance of global political power. During the 18th century, the response to a fuel shortage led to profound economic, technological, and political changes. The introduction of a new source of power, the steam engine, was one of the most important factors in the development of power-driven machines and the Industrial Revolution.

England's rapidly increasing population made it necessary to plant more crops for food. By the 18th century, most of England's forests had been cleared to make way for farmlands. The wood needed to heat homes and the charcoal to fuel fires for the manufacture of iron became scarce.

Since the Middle Ages, people had heated their homes with coal as well as wood. At that time, however, they did not use it in the manufacture of iron. Gradually, ironmakers turned to coal as a cheap source of energy.

As the demand for coal increased, miners dug deeper into the coal deposits. In doing so, they tapped sources of underground water, which filled the mines. At first, pumps worked by horses or donkeys removed the water. But this was an expensive and inefficient procedure.

In 1698, an English engineer named Thomas Savery invented a device that used high-pressure steam to create a vacuum in a metal chamber. Water rushed upward from the mine into the vacuum. Before the cycle could start again, more steam had to be used to remove the water from the chamber.

Fourteen years later, in 1712, Thomas Newcomen, an English ironmonger (seller of iron products) invented a pumping machine that was operated by low-pressure steam. The following diagram demonstrates how Newcomen's machine worked. As in Savery's earlier invention, the steam produced a vacuum. But, in Newcomen's engine, the vacuum set the various parts of the machine in motion. This engine, which could only move downward, was used solely to pump water out of mines.

In the 1760s and 1770s, English inventor James Watt created a more usable engine. Using Newcomen's design as a foundation, he made it possible to power the upstroke as well as the downward stroke of the piston. Capable of a rotary movement, Watt's machine could run machinery, carriage wheels, or riverboat paddles. By the middle of the 19th century, improved versions of the steam engine were running machines in mines and factories and providing power for locomotives and steamships. The steam engine had become the heart of the Industrial Revolution.

Review Questions

1. How was the development of the steam engine a response to a fuel shortage?
2. How did Newcomen and Watt's steam engine help relieve this fuel shortage?
3. How did the steam engine propel the growth of industry and transportation and help bring about the Industrial Revolution?

Diagram of Newcomen's Steam Engine
Water was injected from a tank (A) through a pipe (B) to cool the steam-filled cylinder (C). This process caused atmospheric pressure to push down the piston (D), located in the cylinder. The movement of the piston raised a beam (E) and pumped water from the mine.

9 Yorkshire Cloth Workers' Petition

As the Industrial Revolution progressed, the introduction of new machinery often threatened workers' traditional ways of earning a living. This caused great alarm among the workers.

The following document is a petition by cloth workers in Leeds, a major center of wool manufacture in the Yorkshire region of northeastern England. The petition was published in two Leeds newspapers in 1786.

Greeting to the Merchants, Clothiers and all such as wish well to the Staple Manufactory of this Nation.

The Humble Address and Petition of Thousands, who labor in the Cloth Manufactory.

Sheweth [shows] That the Scribbling-Machines[1] have thrown thousands of your petitioners out of employ, whereby they are brought into great distress, and are not able to [support] their families, and deprived them of the opportunity of bringing up their children to labor: We have therefore to request that prejudice and self-interest may be laid aside, and that you may pay that attention to the following facts, which the nature of the case requires.

The number of Scribbling-Machines extending about seventeen miles south-west of Leeds, exceed all belief, being no less than *one hundred and seventy!* and as each machine will do as much work in twelve hours, as ten men can in that time do by hand (speaking within bounds) and they working night and day, one machine will do as much work in one day as would otherwise employ twenty men.

. . . [T]welve men are thrown out of employ for every single machine used in scribbling; and as it may be supposed the number of machines in all the other quarters [regions] together [are] nearly equal those in the south-west, full four thousand men are left to shift for a living how they can. . . . Allowing one boy to be bound apprentice

[1]**scribbling-machines**—machines that card or separate the strands of wool before the wool is spun into cloth

from each family out of work, eight thousand hands are deprived of the opportunity of getting a livelihood.

We therefore hope that the feelings of humanity will lead those who have it in their power to prevent the use of those machines . . .

This is not all; the injury to the Cloth is great, in so much that in frizzing,[2] instead of leaving a nap upon the cloth, the wool is drawn out and the Cloth is left thread-bare.

Many more evils we could enumerate, but we would hope, that the sensible part of mankind, who are not biased by interest, must see the dreadful tendency of their continuance; a depopulation must be the consequence; trade being then lost, the landed interest will have no other satisfaction but that of being *last devoured* [ruined].

We wish to propose a few queries to those who would plead for the further continuance of these machines:

Men of common sense must know, that so many machines in use, take the work from the hands employed in Scribbling—and who did that business before machines were invented.

How are those men, thus thrown out of employ to provide for their families—and what are they to put their children apprentice to, that the rising generation may have something to keep them at work, in order that they may not be like vagabonds strolling about in idleness? Some say, Begin and learn some other business. — Suppose we do; who will maintain our families, whilst we undertake the arduous task; and when we have learned it, how do we know we shall be any better for all our pains; for by the time we have served our second apprenticeship, another machine may arise, which may take away that business also; so that our families, being half [starved] while we are learning how to provide them with bread, will be wholly so during the period of our third apprenticeship.

But what are our children to do; are they to be brought up in idleness? Indeed as things are, it is no wonder to hear of so many executions; for our parts, though we may be thought illiterate men, our conceptions are, that bringing children up to industry,

[2]**frizing, or frizzing**—raising a nap (downy surface) on cloth

and keeping them employed, is the way to keep them from falling into those crimes, which an idle habit naturally leads to.

These things impartially considered will we hope, be strong [arguments] in our favor; and we conceive that men of sense, religion and humanity, will be satisfied of the reasonableness, as well as necessity of this address, and that their own feelings will urge them to [support] the cause of us and our families—

Signed, in behalf of THOUSANDS, by

Joseph Hepworth   Thomas Lobley
Robert Wood   Thos. Blackburn

Review Questions

1. How did the scribbling machines cause many Yorkshire cloth workers to lose their jobs?
2. a. According to the petitioners, why did the scribbling machines produce an inferior quality of cloth?
   b. Why did the cloth workers include this argument in their petition?
3. What problems did the petition claim would result if laid-off workers tried to learn another trade?
4. What did the petition ask of the cloth manufacturers and merchants?

10 A Woman Coal Mine Worker Tells Her Story

The working conditions in industries and mines during the Industrial Revolution provoked numerous investigations by lawmakers and others interested in protecting the health and morals of workers. In Great Britain, a parliamentary investigation of the coal industry in 1842 produced the document from which the following woman mine worker's story is taken.

Betty Harris, age 37: I was married at 23, and went into a colliery [mine] when I was married. I used to weave when about 12 years old; can neither read nor write. I work for Andrew Knowles, of Little Bolton [Lancashire], and make sometimes 7 [shillings] a week, sometimes not so much. I am a drawer [someone who pulls coal carts], and work from 6 in the morning to 6 at night. Stop about an hour at noon to eat my dinner; have bread and butter for dinner; I get no drink. I have two children, but they are too young to work. I worked at drawing when I was in the family way [pregnant]. I know a woman who has gone home and washed herself, taken to her bed, delivered of a child, and gone to work again under the week.

I have a belt round my waist, and a chain passing between my legs, and I go on my hands and feet. The road is very steep, and we have to hold by a rope; and when there is no rope, by anything we can catch hold of. There are six women and about six boys and girls in the pit I work in; it is very hard work for a woman. The pit is very wet where I work, and the water comes over our clog-tops always, and I have seen it up to my thighs; it rains in at the roof terribly. My clothes are wet through almost all day long. I never was ill in my life, but when I was [recovering from giving birth].

My cousin looks after my children in the day time. I am very tired when I get home at night; I fall asleep sometimes before I get washed. I am not so strong as I was, and cannot stand my work so well as I used to. I have drawn till I have bathe [scraped] skin off me; the belt and chain is worse when we are in the family way. My feller [husband] has beaten me many a times for not being ready. I were not used to it at first, and he had little patience.

I have known many a man beat his drawer. I have known men take liberties with the drawers. . . .

Review Questions

1. What type of work did Betty Harris do in the coal mines?
2. How were women coal mine workers treated?
3. What effect you think the government report had on conditions in the mines?

A Utopian Community

The Industrial Revolution caused many problems in Western Europe and American society. The rise in productivity brought wealth to only certain groups of people. Most workers did not belong to these favored groups. The laws of supply and demand ruled the market for both goods and human labor. The law of supply said that the more plentiful goods were, the less they cost. During the 19th century, labor-saving machines cut the number of workers needed on farms. Factory and mining jobs replaced many traditional jobs. People needing work far outnumbered the jobs available. Therefore, employers could hire workers for very low wages.

Male workers with families often did not earn enough to support them. Women and children had to go to work too. Working conditions were often unsanitary and dangerous. Families lived in crowded apartments. Disease was everywhere. Children often grew up stunted, sickly, and uneducated.

No laws ensured workers' health and safety. No compensation was available to the sick, injured, or elderly. Governments had no power to regulate wages, hours, or working conditions.

Many people were appalled by these conditions. Among the most outspoken critics of industrialization were the Socialists. The Socialists were a group of reformers who originated in France. They believed that society should be reorganized to prevent the miseries suffered by the poor. Cooperation should replace cutthroat competition among the powerful people of the world. To establish this cooperation, governments should engage in economic planning and regulate private property.

One of the early Socialist reformers was the Frenchman Charles Fourier (1772–1825). He dreamed of a utopian, or perfect, society, in which people could lead happy, healthy, and useful lives. This society would be made up of small cooperative farming communities, each inhabited by exactly 1,620 people. There, men, women, and children would share both the work required to keep the community running and the profits of that work. Women would have the same rights and responsibilities as men.

This 1847 German illustration of Fourier's utopian vision shows a peaceful and prosperous community. The older man who seems to be teaching a group of children suggests that in Fourier's utopia, the elderly would be useful and respected, while the young would be both physically and mentally nourished.

Artist's rendering of a Fourier utopian community

Review Questions

1. Why were mid-19th-century employers able to hire workers for very low wages?
2. How did the Socialists wish to reorganize society?
3. What is the meaning of the word "utopia"?
4. How does the illustration depict Fourier's utopian society?

A Manifesto for Revolution

The period that included the French Revolution, the reign of Napoleon Bonaparte, and the French domination of much of Europe (1789–1815) was followed by a period of strong reaction. Many of the revolutionary ideals of social equality, independent national states, and political and social freedom were suppressed, as were the people who advocated them. After 1815, the next generation of rulers of Europe attempted to "turn back the clock" to the time preceding the French Revolution. They reestablished absolute monarchy and privilege, and maintained strict control over the activities and writings of the intellectual class. In Europe, new revolutionary outbreaks in 1830, 1848, and 1870 were followed by periods of reaction and oppression. In the first half of the century, European nationalist movements were successful in gaining a nation's freedom from outside rule only in Belgium and Greece. (In the Americas, however, many of the nations that had been Spanish colonies won their freedom.)

Opposition to reactionary ideas and policies arose early in 19th-century France and Germany. There, younger thinkers proposed new ideas and dreamed of new societies that were not based on inherited wealth or ancient social traditions. (In England, writers like John Stuart Mill proposed a fairer division of the profits of business among the workers, and more rights for women.)

In Germany, groups of young students formed around radical thinkers. A leading member of these groups was Karl Marx (1818–1883). Born into a well-to-do family, Marx was forced to leave Germany because of his radical ideas and associates. He went to Paris in 1843, where he met Frederick Engels (1820–1895). Engels had written about the terrible living conditions of the working class in England, where his prosperous German family had a business. Marx and Engels became lifelong friends. In Paris and London, they joined communistic associations of workingmen.

In 1848, Marx and Engels wrote a small work that would become a major source of much radical thought for the next century. They called it *The Manifesto of the Communist Party,* or as it is better known, *The Communist Manifesto*. This short publication contains the political and social agenda of a secret society called the Communist League. It tells of the "class warfare" that was arising between two classes in 19th-century society. The ruling, or dominant, class was the bourgeoisie, or capitalists. They owned the means of production, such as factories, and controlled the banking system. Their opponents were the proletariat–the great mass of workers who had no property. The proletariat existed by selling its labor to the bourgeoisie. Marx and Engels predicted that a revolution would overthrow the bourgeoisie and set up a communistic society ruled by the proletariat. History was the record of class struggle, they said, of the oppressed fighting their oppressors. In the later 19th and 20th centuries, the *Manifesto* and Marx's other writings (especially *Das Kapital*, or *Capital*) became the basic texts for Marxist revolutionary movements around the world. Excerpts from the *Manifesto* are given below.

The history of all hitherto existing society [recorded or written history] is the history of class struggles. . . .

Our epoch, the epoch of the bourgeoisie [the owners of the means of production], possesses . . . this distinctive feature: It has simplified the class antagonisms. Society as a whole is more and more splitting up into two great hostile camps, into two great classes directly facing each other—bourgeoisie and proletariat [the workers, or laborers, who have no means of production]. . . .

The bourgeoisie has played a most revolutionary role in history. . . . It has resolved personal worth into exchange value, and in place of the numberless . . . chartered freedoms has set up that single . . . freedom—Free Trade. . . .

The bourgeoisie has stripped of its halo every occupation hitherto honored and looked up to with reverent awe. It has converted the physician, the lawyer, the priest, the poet, the man of science, into its paid wage-laborers.

In proportion as the bourgeoisie, i.e., capital [or capitalism], is developed, in the same proportion is the proletariat, the modern working class developed—a class of laborers, who live only so long as they find work, and who find work only so long as their labor increases capital. These laborers, who must sell themselves piecemeal, are a commodity, like every other article of commerce, and are consequently exposed to all the vicissitudes [problems, uncertainties] of competition, to all the fluctuations of the market.

Modern industry has converted the little workshop of the patriarchal master [the workshop owner and teacher; father figure] into the great factory of the industrial capitalist. . . .

No sooner has the laborer received his wages in cash . . . than he is set upon by the other portions of the bourgeoisie, the landlord, the shopkeeper, the pawnbroker, etc.

The lower strata of the middle class—the small tradespeople, shopkeepers, and retired tradesmen generally, the handicraftsmen and peasants—all these sink gradually into the proletariat. . . . The proletariat is recruited from all classes of the population.

The immediate aim of the Communists is the same as that of all other proletarian parties: Formation of the proletariat into a class, overthrow of bourgeois supremacy, conquest of political power by the proletariat. . . .

The distinguishing feature of Communism is not the abolition of property generally, but the abolition of bourgeois property.

To be a capitalist is to have not only a purely personal, but a social status, in production. . . .

Capital is therefore not a personal, it is a social, power.

Communism deprives no man of the power to appropriate [take] the products of society; all that it does is to deprive him of the power to subjugate [enslave, command] the labor of others by means of such appropriation.

. . . The history of all past society has consisted in the development of class antagonisms . . . that assumed different forms in different epochs [time periods]. . . .

We have seen . . . that the first step in the revolution by the working class is to raise the proletariat to the position of ruling class, to establish democracy.

The proletariat will use its political supremacy to wrest [take], by degrees, all capital from the bourgeoisie, to centralize all instruments of production in the hands of the state, i.e., of the proletariat organized as the ruling class; and to increase the total of productive forces as rapidly as possible.

. . . [I]n the most advanced countries, the following will be . . . generally applicable.

1. Abolition of property in land and application of all rents of land to public purposes.
2. A heavy progressive or graduated income tax.
3. Abolition of all right of inheritance.
4. Confiscation of the property of all emigrants and rebels.
5. Centralization of credit in the hands of the state, by means of a national bank with state capital and an exclusive monopoly.
6. Centralization of the means of communication and transport in the hands of the state.
7. Extension of factories and instruments of production owned by the state; the bringing into cultivation of waste lands, . . .
8. Equal obligation of all to work. . . .
9. Combination of agriculture with manufacturing industries. . . .
10. Free education for all children in public schools. Abolition of child factory labor. . . .

Political power . . . is merely the organized power of one class for oppressing another. . . .

In place of the old bourgeois society, with its classes and class antagonisms, we shall have an association, in which the free development of each [person, group] is the condition for the development of all.

The Communists everywhere support every revolutionary movement against the existing social and political order of things.

. . . [T]hey labor everywhere for the union and agreement of the democratic parties of all countries.

The Communists disdain [refuse] to conceal their views and aims. They openly declare that their ends can be attained only by the forcible overthrow of all existing social conditions. Let the ruling classes tremble at a Communist revolution. The proletarians have nothing to lose but their chains. They have a world to win.

Workingmen of all countries, unite!

Review Questions

1. How did Marx and Engels understand the record of history?
2. a. What two classes did Marx and Engels identify in the society of their time?
   b. How did these two classes differ?
3. a. What was to be the immediate aim of the proletariat and the Communists?
   b. How was this to be accomplished?
4. What would happen to bourgeoisie property in the Communist state?
5. How did the ten aims or goals of the Communist Party reveal the party's beliefs and goals?
6. What call did Marx and Engels make at the end of the *Manifesto*?

Dostoyevsky Escapes a Firing Squad

To defenders of the old order in Europe (the small ruling aristocracy and the vast number of poor peasants), the revolutionary spirit that took hold in Europe in the 1840s was a serious threat that had to be crushed without mercy. In Russia, Czar Nicholas I (ruled 1825–1855) sought to halt even the slightest mention among his subjects of such topics as socialism or freeing the serfs. Any Russian who dared to discuss such ideas even in private faced arrest—and perhaps worse.

In 1849, the czar's secret police cracked down on a group of people who gathered on Friday evenings for food, drink, and discussion at the home of a man named Mikhail Petrashevsky. The police knew that Petrashevsky was an admirer of the French socialist Charles Fourier (1772–1837), whose writings advocated a classless agricultural society based on full equality for women and men (see document 11). People in the Petrashevsky group passed around copies of Fourier's writings, which were banned in Russia, and debated his ideas. In the Russia of Nicholas I, such actions were considered a danger to the state.

One of those who occasionally went to Petrashevsky's was a young novelist named Fyodor Dostoyevsky. In his late twenties at the time, Dostoyevsky had not yet written the novels for which he would later become famous—*Crime and Punishment* (1866) and *The Brothers Karamazov* (1879–1880). The young writer was little known outside a small circle of literary admirers. Although he had little interest in Fourier or socialism, Dostoyevsky had made known his support for another dangerous cause—the freeing of Russia's serfs. When the police swept down on the Petrashevsky group, they also went after Dostoyevsky.

The first reading is Dostoyevsky's description of his arrest in April 1849.

A. Dostoyevsky's Arrest (April 23, 1849)

. . . I returned home between three and four in the morning . . . , went to bed and immediately fell asleep. No more than an hour later through my sleep I noticed that some suspicious and strange people had come into my room. A saber [light sword] rattled, having gotten caught on something. What on earth was going on? I struggle to open my eyes and hear a soft, pleasant voice say: "Get up!"

I look around: there is a precinct or district superintendent of police, with gorgeous sideburns. But he was not the one speaking; the one speaking was a gentleman dressed in light blue with a lieutenant-colonel's [shoulder ornaments].

"What is the matter?" I asked, getting up from bed.

"By imperial order . . .

I look around: indeed it was "by imperial order." In the doorway stood a soldier in light blue. He was the owner of the saber that had rattled. . . .

While I was getting dressed they demanded all my books and started rummaging around; they did not find many but they rummaged through everything. My papers and letters they bound neatly with a string. The superintendent of police displayed a great deal of ingenuity in this matter: he climbed up so he could reach into the stove and then groped around in the old ashes with my long-stemmed pipe. At his invitation, the [minor] officer from [military police headquarters] stood on a chair and climbed up over the stove, but he lost hold of the [molding] and crashed down onto the chair making a loud noise and then both fell to the ground. At this point the . . . gentlemen became convinced that there was nothing on top of the stove.

On the table there was a [small coin] which was old and bent. The superintendent of police attentively examined it and finally nodded to the lieutenant-colonel.

"Well, aren't you worried about its being counterfeit?" I asked.

"Hm . . . That, in fact, must be looked into . . ." mumbled the superintendent and he ended up including it in the evidence.

We left. . . . By the entryway a carriage stood waiting; we got in: the soldier, myself, the superintendent and the colonel, then we drove off [to prison]. . . .

Despite the lighthearted talk at his arrest, Dostoyevsky was in very serious trouble. After spending eight months in solitary confinement, he and twenty others were sentenced to death by firing squad. The czar and his officials intended to make an example of these "freethinkers," to let other Russians know how dangerous it was to hold or discuss certain ideas.

The czar never actually intended to have the condemned men executed, however. Rather, he ordered that they be brought to the point of execution and then granted a reprieve. Instead of being shot, they would be sent to prison camps in Siberia.

The condemned prisoners believed they were about to die, and were ready to do so. The sudden news that they would be allowed to live came as a severe shock. Dostoyevsky, while greatly shaken, seems to have drawn lessons and a renewed spiritual strength from the experience. His writings in later years reveal an intense awareness of the death that awaits all people—at a time and place that no one can know for certain.

Dostoyevsky's sentence was four years at hard labor, followed by military service as a common soldier. In the letter that follows, he describes to his brother what it felt like to prepare for a firing squad and in what state of mind he faced his years of exile.

B. Letter to His Brother (December 22, 1849)

. . . Today, December 22, we were taken to Semyonov Square. There we were all read the death sentence, allowed to kiss the cross, had sabers broken over our heads and our pre-death attire put on (white shirts). Then three people were stood against the stakes for the carrying out of the execution. I was the sixth in line, people were summoned by threes, consequently, I was in the second row and had no more than a minute left to live. I remembered you, brother, and all of your family; at the last moment you, only you, were in my mind, only then did I realize how much I love you, my dear brother! I had time also to embrace [two other prisoners] who were nearby, and to say farewell to them. Finally, a retreat was sounded, the ones tied to the stake were led back, and it was announced that His Imperial Majesty was granting us our lives. Then the real sentences followed. . . .

I'm not despondent and I haven't lost heart. Life is everywhere, life is in ourselves, and not outside. There will be people by my side, and to be a *human being* among people and to remain one forever, no matter in what circumstances, not to grow despondent and not to lose heart—that's what life is all about; that's its task. I have come to recognize that. That idea has entered my flesh and blood. But it's the truth! The head that created, lived the higher life of art, that recognized and grew accustomed to the higher demands of the spirit, that head has already been cut from my shoulders. What remains is memory and images. . . . But there remain in me a heart and the same flesh and blood that can also love, and suffer, and pity, and remember, and that's life, too! *On voit le soleil* [One can see the sun]! . . .

Can it be that I'll never [again] take pen in hand? I think that in four years it will be possible. I'll send you everything I write if I write anything. My God! How many images, cast out, created by me anew will perish, will expire in my head or contaminate my blood like a poison! Yes, if I won't be able to write, I'll perish. Better fifteen years of imprisonment and a pen in hand! . . .

But don't grieve, for Heaven's sake, don't grieve about me! Know that I haven't lost heart, remember that hope has not abandoned me. In four years there will be an easing of my lot. I'll be a common soldier—no longer a prisoner, and keep in mind that someday I'll embrace you. After all I was at death's door today, I lived with that thought for three-quarters of an hour, I faced the last moment, and now I'm alive again! . . .

Ten years passed before Dostoyevsky was free to return to St. Petersburg, the Russian capital, and resume his normal life. By then, he had abandoned many of his radical ideas. He considered himself a loyal follower of the new czar, Alexander II (ruled 1855–1881). In 1861, Alexander issued an official decree that freed the Russian serfs.

Review Questions

A. Dostoyevsky's Arrest

1. Why do you think Dostoyevsky was arrested late at night after he had gone to bed?

2. a. What did the men who arrested Dostoyevsky take from his room?
   b. Why do you think these items were taken as evidence?

B. Letter to His Brother

1. Why was Dostoyevsky condemned to death?
2. Why do you think Czar Nicholas issued a reprieve?
3. How did his near-death experience change Dostoyevsky?
4. A French nobleman visiting Russia in the time of Czar Nicholas I wrote: "In Russia, to converse is to conspire; to think is to revolt." Based on Dostoyevsky's experience, do you think the Frenchman was correct?

Irish Peasants Are Evicted From Their Home

From the early 1800s on, British political leaders worked to improve the conditions of the poor working class in England. They were less concerned about conditions in Ireland, however. Although part of 19th-century Great Britain, Ireland might well have been a conquered country. The majority of the Irish were Roman Catholic peasants. They worked the land on great estates owned by Protestant landlords, many of whom lived in England.

Irish peasants were given tiny plots of land in exchange for their work. Potatoes were the best crop to grow on these small fields. A family of four could eat well for a year on the potatoes harvested from one acre.

Unfortunately, the Irish became almost completely dependent on the potato. In 1845, a fungus ruined the potato crop. The potato blight lasted for four long years. Starvation and illness caused by malnutrition killed over a million people. Thousands more emigrated to the United States.

Although the failure of the potato crop affected other parts of Great Britain, it devastated only Ireland. In 1846, England's prime minister, Robert Peel, averted famine in England by repealing the corn laws. These laws had put a high tariff on imported grain. With their repeal, most English people could afford to buy foreign-grown grain. The Irish, however, had been so dependent on the potato that the crop failure wiped out all their financial resources. They were unable to afford even the cheapest grain.

By 1847, the English government had established soup kitchens and emergency work relief for the Irish. In that year, however, a banking crisis in England halted these efforts. The Irish Poor Law system took over famine relief. This system provided workhouses, where the starving and mortally ill had to work to support themselves. Many died in the attempt. Ireland was crippled economically for decades after the famine ended.

The British government not only did not provide effective aid for the starving Irish peasants, it persecuted them as well. When landlords evicted tenant farmers who could not pay their rent, the government sent soldiers to enforce the evictions.

This picture shows an Irish family locked out of its shabby home. The people seem to own nothing but the clothes on their backs and a few tools. This incident, which occurred in the 1880s, shows the long shadow cast by the failure of the potato crops.

Eviction of Irish peasants from their home, 1880s

Review Questions

1. Why did the ruined potato crop cause massive illness and starvation in Ireland?
2. Why were the Irish unable to benefit from the repeal of the corn laws?

3. Why did the British fail to provide more help for the Irish?
4. How does the picture illustrate Britain's lack of support for the Irish peasants after the potato famine?

15 Theodor Herzl Founds the Zionist Movement

Appalled by repeated outbreaks of anti-Jewish violence in Eastern Europe and open discrimination against Jews elsewhere, an Austrian Jew named Theodor Herzl wrote a book in 1896 laying out a plan for resolving "the Jewish question." Herzl's book helped to spark a worldwide movement to create an independent Jewish state. This Jewish nationalist movement was called Zionism. (In the Old Testament, Zion was the hill in ancient Jerusalem where the Hebrews' King David established his capital.)

Even before Herzl's time, some Jews called themselves Zionists and left their homes in Europe to settle in the biblical land of Palestine. But it was Herzl who turned Zionism into a political movement with a specific goal–a Jewish state. In 1897, he called a world congress of Jewish delegates at Basel, Switzerland. The delegates founded the World Zionist Organization, with Herzl as its president.

The following excerpt is from Herzl's 1896 book, *The Jewish State*.

No one can deny the gravity of the Jewish situation. Wherever they live in [considerable] number, Jews are persecuted in greater or lesser measure. Their equality before the law, granted by statute [or law], has become practically a dead letter. They are [prevented] from filling even moderately high offices in the army, or in any public or private institutions. And attempts are being made to thrust them out of business also: "Don't buy from Jews!"

Attacks in parliaments, in assemblies, in the press, in the pulpit, in the street, on journeys—for example, their exclusion from certain hotels—even in places of recreation are increasing from day to day. The forms of persecutions vary according to country and social circle. In Russia, special taxes are [put] on Jewish villages; in Romania, a few persons are put to death; in Germany, they get a good beating occasionally; in Austria, anti-Semites exercise their terrorism over all public life; in Algeria, there are traveling agitators; in Paris, the Jews are shut out of the so-called best social circles and excluded from clubs. . . .

The fact of the matter is, everything tends to one and the same conclusion, which is expressed in the classic Berlin cry: "*Juden 'raus!*" ("Out with the Jews!").

I shall now put the question in the briefest possible form: Shouldn't we "get out" at once, and if so, whither?

Or, may we remain, and if so, how long?

. . . [T]he sins of the Middle Ages are now being visited on the nations of Europe. We are what the ghetto[1] made us. We have without a doubt attained pre-eminence in finance because medieval conditions drove us to it. The same process is now being repeated. We are again being forced into money-lending—now named stock exchange—by being kept out of other occupations. But once on the stock exchange, we are again objects of contempt. At the same time we continue to produce an abundance of mediocre intellectuals who find no outlet, and this endangers our social position as much as does our increasing wealth. Educated Jews without means are now rapidly becoming socialists. Hence we are certain to suffer acutely in the struggle between the classes, because we stand in the most exposed position in both the capitalist and the socialist camps. . . .

The whole plan [of Zionism] is essentially quite simple, as it must necessarily be if it is to be comprehensible to all.

Let sovereignty be granted us over a portion of the globe adequate to meet our rightful national requirements; we will attend to the rest. . . . [*Herzl describes his plan for gradual, voluntary emigration and settlement in the new homeland, and for the development of a sound economy and a modern society.*]

Palestine is our unforgettable historic homeland. The very name would be a marvelously effective rallying cry. If His Majesty the Sultan [the ruler of the Ottoman Empire] were to give us Palestine, we could in return undertake the complete management of the finances of Turkey. We should there form a part of a wall of defense for Europe in Asia, an outpost of civilization against barbarism. We should as a neutral state remain in contact with all Europe, which would have to guarantee our existence. The holy places of

---

[1]**ghetto**—area of a city in which Jews were required to live

Christendom could be placed under some form of international extraterritoriality.[2] We should form a guard of honor about these holy places, answering for the fulfillment of this duty with our existence. The guard of honor would be the great symbol of the solution of the Jewish question after what were for us eighteen centuries of affliction. . . .

We shall live at last as free men on our own soil, and in our own homes peacefully die.

The world will be liberated by our freedom, enriched by our wealth, magnified by our greatness.

And whatever we attempt there for our own benefit will [contribute] mightily and beneficially to the good of all mankind.

When Herzl died in 1904, the Zionist movement was still in its infancy. Many decades would pass before it finally achieved its goal: the creation of the state of Israel in 1949. That same year, Herzl's remains were flown to Israel and entombed in Jerusalem on a hill now known as Mount Herzl.

Review Questions

1. How did the writings of Theodor Herzl create the Zionist movement?
2. Why did Herzl feel that Jews needed to leave the nations in which they were living?
3. Why did Herzl feel that the creation of a Jewish state would solve the problems that Jews were having?
4. Why did Herzl believe that the future Jewish state should be in Palestine?
5. Why did Herzl believe that other nations would support the creation of a Jewish state?

---

[2] **extraterritoriality**—an arrangement by which a place is exempted from local laws and jurisdiction

16 Zapata Fights in the Mexican Revolution

The Mexican Revolution, which began in 1910, was a long and messy affair. Factions formed and reformed. One-time allies became enemies. Assassination of opponents served as a tool of politics. The underlying causes of the revolution included a growing gap between rich and poor and the fact that a small number of wealthy families owned the land, while most of the rural people had no land and were desperately poor.

The revolution began with a revolt against Porfirio Díaz, who had ruled as dictator since 1876. Revolutionaries formed armies and battled against first Díaz and then, when he fled, his successors. The first of those successors was Francisco Madero, a northern landowner and political moderate who was elected president of Mexico in November 1911.

Emiliano Zapata led an army of the landless in southern Mexico. At first, Zapata and his followers sided with Madero, but they soon turned against him. The *zapatistas* (as Zapata and his followers came to be known) demanded immediate steps to take land from the rich and distribute it to the landless. In December 1911, they set forth their political goals in the *Plan of Ayala*. This was named for the town of Villa de Ayala, in southern Mexico, near the village where Zapata had grown up.

Ayala, November 21, 1911

We who undersign, constituted in a revolutionary junta to sustain and carry out the promises which the revolution of November 20, 1910, just past, made to the country, declare solemnly before the face of the civilized world which judges us and before the nation to which we belong . . . , propositions which we have [formed] to end the tyranny which oppresses us and redeem the fatherland from the dictatorships which are imposed on us. . . .

. . . The revolutionary junta . . . will admit no transactions or compromises until it achieves the overthrow of the dictatorial elements of Porfirio Díaz and Francisco I. Madero, for the nation is tired of false men and traitors who make promises like liberators and who on arriving in power forget them and [establish] themselves as tyrants. . . .

As an additional part of the plan we invoke, we give notice: that [regarding] the fields, timber, and water which the landlords, [political leaders], or bosses have [taken over], the pueblos [villages] or citizens who have the titles corresponding to those properties will immediately enter into possession of that real estate of which they have been [robbed] by the bad faith of our oppressors. . . .

In virtue of the fact that the immense majority of Mexican pueblos and citizens are owners of no more than the land they walk on, suffering the horrors of poverty without being able to improve their social condition in any way or to dedicate themselves to Industry or Agriculture, because lands, timber, and water are monopolized in a few hands, for this cause there will be [seized one third] of those monopolies from the powerful proprietors of them, with prior [repayment] in order that the pueblos and citizens of Mexico may obtain *ejidos,*[1] colonies, and foundations for pueblos, or fields for sowing or laboring, and the Mexicans' lack of prosperity and well-being may improve in all and for all. . . .

[Regarding] the landlords, [political leaders], or bosses who oppose the present plan directly or indirectly, their goods will be nationalized [taken over by the government] and the two third parts which [otherwise would] belong to them will go for [compensation for] war, pensions for widows and orphans of the victims who [fall] in the struggle for the present plan. . . .

Once [the revolution is] triumphant, . . . a junta of the principal revolutionary chiefs from the different States will name a temporary President of the Republic, who will [hold] elections for the organization of the federal powers. . . .

The principal revolutionary chiefs of each State will designate in junta the Governor of the State to which they belong, and this

[1]**ejidos**—communities in which people own land in common, as among native people in pre-Spanish times

appointed official will convoke elections for the due organization of the public powers. . . .

[W]e are not [egotists intent on gaining power], we are [supporters] of principles and not of men!

Mexican People, support this plan with arms in hand and you will make the prosperity and well-being of the fatherland.

Liberty, Justice, and Law

Signed, General in Chief Emiliano Zapata; Generals Eufemio Zapata, Francisco Mendoza, Jesús Morales [and many more names]. . . .

[This] is a true copy taken from the original. Camp in the Mountains of Puebla, December 11, 1911. *Signed,* General in Chief Emiliano Zapata.

Review Questions

1 Why did the *zapatistas* dislike Porfiro Diaz and Francisco I. Madero?

2. a. What did the *zapatistas* believe caused widespread poverty in Mexico?
   b. How did they plan to eliminate poverty?
3. a. What does the word "nationalize" mean?
   b. Why did the *zapatistas* favor nationalizing the property of their opponents?
4. What type of government did the *zapatistas* promise to establish if their revolution was successful?

Unit V Document-Based Question

Write a well-organized essay that includes an introduction, several paragraphs, and a conclusion. Use evidence from at least ***four*** *documents from the unit in the body of your essay. Support your response with relevant facts, examples, and details. Include additional outside information.*

Historical Context

From 1750 to 1914, nations of the world were exposed to many new ideas and were forced to address many issues, such as intellectual freedom, the right to humane working and living conditions, nationalism, and human rights.

Task: Using the documents and questions in the unit, along with your knowledge of global history, write an essay in which you:

- Demonstrate how **three** of the issues mentioned above were addressed from 1750 to 1914
- Evaluate the extent to which **one** of those issues was successfully achieved

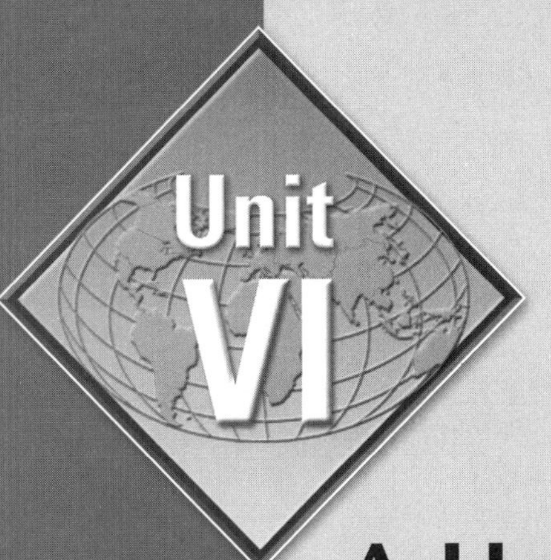

A Half-Century of Crisis and Achievement

(1900–1945)

Woodrow Wilson's Fourteen Points

The war that broke out in Europe in August 1914 was worldwide in its scope and effect. But the United States did not enter World War I until April 6, 1917, after more than two and a half years of European bloodletting. The Americans joined the side of Britain, France, and Russia (known as the Allies). By 1918, the tide of battle turned against Germany and the other Central Powers.

U.S. President Woodrow Wilson did not support all of the war aims of Britain and France. Those European powers were fiercely anti-German and had made a number of secret agreements about breaking off parts of Germany and the territory of other enemies. Wilson spoke out against such agreements, insisting instead on the principal of *self-determination* of peoples. By that he meant that ethnic and national groups like Croats and Poles should be able to decide their future for themselves—whether to remain part of an existing country, agree to be annexed by another country, or set up their own independent government.

Self-determination formed a central part of a peace plan that Wilson announced in a speech to Congress in January 1918. His so-called Fourteen Points were designed to state Allied war aims in such a way as to win maximum possible support for the alliance. The fate of "subject peoples" was being hotly debated at the time. Also, Russia, one of the Allies, after severe defeats, had signed an armistice with Germany and was negotiating for a peace treaty (finally signed in March 1918). Since the Bolshevik Revolution of November 1917, Russia had been ruled by a Communist government that was stirring up hopes of self-determination among "subject peoples."

Wilson's Fourteen Points were much debated at the Paris Peace Conference that followed the war. Nonetheless, many of the points were left out of the final treaties.

The following excerpts from the Fourteen Points show how Wilson hoped to bring about a peaceful and tolerant world.

. . . It will be our wish and purpose that the processes of peace, when they are begun, shall be absolutely open and that they shall involve and permit henceforth no secret understandings of any kind. The day of conquest and [enlarging one's state at the expense of others] is gone by; so is also the day of secret covenants [agreements] entered into in the interest of particular governments and likely at some unlooked-for moment to upset the peace of the world. . . .

We entered this war because violations of right had occurred which touched us to the quick and made the life of our own people impossible unless they were corrected and the world secured once [and] for all against their recurrence. What we demand in this war, therefore, is nothing peculiar to ourselves. It is that the world be made fit and safe to live in; and particularly that it be made safe for every peace-loving nation which, like our own, wishes to live its own life, determine its own institutions, be assured of justice and fair dealing by the other peoples of the world as against force and selfish aggression. All the peoples of the world are in effect partners in this interest, and for our own part we see very clearly that unless justice be done to others it will not be done to us. The program of the world's peace, therefore, is our program; and that program, the only possible program, as we see it, is this:

I. Open covenants [agreements] of peace, openly arrived at, after which there shall be no private international understandings of any kind but diplomacy shall proceed always frankly and in the public view.

II. Absolute freedom of navigation upon the seas, outside territorial waters, alike in peace and in war, except as the seas may be closed in whole or in part by international action for the enforcement of international covenants.

III. The removal, so far as possible, of all economic barriers and the establishment of an equality of trade conditions among all the nations consenting to the peace and associating themselves for its maintenance.

IV. Adequate guarantees given and taken that national armaments will be reduced to the lowest point consistent with domestic safety.

V. A free, open-minded, and absolutely impartial [fair] adjustment of all colonial claims, based upon a strict observance of the principle that in determining all such questions of sovereignty [control] the interests of the populations concerned must have equal weight with the equitable claims of the government whose title is to be determined.

VI. The evacuation of all Russian territory [by the Central Powers] and such a settlement of all questions affecting Russia as will secure the best and freest cooperation of the other nations of the world. . . . The treatment accorded Russia by her sister nations in the months to come will be the acid test of their good will, of their comprehension of her needs as distinguished from their own interests, and of their intelligent and unselfish sympathy. . . .

[Articles VII–XIII describe in detail Wilson's proposals for establishing the independence and integrity of specific nations.]

XIV. A general association of nations must be formed under specific covenants for the purpose of affording mutual guarantees of political independence and territorial integrity to great and small states alike. . . .

An evident principle runs through the whole program I have outlined. It is the principle of justice to all peoples and nationalities, and their right to live on equal terms of liberty and safety with one another, whether they be strong or weak. Unless this principle be made its foundation no part of the structure of international justice can stand. . . .

Review Questions

1. What secret agreements did Britain and France make before the Versailles Conference?
2. Why did Wilson propose "open covenants of peace"?
3. What did Wilson mean by the principle of "self-determination"?
4. Why did the Bolshevik Revolution stir up hopes of subject peoples?
5. According to Wilson, why did the United States enter World War I?
6. a. What was Wilson's main goal in proposing a "general association of nations"?
   b. Why do you think the idea of an "association of nations" was appealing to the rest of the nations attending the Versailles Peace Conference?

The Balfour Declaration

An early step toward the creation of the nation-state of Israel occurred in 1917, during World War I. At the time, Britain was eager to win Jewish support for its war goals and for a British takeover of Palestine from the Ottoman Empire. About 10 percent of Palestine's population was Jewish and the rest mainly Arab.

On November 2, 1917, James Balfour, the British foreign secretary, issued what became known as the Balfour Declaration. The declaration was prepared after extensive consultation with Zionists. In fact, British Zionists prepared drafts of the statement for the consideration of the British government.

The documents below include two drafts prepared by Zionists and the statement finally issued by Balfour. The first document is an early draft that included wording sought by the Zionists. Advised by British officials that the statement was too long and too specific, the Zionists made it shorter. The British cabinet considered the shorter version, changed its wording, and authorized Balfour to issue it. As it finally emerged, the Balfour Declaration was a single paragraph enclosed in a letter to the second Baron Rothschild, a British member of a prominent banking family who was a supporter of the Zionist movement.

Zionist Draft of July 12, 1917

His Majesty's Government, after considering the aims of the Zionist Organization, accepts the principle of recognizing Palestine as the National Home of the Jewish people and the right of the Jewish people to build up its national life in Palestine under a protection to be established at the conclusion of peace following upon the successful issue of the war.

His Majesty's Government regards as essential for the realization of this principle the grant of internal autonomy [independence] to the Jewish nationality in Palestine, freedom of immigration for Jews, and the establishment of a Jewish National Colonizing Corporation for the resettlement and economic development of the country.

The conditions and forms of the internal autonomy and a charter for the Jewish National Colonizing Corporation should, in the view of His Majesty's Government, be [worked out] in detail and determined with the representatives of the Zionist Organization.

Zionist Draft of July 18, 1917

1. His Majesty's Government accepts the principle that Palestine should be reconstituted [established] as the National Home of the Jewish people.

2. His Majesty's Government will use its best endeavors to secure the achievement of this object and will discuss the necessary methods and means with the Zionist Organization.

Balfour Declaration, November 2, 1917

Dear Lord Rothschild:

I have much pleasure in conveying to you, on behalf of His Majesty's government, the following declaration of sympathy with Jewish Zionist aspirations which has been submitted to, and approved by, the Cabinet:

His Majesty's Government view with favor the establishment in Palestine of a national home for the Jewish people, and will use their best endeavors to [advance] the achievement of this object, it being clearly understood that nothing shall be done which may [damage] the civil and religious rights of existing non-Jewish communities in Palestine, or the rights and political status enjoyed by Jews in any other country.

I should be grateful if you would bring this declaration to the knowledge of the Zionist Federation.

Yours,
Arthur James Balfour

Within a year of the Balfour Declaration, British and Arab armies had succeeded in taking control of Palestine and surrounding areas from the Ottoman Empire. In 1920 the League of Nations gave Britain a mandate to rule Palestine, with encouragement for Jewish immigration (see document 3). During the 1920s and 1930s, especially after Hitler came to power in Germany, Jewish immigrants poured into Palestine. By 1947, 35 percent of Palestine's population was Jewish.

Relations between Jews and Arabs in Palestine became increasingly bitter under the British mandate. British officials tried to appease both sides, but met resistance from secret Arab and Jewish armies and terrorist groups. Unable to persuade Arabs and Jews to agree to a joint Arab-Jewish state in Palestine, the British finally gave up. They asked the United Nations to decide what to do. On November 29, 1947, after extensive study and debate, the United Nations General Assembly approved a plan for the partition (division) of Palestine into a Jewish and an Arab state, joined in an economic union.

Review Questions

1. How was the tone of the second Zionist draft (July 18) different from that of the first draft (July 12)?
2. Why did the official Balfour Declaration of November 2, 1917, discuss "non-Jewish communities in Palestine"?
3. How was the Balfour Declaration an attempt by Great Britain to serve its own interests?
4. To what extent did the final version of the declaration meet the expectations of the two Zionist drafts?

The League of Nations System of Mandates

The League of Nations that emerged from the Paris Peace Conference was not entirely to U.S. President Woodrow Wilson's liking. Moreover, because of disputes in Congress, the United States never joined the League. The United States cooperated with the League in many ways, but not as a member.

At Wilson's insistence, the Paris Peace Conference imposed limits on the right of the war's victors to claim control of colonies and other territories taken from Germany and the Ottoman Empire. The territories went to the victors, who had to agree to a system of supervision by the new League of Nations. In addition, they had to agree to govern the territories according to certain principles.

In effect, the defeated powers turned the territories over to the League of Nations, which granted nations like Britain, France, and Belgium the authority to rule them. This grant of authority is called a *mandate*. In theory, the mandates were to last for a limited time, with the subject peoples eventually gaining the right to rule themselves. In practice, however, the powers that took over the mandates sometimes ruled them in much the same manner as they ruled their other colonies.

This document is part of the Covenant of the League of Nations—the formal treaty that created the League.

Article 22. Mandatory System

1. To those colonies and territories . . . which are inhabited by peoples not yet able to stand by themselves [in] the modern world, there should be applied the principle that the well-being and development of such peoples form a sacred trust of civilization, and that [guarantees] for the performance of this trust should be embodied in this Covenant.

2. The best method of [carrying out] this principle is that the [guardianship] of such peoples should be entrusted to advanced nations who by reason of their resources, their experience, or their geographical position can best undertake this responsibility, and who are willing to accept it, and that this tutelage [education] should be exercised by them as Mandatories [those who have been granted governing authority] on behalf of the League.

3. The character of the mandate must differ according to the stage of the development of the people, the geographical situation of the territory, its economic conditions and other similar circumstances.

4. Certain communities formerly belonging to the Turkish Empire have reached a stage of development where their existence as independent nations can be . . . recognized subject to the . . . administrative advice and assistance by a Mandatory until such time as they are able to stand alone. The wishes of these communities must be a principal consideration in the selection of the Mandatory.

5. Other peoples, especially those of Central Africa, are at such a stage that the Mandatory must be responsible for the administration of the territory under conditions which will guarantee freedom of conscience and religion, subject only to the maintenance of public order and morals; the prohibition of abuses such as the slave trade, the arms traffic, and the liquor traffic; and the prevention of the establishment of fortifications or military and naval bases and of military training of the natives for other than police purposes and the defense of territory, and will also secure equal opportunities for the trade and commerce of other Members of the League.

6. There are territories, such as Southwest Africa and certain of the South Pacific Islands, which, owing to their [small] population, their small size, or their remoteness from civilization, or their geographical [closeness] to the territory of the Mandatory, . . . can be best administered under the laws of the Mandatory as integral portions of its territory. . . .

7. In every case of mandate, the Mandatory shall [give] to the Council an annual report [about] the territory committed to its charge. . . .

The mandates fell into three categories, labeled A (most advanced), B, and C (least advanced). The following table lists the mandates in each category.

Mandates of the League of Nations

	Country or Region	Mandatory Power
Class A	Palestine, Transjordan, Iraq	Britain
	Syria/Lebanon	France
Class B	Tanganyika; part of Togoland; part of Cameroons	Britain
	part of Togoland, part of Cameroons	France
	Ruanda-Burundi	Belgium
Class C	South-West Africa	Union of South Africa
	Western Samoa	New Zealand
	Nauru	Britain/New Zealand/ Australia
	New Guinea	Australia
	North Pacific islands	Japan

Review Questions

1. What happened to the colonies of the defeated nations after World War I?
2. a. How was a mandate supposed to differ from a colony?
   b. How did the theory of governing a mandate differ from the actual practice?
3. Why was the word "tutelage" used in Section 2?
4. Why were three different classes of mandates created?

Germany Emerges From World War I

As World War I neared an end in the fall of 1918, Germany stood face to face with defeat. Its people were hungry and disillusioned. The emperor, Kaiser Wilhelm II, agreed to make Germany's government more democratic, but the changes were not enough for the leaders of Germany's enemies. U.S. President Woodrow Wilson, in particular, refused to sign an armistice as long as the emperor remained in power.

Meanwhile, revolution was in the air. Inspired by the Bolshevik Revolution in Russia the year before, German leftists staged street demonstrations and plotted to seize power. In late October, German sailors mutinied. Many soldiers put on red armbands and declared themselves in favor of revolution. With chaos threatening and Allied soldiers advancing on Germany, the emperor gave up his throne and went into exile. Germany became a republic, governed by a coalition of moderate and leftist parties. Two days later, on November 11, an armistice ended the war and the guns fell silent.

We get glimpses of the chaotic aftermath of the war in Berlin, the German capital, in the following passages. They are from the diary of a German nobleman, Count Harry Kessler. Active in one of Germany's centrist, or moderate, political parties, Kessler sympathized with some of the revolutionaries' goals and was strongly critical of the departed emperor. His writings show the profound shock of the defeat on the German people and describe the political chaos that followed the war. Not until 1924 did Germany enter a period of stability. This period would be cut short by the rise to power of Adolph Hitler and the Nazis in 1933.

Saturday, 9 November 1918

The Emperor has abdicated [given up his power]. Revolution has won the day in Berlin. This morning, as I left home, I saw a soldier [preaching to] a crowd. . . .

At ten o'clock [p.m. I went] with . . . [two others] to the Reichstag[1]. . . . In front of the main entrance, and in an arc of [light] provided by the headlights of several army vehicles, stood a crowd waiting for news. . . .

[Inside] [g]roups of soldiers and sailors stood and lay about on the enormous red carpet and among the pillars of the lobby. Rifles had been stacked. Here and there some individual was stretched full length and asleep on a bench. It was like a film of the Russian Revolution. . . .

We . . . climbed two or three floors to a committee room where a woman, apparently the wife of a Reichstag member, was issuing identification papers. I received . . . a card according to which, as "bearer of this credential," I am authorized "to maintain order and security in the streets of the city." . . . I have become, so to speak, a policeman in the Red Guard. I was also given an identity card certifying on the part of the Workers' and Soldiers' Council that I am "trustworthy and free to pass." . . .

I . . . walked in the direction of the palace, from which the sound of isolated shots still came. . . . Patrols all around; they challenged and let me through. . . . A sentry told me that "young rascals" are still hidden in the palace and the stables. There are secret passages through which they disappear and reappear. A couple of officers and a few loyalist soldiers were still firing from a house. . . . At [an intersection] I saw [small mobs] . . . which reassembled as often as the [soldiers] broke [them] up. A sergeant said they were waiting for the chance to [loot]; they must be cleared out. Slowly I made my way home.

. . . It was close to one o'clock when I got home. So closes this first day of revolution which has witnessed in a few hours the downfall of the Hohenzollerns [royal family], the [breakup] of the German Army, and the end of the old order of society in Germany. One of the most memorable and dreadful days in German history. . . .

Monday, 11 November 1918

Today the dreadful armistice terms have been signed. Langwerth [a German diplomat] says that anything else was out of the question: our Front has cracked completely. The Emperor has fled to Holland.

---

[1]**Reichstag**—the building in which the German parliament met

Tuesday, 12 November 1918

. . . In the city everything is peaceful today and the factories are working again. . . . Noteworthy is that during the days of revolution, the [streetcars] . . . ran regularly. Nor did the electricity, water, or telephone services break down for a moment. The revolution never created more than [a swirl] in the ordinary life of the city which flowed calmly along on its customary course. Moreover, though there was so much shooting, there were remarkably few dead or wounded. The colossal, world-shaking upheaval has scurried across Berlin's day-to-day life much like an incident in a crime film. . . .

Thursday, 14 November 1918

. . . At one o'clock as I was walking down Unter den Linden, the palace guard approached . . . carrying revolutionary flags. . . . [A second tune they played] sounded like a funeral march and cut me to the quick. I thought of lost Alsace[2] and the French left bank of the Rhine. How are our feelings about that ever to be salved? However fine the League of Nations may prove to be, this is a wound it can but [keep open]. . . .

Sunday, 16 February 1919

Today's newspapers publish the Entente's[3] League of Nations plan. A bundle of barren legal paragraphs animated by the old spirit and barely disguising the imperialist intention of a number of states to enslave and [make] their defeated enemies [poor]. What should our reaction be? Rejection would only be possible on the basis of a better plan which dealt with the whole question from a broader and more profound aspect, from a human and not merely judicial [legal] angle, and provided a convincing solution. A mistake that leaps to the eye is that the plan has originated with states . . . that are by nature rivals. . . .

---

[2]**Alsace**—region on the French-German border that Germany took from France in 1871 and lost in World War I

[3]**Entente**—alliance led by Britain and France against Germany

Easter Sunday, 20 April 1919

. . . Yesterday's arrival of the Entente's impertinent summons [demanding immediate German acceptance of the Treaty of Versailles on a take-it-or-leave-it basis] and our contemptuous answer have created so critical a situation that the government must make some positive counter-proposals immediately. . . .

Sunday, 22 June 1919

[The head of Germany's government has] resigned. The new Bauer Cabinet proposes to sign the peace treaty under protest and with reservations. These relate to acknowledgment of Germany's sole war-guilt and [the handing over for trial] of the Emperor as well as other so-called criminals.

The German Navy . . . has scuttled its ships.

This evening I have been indescribably depressed, as though the entire sap of life has dried up inside me.

Monday, 23 January 1919

This morning students and sailors removed the French flags we are supposed to surrender from the Arsenal and burned them in front of the statue of Frederick the Great.

This afternoon, since the Entente has declined to accept our signature under reservation, the military leaders have announced their resistance to the Government, the Center Party has withdrawn its agreement to signature, and the Government has decided to resign. This evening the ultimatum [a demand by the Entente that Germany sign at once] expires. The tension is terrific. Very oppressive weather. Counter-revolution, war, insurrection threaten us like a nearing thunderstorm. . . .

Saturday, 10 January 1920

Today the Peace Treaty was ratified at Paris; the war is over. A terrible era begins for Europe, like the gathering of clouds before a storm, and it will end in an explosion probably still more terrible than that of the World War. In Germany there are all the signs of a continuing growth of nationalism.

Review Questions

1. Why did the German emperor give up his throne?
2. Why did Harry Kessler call the first day of the revolution "one of the most memorable and dreadful days in German history"?
3. Why was Kessler critical of the plan for the League of Nations?
4. What was meant by "sign the peace treaty under protest and with reservations"?
5. What was Kessler's prediction about the effect of the peace treaty on Germany and its people?

5 Emma Goldman on the Russian Revolution

The Russian Revolution of 1917 shocked the world. Russia entered into a new era of turmoil and uncertainty. Actually, there were two revolutions. The first, in March, overthrew the czar (emperor) and led to a parliamentary republic with a democratic form of government. But in a second revolution, on November 7, 1917, Bolsheviks led by Vladimir Lenin overthrew the democratic government and established a new Communist state. While the democratic government had remained in World War I, fighting on the side of the Allies, Lenin sought peace. And Germany imposed very harsh terms. Under a treaty signed in March 1918, Russia withdrew from the war and granted independence to many surrounding areas, including Finland, the Baltic states, Poland, and Ukraine.

Leftists (including many Socialists) in the rest of the world generally welcomed the Bolshevik Revolution. Many of them expected Russia to become a democratic Socialist state that would serve as a model for leftist revolutionaries in Germany and other nations. Leftists flocked to Russia to see what was happening and to help if they could.

Emma Goldman, a well-known American anarchist, was one of those leftists. Born in Lithuania (one of the Baltic states that were part of the Russian empire), she had lived in the Russian capital, St. Petersburg. In 1886, she emigrated to the United States. Goldman worked in clothing factories and took an active part in union organizing and in anarchist activities. She became a U.S. citizen, but the government later revoked her citizenship. Like many other leftists, she opposed U.S. involvement in World War I and lectured against the draft. After serving a two-year prison term for her antidraft activities, she was deported in December 1919—along with 248 others—during the postwar "Red Scare."

Arriving in Russia, Goldman found a nation plagued by hunger in the midst of a bitter civil war. Although she volunteered her services to the revolution, Goldman quickly became critical of the Bolsheviks. Among other things, she was appalled to find that Russia's Bolshevik leaders treated Russian anarchists as enemies of the revolution. In December 1921, Goldman left Russia for Western Europe. The following excerpts are from a book Goldman wrote in 1923, *My Disillusionment in Russia*.

The population of Petrograd [name given St. Petersburg at the start of World War I] before the war was almost two million; in 1920 it had dwindled to five hundred thousand. The people walked about like living corpses; the shortage of food and fuel was slowly sapping the city; grim death was clutching at its heart. Emaciated and frost-bitten men, women, and children were being whipped by the common lash, the search for a piece of bread or a stick of wood. . . .

Each day brought new conflicting thoughts and emotions. The feature which affected me most was the inequality I witnessed in my immediate environment. I learned that the rations issued to the tenants of the First House of the Soviet[1] . . . were much superior to those received by the workers in the factories. To be sure, they were not sufficient to sustain life—but no one in the Astoria lived from these rations alone. The members of the Communist Party, quartered in the Astoria, worked in Smolny[2] and the rations in Smolny were the best in Petrograd. . . .

The rations were distributed at the Commissary, but one had to fetch them himself. One day, while waiting my turn in the long line, a peasant girl came in and asked for vinegar. "Vinegar! who is it calls for such a luxury?" cried several women. It appeared that the girl was Zinoviev's servant.[3] She spoke of him as her master, who worked very hard and was surely entitled to something extra. At once a storm of indignation broke loose. "Master! is that what we made the Revolution for, or was it to do away with masters? Zinoviev is no more than we, and he is not entitled to more."

[1]**Soviet**—the Russian word soviet means "council"; Russia's Communists referred to their representative governments as soviets
[2]**Smolny**—the Smolny Institute at Petrograd's eastern edge served as Lenin's headquarters in the period of the revolution
[3]**Zinoviev**—Grigory Zinoviev, high-ranking Bolshevik and a close associate of Lenin

These working women were crude, even brutal, but their sense of justice was instinctive. The Revolution to them was something fundamentally vital. They saw the inequality at every step and bitterly resented it. I was disturbed. I sought to reassure myself that Zinoviev and the other leaders of the Communists would not use their power for selfish benefit. It was the shortage of food and the lack of efficient organization which made it impossible to feed all alike, and of course the blockade and not the [Bolsheviks] was responsible for it. The Allied Interventionists, who were trying to get at Russia's throat, were the cause.

Every Communist I met [repeated] this thought; even some of the Anarchists insisted on it. . . . But how reconcile the explanation given to me with some of the stories I learned every day—stories of systematic terrorism, of relentless persecution, and suppression of other revolutionary elements? . . .

Was this the Revolution I had believed in all my life, yearned for, and strove to interest others in, or was it . . . a hideous monster that had come to jeer and mock me? The Communists I had met daily during six months—self-sacrificing, hard-working men and women imbued with a high ideal—were such people capable of the treachery and horrors charged against them? Zinoviev, Radek, Zorin, Ravitch[4] and many others I had learned to know—could they in the name of an ideal lie, defame, torture, kill? But, then—had not Zorin told me that capital punishment had been abolished in Russia [when it was in fact still in use]? . . .

Why did Zorin resort to lies? Surely he must have known that I would not remain in the dark very long. And then, was not Lenin also guilty of the same methods? "Anarchists of ideas . . . are not in our prisons," he had assured me. Yet at that very moment numerous Anarchists filled the jails of Moscow and Petrograd and of many other cities in Russia. In May 1920, scores of them had been arrested in Petrograd, among them two girls of seventeen and nineteen years of age. None of the prisoners was charged with counter-revolutionary activities: they were "Anarchists of ideas," to use Lenin's expression. Several of them had issued a [proclamation] for the First of May, calling attention to the appalling conditions in the factories of [Russia] . . . . The two young girls who had circulated a handbill

[4]**Radek et al**—Bolshevik leaders

against the "labor book,"[5] which had just then gone into effect, were also arrested. . . .

The [halo] was falling from the Communists. All of them seemed to believe that the end justified the means. . . .

In short, I had come to see that the [Bolsheviks] were social puritans who sincerely believed that they alone were ordained to save mankind. . . .

Review Questions

1. How did Emma Goldman originally feel about the Bolshevik Revolution?
2. a. What conditions did Goldman find in Petrograd in 1920?
   b. What excuse did the Communists make for these conditions?
3. Why did Goldman become critical of the Bolsheviks?
4. What did Goldman mean when she questioned whether the revolution was a "hideous monster that had come to jeer and mock [her]"?
5. Why did Goldman feel that "a halo was falling from the Communists. All of them seemed to believe that the end justified the means"? Explain her reaction.

[5]**labor book**—a document required for changing one's job or one's place of residence

Gandhi Introduces Civil Disobedience to India

Mohandas K. Gandhi was a central figure in India's efforts to free itself from British imperial rule. His emphasis on nonviolent methods of resistance and struggle influenced people far beyond the boundaries of India. For example, leaders of the U.S. civil rights movement in the 1950s and 1960s, such as Bayard Rustin and Dr. Martin Luther King, Jr., were inspired to follow Gandhi's methods.

Born in 1869 into a Hindu family in what is now the western Indian state of Gujarat, Gandhi went to London to study law. In 1893, he took a job in white-ruled South Africa, where the large Indian community was subject to many forms of discrimination. Gandhi became a leader in efforts to better his people's conditions there. He developed the methods that he would later use in India itself, including the technique he called *satyagraha* ("firmness in truth"). This included public demonstrations, fasting, civil disobedience (peacefully disobeying laws and then submitting to arrest and punishment), and negotiations.

Returning to India in 1914, Gandhi joined the Congress Party in its struggle for independence from Britain. But political independence was only one of Gandhi's goals. He also worked to improve relations between upper-caste and lower-caste Hindus and between Hindus and Muslims. And he tried to improve the lives of India's desperately poor peasants. He spoke out against powerful economic interests and encouraged Indians to become self-sufficient by such methods as spinning their own cloth and making their own clothing.

Gandhi's first use of civil disobedience in India occurred in April 1917 in the district of Champaran, in India's far north. Local peasants had invited him to the district. They complained that the English landlords treated them unjustly and required them to grow huge quantities of indigo (a plant used to make dye), which they were unable to do. Gandhi set out to visit peasant dwellings and assess the situation. But he was soon arrested. In his autobiography, Gandhi describes his part in his trial and its result.

The trial began. The government pleader [prosecutor], the magistrate and other officials were . . . at a loss to know what to do. The government pleader was pressing the magistrate to postpone the case. But I interfered and requested the magistrate not to postpone the case, as I wanted to plead guilty to having disobeyed the order to leave Champaran, and read a brief statement as follows:

> . . . I have entered the [district] with motives of rendering humanitarian and national service. I have done so in response to a pressing invitation to come and help the ryots [peasants], who urge they are not being fairly treated by the indigo planters. I could not render any help without studying the problem. I have, therefore, come to study it with the assistance, if possible, of the [British colonial] Administration and the planters. I have no other motive, and cannot believe that my coming can in any way disturb public peace and cause loss of life. . . . As a law-abiding citizen my first instinct would be, as it was, to obey the order served upon me. But I could not do so without doing violence to my sense of duty to those for whom I have come. I feel that I could just now serve them only by remaining in their midst. I could not, therefore, voluntarily [leave]. Amid this conflict of duties I could only throw the responsibility of removing me from them on the Administration. . . . It is my firm belief that in the complex constitution under which we are living, the only safe and honorable course for a self-respecting man is . . . to do what I have decided to do, that is, to submit without protest to the penalty of disobedience.
>
> . . . I have disregarded the order served upon me not for want of respect for lawful authority, but in obedience to the higher law of our being, the voice of conscience.

There was now no occasion to postpone the hearing, but as both the magistrate and the government pleader had been taken by surprise, the magistrate postponed judgment. Meanwhile, I had wired full details to the Viceroy [the top British official in colonial India] . . . as also to . . . others.

Before I could appear before the court to receive the sentence, the magistrate sent a written message that the Lieutenant Governor had ordered the case against me to be withdrawn, and [another official] wrote to me saying that I was at liberty to conduct the proposed inquiry, and that I might count on whatever help I needed from the officials. None of us was prepared for this prompt and happy [result]. . . . The country thus had its first direct object-lesson in civil disobedience.

After his release from custody, Gandhi went ahead with his investigation. Often he was surrounded by admiring crowds of poor people. As a result of Gandhi's efforts, the government appointed a commission to investigate further, with Gandhi as one of the members. The commission ultimately called for an end to compulsory indigo-growing. Money payments were made to the local peasants. This was a notable victory for Gandhi and his methods.

Gandhi continued his campaigns. One of his most dramatic efforts came in 1930, when he led hundreds of Indian followers on a march to the sea. They were protesting a tax on salt that placed heavy burdens on the poor. By letting sea water evaporate, the marchers made their own salt—in violation of the law. Gandhi and many followers were arrested.

Independence finally came to India in 1947, under a plan that created two separate nations, Pakistan (mainly for Muslims) and India (mainly for Hindus). Gandhi continued to work to improve Muslim-Hindu relations. In 1948, however, at the age of 78, he was assassinated by a radical Hindu who considered him pro-Muslim.

Review Questions

1. Why did Mohandas Gandhi wish to study the complaints of the peasants of Champaran?

2. Why did Gandhi refuse to obey the British order to leave Champaran?
3. Why was Gandhi willing to go on trial and accept the penalty for disobeying the law?
4. In what way did Gandhi's actions in Champaran bring about a solution to the peasants' problems?
5. In what way did Gandhi influence leaders of the civil rights movement in the United States?

7 Sigmund Freud on Childhood Memories

Sigmund Freud (pronounced FROYD) (1856–1939) was a pioneer in the understanding and treatment of mental illness. He lived and practiced in Vienna, Austria. Freud's theories about the mental processes by which people remember the past—and by which he said they unconsciously repress (forget) certain significant or painful memories—attracted a wide following in the early 20th century. By the 1920s Freudian terms like "repression" and "ego" had become part of everyday language.

Freud's principal method of treatment was psychoanalysis. This involved a dialog between doctor and patient in which the patient was encouraged to remember past events and feelings. The goal was to help patients recover repressed memories, reach a deeper understanding of themselves, and thereby come to terms with their feelings of guilt and desire.

Because Freud's theories challenged many popular ideas, they attracted harsh criticism and contempt—among doctors, political leaders, and religious leaders. His emphasis on the importance of sexual feeling seemed especially shocking to many people.

The following document, concerning his theory of repressed childhood memories, is taken from a book he published in 1901.

[T]he earliest recollections of a person often . . . [seem] to preserve the unimportant and accidental, whereas (frequently though not universally!) not a trace is found in the adult memory of the weighty and [emotion-laden] . . . impressions of this period. . . . The indifferent childhood memories owe their existence to a process of displacement [that is, one memory takes the place of another]. It may be shown by psychoanalysis that . . . [the displaced memories] represent the substitute for other really significant impressions, whose direct reproduction is hindered by some resistance. . . .

I believe we accept too [unquestioningly] the fact of infantile amnesia—that is, the failure of memory for the first years of our lives—and fail to find in it a strange riddle. We forget of what great intellectual accomplishments and of what complicated emotions a child of four years is capable. We really ought to wonder why the memory of later years has, as a rule, retained so little of these psychic [emotional and mental] processes, especially as we have every reason for assuming that these same forgotten childhood activities have not glided off without leaving a trace in the development of the person, but that they have left a definite influence for all future time. Yet, in spite of this unparalleled effectiveness they were forgotten! . . .

Powerful forces from a later period have molded the memory capacity of our infantile experiences, and it is probably due to these same forces that the understanding of our childhood is generally so very strange to us. . . .

Various sources force us to assume the so-called earliest childhood recollections are not true memory traces but later elaborations of the same, elaborations which might have been subjected to the influences of many later psychic forces. Thus the "childhood reminiscences" [memories] of individuals altogether advance to the signification of "concealing memories.". . .

A twenty-four-year-old man preserved the following picture from the fifth year of his life: In the garden of a summer-house, he sat on a stool next to his aunt, who was engaged in teaching him the alphabet. He found difficulty in distinguishing the letter *m* from *n*, and he begged his aunt to tell him how to tell one from the other. His aunt called his attention to the fact that the letter *m* had one whole portion (a stroke) more than the letter *n*. There was no reason to dispute the reliability of this childhood recollection; its meaning, however, was discovered only later, when it showed itself to be the symbolic representation of another boyish inquisitiveness. For just as he wanted to know the difference between *m* and *n* at that time so he concerned himself later about the difference between boy and girl, and he would have been willing that just this aunt should be his teacher. He also discovered that the difference was a similar one; that the boy again had one whole portion more than the girl, and at the time of this recognition, his memory awoke to the responding childish inquisitiveness.

Review Questions

1 a. How does Sigmund Freud account for the displaced memories of childhood?
  b. How did this conflict with the prevailing belief of his time in "infantile amnesia"?
2. What did Freud mean by the term "repression"?
3. How does the story of the 24-year-old man explain Freud's belief in repression and sexuality in early childhood?

Carl Jung on Psychoanalysis

Swiss-born Carl Jung (1875–1961) was an early follower of Freud who broke with him in 1912 and pioneered his own methods of psychoanalysis. Jung (pronounced YOONG) introduced such terms as the *collective unconscious*, meaning a common stock of human ideas drawn from stories and myths shared by many different cultures across the ages. Like Freud, he wanted to help patients understand the fears and drives that grew out of their past experiences. He also wanted to help patients take charge of setting their own goals for the future.

In this document, Jung compares psychoanalysts to priests who hear the confessions of their flock. Jung sees significant differences in the two roles, however. He says the role of analysts is to wean patients away from the habit of looking to a substitute parent like a priest or analyst for guidance. He describes his goal as encouraging patients to become fully independent human beings.

Nothing makes people more lonely, and more cut off from the fellowship of others, than the possession of an anxiously hidden and jealously guarded personal secret. Very often it is "sinful" thoughts and deeds that keep them apart and [cause them to withdraw] from one another. Here [religious] confession sometimes has a truly redeeming effect. The tremendous feeling of relief which usually follows a confession can be attributed to the readmission of the lost sheep into the human community. His moral isolation and seclusion, which were so difficult to bear, cease. Herein lies the chief psychological value of confession.

Besides that, however, it has other consequences: through the transference of his secret and all the unconscious fantasies underlying it, a moral bond is formed between the patient and his father confessor. We call this a "transference relationship." Anyone with psychoanalytic experience knows how much the personal significance of the analyst is [increased] when the patient is able to confess his secrets to him. The change this [brings about] in the patient's behavior is often amazing.

[A] modern, mentally developed person strives, consciously or unconsciously, to govern himself and stand morally on his own feet. He wants to take the helm in his own hands; the steering has too long been done by others. He wants to understand; in other words, he wants to be an adult. It is much easier to be guided, but this no longer suits intelligent people today, for they feel that the spirit of the age requires them to exercise moral [independence]. Psychoanalysis has to [consider this need], and has therefore to reject the demand of the patient for constant guidance and instruction. The analyst knows his own shortcomings too well to believe that he could play the role of father and guide. His highest ambition must consist only in educating his patients to become independent personalities, and in freeing them from their unconscious bondage to infantile limitations. He must therefore analyze the transference, a task left untouched by the priest. Through the analysis, the unconscious—and sometimes conscious—tie to the analyst is cut, and the patient is set upon his own feet. That, at least, is the aim of the treatment.

Review Questions

1. Define what Carl Jung meant by the term "collective unconscious."
2. How did Jung explain the value of the "transference relationship"?
3. According to Jung, what is the role of the psychoanalyst?
4. How are the views of Freud and Jung similar?

Albert Einstein on Tolerance

Albert Einstein (1879–1955) was perhaps the most famous scientist of the early 20th century. His *Special Theory of Relativity* (1905) and *General Theory of Relativity* (1915) set physics on a new foundation and paved the way for the development of nuclear weapons and nuclear energy.

By 1914, Einstein held a distinguished scientific position in the German capital, Berlin. In 1921, he won the Nobel Prize for Physics. But after Hitler's rise to power in 1933, Einstein's Jewish background made him unwelcome in Germany. He spent the last 22 years of his life on the faculty of the Institute for Advanced Studies in Princeton, New Jersey.

Einstein supported many causes over the years. He spoke out in favor of Zionism and worked for more peaceful relations among nations. Both before and after he became famous, Einstein was known for his kindness and thoughtfulness.

In the following document, written in 1934, he expresses his views on tolerance and on the importance of the individual.

As I now ask myself what tolerance really is, there comes to mind the amusing definition that the humorist Wilhelm Busch[1] gave of "abstinence" [voluntarily denying oneself of something]:

> Abstinence is the pleasure we net
> From various things we do not get.

I could say [comparably] that tolerance is the [good-natured] appreciation of qualities, views, and actions of other individuals which are foreign to one's own habits, beliefs, and tastes. Thus being tolerant does not mean being indifferent toward the actions and feelings of others. Understanding and empathy [feeling] must also be present. . . .

Whether it be a work of art or a significant scientific achievement, that which is great and noble comes from the solitary person-

[1]**Wilhelm Busch**—German poet and caricaturist (lived 1832–1908), who has been called "the father of the modern comic strip"

ality. European culture made its most important break away from stifling stagnation when the Renaissance offered the individual the possibility of [free] development.

The most important kind of tolerance, therefore, is tolerance of the individual by society and the state. The state is certainly necessary, in order to give the individual the security he needs for his development. But when the state becomes the main thing and the individual becomes its weak-willed tool, then all finer values are lost. Just as the rock must first crumble for trees to grow on it, and just as the soil must first be loosened for its fruitfulness to develop, so too can valuable achievement sprout from human society only when it is sufficiently loosened so as to make possible to the individual the free development of his abilities.

Review Questions

1. How did Einstein define the concept of "tolerance"?
2. What, according to Einstein, is the most important kind of tolerance?
3. According to Einstein, what should the state provide the individual?
4. How might the rise of Nazism in Germany have influenced Einstein's concerns about the tolerance of the state toward individuals?

10 George Orwell on the Spanish Civil War

The Spanish Civil War of 1936–1939 is often viewed as a preview of World War II, which broke out in 1939. The war in Spain began as a revolt by right-wing military leaders commanded by Francisco Franco against Spain's Socialist-led government. It soon turned into a wider battle between Fascists and anti-Fascists.

Outsiders took a keen interest in the outcome of the Spanish war, and both sides received foreign assistance. Fascist Germany and Italy poured arms and soldiers into Spain in support of Franco's forces. Spain's government, in contrast, received mainly verbal support from leaders of the democratic nations. The government (or Republican) side did get help from other sources. Volunteer soldiers—mainly leftists—arrived from many nations, including the United States. The Communist leadership of the Soviet Union sent money and military supplies.

George Orwell was an English novelist and journalist who went to Spain in 1936 and fought for the Republican side. A Communist sympathizer, he signed up with one of the many militias that had been formed by Spanish trade unions and political parties. But he quickly became disillusioned with the Communists. In his book *Homage to Catalonia*, which was published in 1938 while the Spanish war was still raging, he described his experiences as a soldier in Spain. (Orwell had left Spain after being seriously wounded in battle.) According to Orwell, Soviet Communists manipulated their aid-giving so as to impose their will on the Spanish Republicans. Rather than support revolutionary change in Spain that might have improved the lives of the poorest classes, the Soviets helped to maintain Spain's existing capitalist system, Orwell claimed. Historians today generally agree with him.

At least four political groups played a role on the side of the Spanish Republicans. The Socialists (moderate leftists) controlled the government at the start of the war. Spanish

Communists (more radical leftists) were also well organized. Both Socialists and Communists had influence within the trade unions. But another radical group, the Anarchists, were the strongest element within the unions. Both Socialists and Anarchists favored a thoroughgoing social revolution. Communists, in contrast, followed the official Soviet line, arguing that revolution would have to wait until the war had been won. This line aimed to keep from alienating the fourth political group, the conservatives—often middle-class people and business owners who supported Spain's parliamentary democracy. (In Orwell's book, such people are called *liberals*, in keeping with European terminology.)

The selection that follows is from Orwell's *Homage to Catalonia*. Catalonia is a region in northern Spain, where many people today speak the Catalan language as well as Castilian Spanish. Its capital is Barcelona. Orwell enlisted in Barcelona and served mainly with Catalan-speaking soldiers.

[I]t would be quite impossible to write about the Spanish war from a purely military angle. It was above all things a political war. . . .

To understand . . . one has got to remember how the war started. When the fighting broke out on 18 July [1936] it is probable that every anti-Fascist in Europe felt a thrill of hope. For here at last, apparently, was democracy standing up to Fascism. . . . [W]hen Franco tried to overthrow a mildly left-wing government, the Spanish people, against all expectation, had risen against him. . . .

[Franco's] rising was a military mutiny backed up by the aristocracy and the Church, and in the main, especially at the beginning, it was an attempt not so much to impose Fascism as to restore feudalism. This meant that Franco had against him not only the working class but also various sections of the liberal [middle classes and business owners]—the very people who are the supporters of Fascism when it appears in a more modern form. More important than this was the fact that the Spanish working class did not . . . resist Franco in the name of "democracy" and the status quo [established order]; their resistance was accompanied by—one might almost say it consisted of—a definite revolutionary outbreak. Land was seized by the peasants; many factories and most of the transport were seized by the trade unions; churches were wrecked and the priests driven out or killed. The [London] *Daily Mail,* amid the cheers of the Catholic clergy, was able to represent Franco as a patriot delivering his country from hordes of fiendish "Reds."

For the first few months of the war Franco's real opponent was not so much the Government as the trade unions. As soon as the rising [by Franco] broke out the organized town workers replied by calling a general strike[1] and then by demanding—and, after a struggle, getting—arms from the public arsenals. If they had not acted spontaneously and more or less independently it is quite conceivable that Franco would never have been resisted. . . . When the trouble started . . . [the government's] attitude was weak and hesitant. . . . Moreover, the one step that could save the immediate situation, the arming of the workers, was only taken unwillingly and in response to violent popular clamor. However, the arms were distributed, and in the big towns of eastern Spain the Fascists were defeated by a huge effort, mainly of the working class. . . . It was the kind of effort that could probably only be made by people who were fighting with a revolutionary intention—i.e., believed that they were fighting for something better than the *status quo.* In the various centers of revolt it is thought that three thousand people died in the streets in a single day. Men and women armed only with sticks of dynamite rushed across the open squares and stormed stone buildings held by trained soldiers with machine-guns. Machine-gun nests that the Fascists had placed at strategic spots were smashed by rushing taxis at them at sixty miles an hour. Even if one had heard nothing of the seizure of the land by the peasants, the setting up of local soviets[2], etc., it would be hard to believe that the Anarchists and Socialists who were the backbone of the resistance were doing this kind of thing for the preservation of capitalist democracy, which especially in the Anarchist view was no more than a centralized swindling machine. . . .

The thing that had happened in Spain was, in fact, not merely a civil war, but the beginning of a revolution. . . .

---

[1]**general strike**—a strike in which all working people are called on to stop work, usually as a political protest

[2]**soviets**—elected councils (after the Russian model)

[E]xcept for the small revolutionary groups which exist in all countries, the whole world was determined upon preventing revolution in Spain. In particular the Communist Party, with Soviet Russia behind it, had thrown its whole weight against the revolution. It was the Communist thesis that revolution at this stage would be fatal and that what was to be aimed at in Spain was not workers' control, but bourgeois democracy.[3] . . .

The general swing to the Right [that is, against revolution] dates from about October–November 1936, when the U.S.S.R. began to supply arms to the Government and power began to pass from the Anarchists to the Communists. . . .

The whole of Comintern[4] policy is now [focused on] the defense of the U.S.S.R., which depends upon a system of military alliances. In particular, the U.S.S.R. is in alliance with France, a capitalist-imperialist country. The alliance is of little use to Russia unless French capitalism is strong; therefore, Communist policy in France has got to be antirevolutionary. . . . In Spain the Communist "line" was undoubtedly influenced by the fact that France, Russia's ally, would strongly object to a revolutionary neighbor. . . . The *Daily Mail*, with its tales of red revolution financed by Moscow, was even more wildly wrong than usual. In reality it was the Communists above all others who prevented revolution in Spain.

General Franco's forces won the Spanish Civil War. They sealed their victory with the capture of Barcelona in January 1939 and Madrid in March. Franco restored the Spanish royal family, which had lost its status when Spain became a presidential republic in 1931. Franco ruled as Spain's dictator until his death in 1975. He imposed a rigid centralized government that denied self-rule to Catalonia and other Spanish regions. Since Franco's death, Spain has evolved into a traditional constitutional, or parliamentary, democracy, with two legislative houses. Regional governments have a great deal of freedom from government regulations. Today, as in the Franco era, a king is Spain's official head of state.

---

[3]**bourgeois democracy**—parliamentary democracy in a capitalist system

[4]**Comintern**—central government body of world communism, controlled by the Soviet Union

Review Questions

1. a. Who were the combatants and what were their purposes in the Spanish Civil War?
   b. Why did Orwell believe that the civil war was not just a military situation but one of great political conflict?
2. Why did Orwell come to oppose the Communist Party in the war?
3. What was the result of the Spanish Civil War?

The Bombing of Guernica

From 1936 to 1939, General Francisco Franco, a Spanish military officer, led a successful revolt against the democratically elected Spanish government. As George Orwell pointed out in *Homage to Catalonia*, Spain's civil war became a battleground for competing ideologies. The Communist Soviet Union helped the Spanish Loyalists defend the established government, while Germany and Italy supported Franco's Fascist regime.

Other Fascist leaders welcomed the Spanish war. Not only did it give them a strong ally. It also provided the opportunity to test military tactics and weapons that they would use a few years later in full-scale war.

In 1937, German planes bombed the small Basque town of Guernica for three and a half hours. The apparent object of this bombardment was to cut off the retreat of Loyalist troops. A lesser amount of bombing, however, would have done that. It seemed as if the Germans were determined to kill as many civilians as possible. The bombing was an act of terrorism, an announcement of a new ruthlessness in the conduct of war. A few years later, the German army committed even more brutal acts against innocent people all over Europe.

The Spanish artist Pablo Picasso seems to have sensed that the attack on Guernica was an omen of even greater evils to come. In May and June of 1937, he painted the mural *Guernica* as a response to the event. Picasso's aim was to express the horror of unarmed, defenseless people being killed by an unseen, impersonal force. Distorted figures scream, lie limp and broken, or stare in shock. The two animals, a bull and a horse, are symbols, Picasso said. The bull stands for "brutality and darkness." The wounded horse represents "the people" (by which he probably meant humankind).

It is not necessary to know what each figure in the work symbolizes. It is more important to react emotionally to the work than to understand it. For Picasso, the destruction of

Guernica was not just a news event printed in the newspaper. He presents it as an immediate experience. The painting is an assault on its viewers. Bright, jagged areas flash out its dark background. In the harsh light, fragmented figures writhe or stiffen. This is how the victims in their confusion must have perceived one another. If viewers allow themselves to be drawn into the work, they cannot help identifying with the victims' pain and fear.

Guernica, by Pablo Picasso (1937)

Review Questions

1. Why did the Germans attack the Spanish Basque town of Guernica?
2. How did Pablo Picasso use the medium of painting to express the brutality of the German attack on Guernica?

"Spineless Democracies"

During his early years in political power in Germany, Adolf Hitler hid his aggressive intentions from other European leaders. The 1919 Treaty of Versailles had limited the German army to only a hundred thousand soldiers. Hitler knew that, if the democratic leaders realized what he planned to do, they would easily have stopped him.

By 1933, however, Hitler felt more confident. He indicated his plans to rearm Germany by walking out of a 60-nation disarmament conference. That same year, he resigned from the League of Nations.

In March 1935, Hitler openly rebelled against the disarmament clauses of the Treaty of Versailles. He established a general military draft in Germany. The rest of Europe began to sense danger. Led by France, Italy and Great Britain protested against German rearmament.

United opposition to Hitler was short-lived. Fearing another world war, Britain tried to negotiate with Hitler. It signed a naval agreement with Germany in 1935. A year later, German troops marched into and occupied the Rhineland. This German region had been *demilitarized* by the Versailles Treaty. (No army was to be allowed there.) Hitler had ordered his troops to turn back if they met resistance from France. But without Britain's backing, France could do nothing. Britain refused to help on the grounds that German forces had a right to occupy German soil.

One important reason for Britain's policy of *appeasement* (giving in to an aggressor's demands in order to avoid conflict) was the memory of the "Great War" of 1914–1918. British leaders were willing to pay almost any price to avoid another such disaster. Then, too, British leaders shared Hitler's dislike of communism. They hoped that Hitler, who had suppressed all forms of socialism in Germany, would prove an ally against the Soviet Union and its economic and political beliefs.

Confident that Britain would not protest, Hitler next forced the leader of Austria to accept a Nazi German government. British Prime Minister Neville Chamberlain, convinced that he was achieving peace, allowed Germany to move into the Sudetenland in 1938. This was a large area of Czechoslovakia with a German-speaking population. When Hitler next targeted Danzig, a German-speaking area of Poland, Chamberlain at last took a stand against the Nazi leader. He threatened that France and Britain would fight to prevent an invasion of Poland.

The English cartoonist David Low shows the humiliation that the democracies brought on themselves by underestimating Hitler. Low's 1938 cartoon shows how their "spineless" behavior endangered the entire free world.

David Low, "Spineless Democracies"

Review Questions

1. Why did Britain adopt a policy of appeasement toward Hitler?
2. How did cartoonist David Low ridicule the democracies' policy of appeasement?

Massacre in Nanjing

The1930s saw the beginning of another terrible world war, which would cause untold suffering in many nations. This document focuses on Japan's capture in 1937 of China's capital city, Nanjing (also called Nanking).

The fall of Nanjing occurred during the Sino-Japanese War of 1937–1945. After years of friction caused by Japanese pressure on China, full-scale war broke out in the summer of 1937. Invading Japanese forces attacked the port city of Shanghai and advanced on Nanjing, which lay west of Shanghai on the Yangtze River. Surrounded and unable to escape, 300,000 Nationalist Chinese soldiers surrendered and Japanese soldiers entered Nanjing on December 13.

The scenes that followed shocked even some Japanese observers. Unable or unwilling to deal with up to 300,000 prisoners of war, the Japanese slaughtered their captives mercilessly. Treatment of civilians was equally brutal, as tens of thousands of men and women were bayoneted, raped, beheaded, or otherwise mistreated. The mayhem continued into January 1938. These events are now known as the Nanjing Massacre, or the Rape of Nanjing. The toll of dead has been estimated at between 100,000 and 300,000.

The first document is by a Japanese military correspondent covering the war.

A. The Massacre

On Hsiakwan wharves, there was the dark silhouette of a mountain made of dead bodies. About fifty to one hundred [Chinese] people were toiling there, dragging bodies from the mountain of corpses and throwing them into the Yangtze River. The bodies dripped blood, some of them still alive and moaning weakly, their limbs twitching. The laborers were busy working in total silence, as in a pantomime [a play in which the actors substitute body movement for speech]. In the dark one could barely see the opposite bank of the river. On the pier was a field of glistening mud under the moon's dim light. Wow! That's all blood!

After a while, the . . . [laborers] had done their job of dragging corpses and the soldiers lined them up along the river. Rat-tat-tat machine-gun fire could be heard. The . . . [laborers] fell backwards into the river and were swallowed by the raging currents. The pantomime was over.

A Japanese officer at the scene estimated that 20,000 persons had been executed.

The second document is from a diary kept by John Rabe, a German resident of Nanjing who became the unofficial leader of the city's foreign community in protesting against Japanese actions. Rabe was a Nazi party member who reported directly to Hitler, yet he was unsparing in his criticism of the Japanese.

B. A Foreigner's Reaction

December 24, 1937

I have had to look at so many corpses over the last few weeks that I can keep my nerves in check even when viewing these horrible cases. It really doesn't leave you in a "Christmas" mood; but I wanted to see these atrocities with my own eyes, so that I can speak as an eyewitness later. A man cannot be silent about this kind of cruelty!

Japanese military leaders involved in the massacre were charged with war crimes and put on trial by the Allies at the end of World War II. Matsui Iwane, who held command over the armies that captured the city, was convicted and executed. So was Tani Hisao, a lieutenant general.

Review Questions

A. The Massacre

1. What did the Japanese military order the Chinese laborers to do?
2. What eventually happened to the Chinese laborers?

3. Why do you think the books from which this document was excerpted refer to the fall of Nanjing (Nanking) as a "rape" and a "forgotten Holocaust"?

B. A Foreigner's Reaction

1. Why did John Rabe feel that he had to see the atrocities that the Japanese had committed against the people of Nanjing?
2. Why did Rabe refer to a "Christmas mood"?
3. Why did later atrocities make Rabe's criticism of the Japanese ironic?

Soviet Wartime Poster Recalls Past Russian Glories

The Soviet Union was a latecomer to the fight against fascism. In 1939, Soviet leader Joseph Stalin signed a Non-Aggression Pact with Hitler. The agreement, however, was a trick Hitler used to keep the Russians out of the war until he had gained enough military strength to attack them.

After conquering Western Europe, Hitler felt able to defeat Russia. He began an invasion of that country on June 22, 1941. Though large, the Soviet army was unprepared to stop the invasion. Its leadership was weak and inexperienced. During the 1930s, Stalin, fearing a revolt from within, had imprisoned, killed, or fired thousands of army officers. Stunned by Hitler's unexpected move, Stalin could not at first respond. Finally, on July 3, he announced his alliance with England and France.

Russia remained at a disadvantage for months. During that time, the Germans advanced through western Russia on their way to Moscow. By the time they reached Moscow, however, the Soviets had rallied. The Red Army now had fighting experience. Russian civilians, intent on saving their country and outraged by the German slaughter of noncombatants, also pitched in. Russian farmers destroyed crops and animals that the Germans might use for food. The women of Moscow dug trenches throughout the city to slow the progress of German tanks.

This fierce resistance delayed the Germans and left them open to the bitter Russian winter. Expecting a rapid victory, they were not equipped for harsh weather. And the 1941 winter was unusually severe, even for Russia. The Soviets counterattacked in early December. Weakened, the Germans retreated. Unable to get supplies from the countryside, many soldiers perished as they fled. By February, the Germans had suffered over a million casualties.

The Russian people's determination to defend their homeland fired their courage. Soviet leaders encouraged this nationalistic spirit by exhibiting propaganda posters such as the one shown here. Notice in the background the heroic, sword-carrying warrior from Russia's medieval past. This figure connects the modern soldier in the foreground with centuries of Russian military glory and spurs him on to victory.

Hitler launched a second invasion of Russia in 1942. This campaign also failed, and Hitler's offensive against Russia was over. The Soviet army began moving into Eastern Europe and finally drove the Germans out, thus aiding the Allied victory.

Soviet wartime poster

Review Questions

1. How was Stalin fooled by Hitler?
2. Why does the Soviet poster show both a modern-day soldier and a medieval Russian warrior?

In a Polish Ghetto

Nazi Germany's attempt to exterminate Europe's Jews—along with millions of Gypsies, Slavs, homosexuals, and people with disabilities—is called the *Holocaust*. As World War II raged between 1939 and 1945, the Nazis uprooted Jewish families and herded them into ghettos—walled-off sections of cities where Jews were forced to live as best they could. Later, German units raided the ghettos and sent Jews off to be murdered in special death camps such as Auschwitz.

In carrying out their atrocities against Jews and others, the Nazis were often aided by local henchmen. These people acted sometimes out of hatred for Jews and sometimes out of fear for their own lives and families. The following document tells of an encounter between two acquaintances who found themselves on opposite sides in a roundup of Polish Jews. It is taken from the book *Alicia: My Story*, by Alicia Appleman-Jurman. The author was nine years old in 1939, when the war first came to her village in eastern Poland. There, Polish Jews had lived side by side with Christians of Polish and Ukrainian background. First the Russians and then the Germans occupied the village. By 1942, the author had lost a father and two brothers and was living in a ghetto with her mother and a younger brother.

All of my nightmares became reality one late afternoon in December 1942, about four o'clock. I had just returned from pumping water for our tiny household. I had set the water buckets down in their usual place in the hall and pushed the front door shut, when suddenly there was a heavy knock. I still had my gloves on, and my heavy shawl was wrapped high around my head, covering my nose and mouth against the bitter outside cold.

I opened the door and saw a Ukrainian policeman. He held a pencil and a small notebook, and seemed to be checking things off some sort of list. "Frieda Jurman?" he asked.

I swallowed hard, and a wave of sickness swept over me. "Yes," I said.

He made a check in his little book. "Come with me."

And so I went. I said nothing, fearing he would realize that my voice was too high and childlike to belong to a woman. It may seem strange that he thought me an adult, but I was tall for a twelve-year-old, about five feet six inches, and the coat and shawl disguised my body well. The thing I most feared had happened. They had come for my mother. I wanted to get away from our house as soon as possible, so I walked quickly in the direction the policeman indicated.

He brought me directly to the police station, where I was put into a cell with many others. It was a bare cell. The people were sitting on the stone floor all huddled together. I found a corner and sat down, pulling my legs up and encircling them with my arms. I put my head down and closed my eyes. I made up my mind that I wasn't going to cry or think about what was going to happen to all of us. . . .

Dawn was just breaking, when a prison guard came and unlocked the door to our cell. "Everybody line up and go upstairs into the waiting room," he called out. The people who had remained awake were heavy with fatigue. I, like some others, had taken the opportunity to get some sleep; I knew I would need to be alert later.

As the line moved, I could see that the people were stooping and writing their names on a yellow ledger in front of a policeman seated behind a table. I blinked hard when I realized that I knew the policeman. I felt ill inside.

This man, who was helping murder my people, was the father of my childhood friend, Olga. As I came nearer, I watched him silently. He did not look much at the people who approached him, but kept his eyes on the ledger.

When it was my turn I stepped up, took the pencil, and wrote "Alicia Jurman" on the yellow paper. I did not sign my mother's name, as I feared Olga's father would recognize me, realize what had happened, and send for my mother. His eyes widened as he recognized the name. "Alicia"—he looked at me—"what are you doing here?"

I straightened my shoulders. "I was taken here like the others," I said. He seemed baffled; clearly there had been a mistake. All of the others were adults; they had not meant to include children in this action.

Olga's father looked around to see if any of the other policemen had noticed his outburst, then motioned for me to come closer.

"Look," he said, "the Germans will be here soon to take you away. When they get here, I want you to get down on your knees and beg for your life."

He searched my face for a nod or some other sign of acknowledgment, but I only stared back. His words "beg for your life" were still ringing in my ears. He looked uncomfortable under my gaze. "All right," he said. "Move on."

I took my place with the others. I still couldn't believe that Olga's father could be part of this. I still remembered when he had told his daughter how fortunate she was to have me help her with her homework and how glad he was that we were friends. Friends, I thought bitterly, and hatred began to settle into my heart. Will he accompany the Germans and help them shoot us? Will his bullet find its target in my heart or head?

It wasn't long before the Germans came. I could see by their uniforms that they were not the usual SS[1] men, known to us as Hitler's most brutal killers, or even the Wehrmacht (army). They were the local German police.

As one of them explained that we were to be loaded into sleighs for a journey to another city, I watched Olga's father. Our eyes met. I could almost hear his thoughts. Say it! Do it now! I looked back at the German. He was winding down his talk; time was running out. Olga's father looked at the German, then at me again. Beg for your life, his eyes commanded me.

But I would not. Never! Never! I was frightened but angry at him, at the Germans, at the whole world. I wanted desperately to live, but I didn't think for a moment that going down on my knees before a heartless German murderer would save my life. If they released me, would they look for my mother again? Call it what you will, anger, dignity, courage, or just hatred, I couldn't beg, and the moment passed.

Finally the German finished. The doors opened, and the people were being pushed outside. Suddenly Olga's father stood up and came over to me. Swiftly he swung his open hand at me. The blow caught me on the cheek, throwing my head to one side. Then his hand swung back, connecting against my other cheek. The force of

---

[1]**SS**—abbreviation for Shutzstaffel, a special unit of German troops

his slap threw me off my feet, onto the crowd of the people. Hands reached out to catch me, and I was quickly steadied.

Olga's father stood in the middle of the room, his body stiff, his eyes glaring at me. Then something seemed to break inside him. He turned and went back to the table, where he sat down. He folded his hands in front of him and studied them. He did not look up again as we left the room.

Taken to prison in a nearby town, Alicia suffered beatings and other mistreatment. She was thrown unconscious onto a pile of corpses. When Jewish gravediggers discovered that she was alive, they revived her, and eventually she was able to rejoin her mother and brother. Her book tells of further harrowing adventures, and of the eventual capture and execution of her mother and brother. Somehow, Alicia survived the Holocaust and the war. In 1948, she managed to reach Palestine, where she fought in the Israeli navy during the first Arab-Israeli war. She eventually married an American, became a U.S. citizen, and moved to California, where she wrote her book.

Review Questions

1. Why did Alicia go with the Ukrainian police officer?
2. a. How did Alicia feel when she was in the cell?
   b. How did she react when she recognized the police officer in charge of the prison ledger?
3. Why did Alicia refuse to beg for her life?
4. Who were the SS?
5. Why did the officer in charge of the ledger slap Alicia?
6. What eventually became of Alicia?

16 The Horror of Auschwitz I: From *Night*, by Elie Wiesel

Some of the most powerful writings about the Holocaust have come from Elie Wiesel (pronounced EL-ee vee-ZEL), who was 15 years old in May 1944 when the Nazis sent him and his family to Auschwitz. His mother, younger sister (named Tzipora), and father died in Nazi camps, but Elie and two older sisters survived. After a career as a journalist, he began to write books about his experiences in and reflections on the Holocaust. Those books made him famous, as did his lectures on behalf of victims of oppression in the Soviet Union, South Africa, Vietnam, and other nations. In 1986, Wiesel was awarded the Nobel Peace Prize. Since 1963, he has been a U.S. citizen.

Born in the small Romanian town of Sighet, Wiesel spent the early years of his life in a close-knit Jewish community. In 1940, Sighet became part of Hungary, and four years later Nazi storm troopers arrived to ship all Sighet's Jews to concentration camps. The document that follows is taken from Wiesel's book *Night*, a combination memoir and novel. It begins as the people of Sighet leave the railroad car that had carried them to Auschwitz. German soldiers had taken all their possessions from them on the train.

The cherished objects we had brought with us thus far were left behind in the train, and with them, at last, our illusions.

Every two yards or so an SS man held his tommy gun trained on us. Hand in hand we followed the crowd.

An SS noncommissioned officer came to meet us, a [club] in his hand. He gave the order:

"Men to the left! Women to the right!"

Eight words spoken quietly, indifferently, without emotion. Eight short, simple words. Yet that was the moment when I parted from my mother. I had not had time to think, but already I felt the pressure of my father's hand: we were alone. For a part of a second I glimpsed my mother and my sisters moving away to the right. Tzipora held Mother's hand. I saw them disappear into the distance; my mother was stroking my sister's fair hair, as though to protect her, while I walked on with my father and the other men. And I did not know that in that place, at that moment, I was parting from my mother and Tzipora forever. I went on walking. My father held onto my hand.

Behind me, an old man fell to the ground. Near him was an SS man, putting his revolver back in its holster.

My hand shifted on my father's arm. I had one thought—not to lose him. Not to be left alone.

The SS officers gave the order:

"Form fives!"

Commotion. At all costs we must keep together.

"Here, kid, how old are you?" It was one of the prisoners [already in Auschwitz] who asked me this. I could not see his face, but his voice was tense and weary.

"I'm not quite fifteen yet."

"No. Eighteen."

"But I'm not," I said. "Fifteen."

"Fool. Listen to what *I* say."

Then he questioned my father, who replied:

"Fifty."

The other grew more furious than ever.

"No, not fifty. Forty. Do you understand? Eighteen and forty."

He disappeared into the night shadows. A second man came up, spitting oaths at us.

"What have you come here for, you sons of bitches? What are you doing here, eh?"

Someone dared to answer him.

"What do you think? Do you suppose we've come here for our own pleasure? Do you think we asked to come?"

A little more, and the man would have killed him.

"You shut your trap, you filthy swine, or I'll squash you right now! You'd have done better to have hanged yourselves where you were than come here. Didn't you know what was in store for you at Auschwitz? Haven't you heard about it? In 1944?"

No, we had not heard. No one had told us. He could not believe his ears. His tone of voice became increasingly brutal.

"Do you see that chimney over there? See it? Do you see those flames? (Yes, we did see the flames.) Over there—that's where you're going to be taken. That's your grave, over there. Haven't you realized it yet? You dumb bastards, don't you understand anything? You're going to be burned. Frizzled away. Turned into ashes."

He was growing hysterical in his fury. We stayed motionless, petrified. Surely it was all a nightmare? An unimaginable nightmare?

I heard murmurs around me.

"We've got to do something. We can't let ourselves be killed. We can't go like beasts to the slaughter. We've got to revolt."

There were a few sturdy young fellows among us. They had knives on them, and they tried to incite [rouse] the others to throw themselves on the armed guards.

One of the young men cried:

"Let the world learn of the existence of Auschwitz. Let everybody hear about it, while they can still escape. . . ."

But the older ones begged their children not to do anything foolish:

"You must never lose faith, even when the sword hangs over your head. That's the teaching of our sages. . . ."

The wind of revolt died down. We continued our march toward the square. In the middle stood the notorious Dr. Mengele (a typical SS officer: a cruel face, but not devoid of intelligence, and wearing a monocle); a conductor's baton in his hand, he was standing among the other officers. The baton moved [constantly], sometimes to the right, sometimes to the left.

I was already in front of him:

"How old are you?" he asked, in an attempt at a paternal tone of voice.

"Eighteen." My voice was shaking.

"Are you in good health?"

"Yes."

"What's your occupation?"

Should I say I was a student?

"Farmer," I heard myself say.

This conversation cannot have lasted more than a few seconds. It had seemed like an eternity to me.

The baton moved to the left. I took half a step forward. I wanted to see first where they were sending my father. If he went to the right, I would go after him.

The baton once again pointed to the left for him too. A weight was lifted from my heart.

We did not yet know which was the better side, right or left; which road led to prison and which to the crematory [place where bodies were burned]. But for the moment I was happy; I was near my father.

Review Questions

1. What did Elie Wiesel mean when he wrote, "The cherished objects we had brought with us this far were left behind on the train, and with them, at last, our illusions"?
2. a. What were the "eight simple words" Wiesel wrote about?
   b. Why did he write about these words?
3. Why did the prisoner tell Elie and his father to lie about their ages?
4. How was Elie Wiesel's experience similar to Alicia Jurman's?
5. How has Wiesel used his experiences as a Holocaust survivor to help people today?

The Horror of Auschwitz II: Testimony of Rudolf Höss

After the war, the Allied nations put German and Japanese leaders on trial for war crimes, including the operation of death camps such as Auschwitz. In the Nuremberg Trials of 1945–1946, held in the German city of Nuremberg, 19 top Germans were convicted, and 10 were executed by hanging.

Among Germans who submitted evidence for the Nuremberg Trials was a man named Rudolf Höss (also spelled Hoess), who served as commandant at Auschwitz for two and a half years. (Höss should not be confused with Rudolf Hess, a close confidant of Hitler's who was a defendant at Nuremberg. Hess received a life sentence and died in prison in 1987.)

The document below is an affidavit, or sworn statement, submitted by Höss to the Nuremberg tribunal.

1. I am forty-six years old, and have been . . . a member of the SS since 1934. . . .

2. . . . I commanded Auschwitz until 1 December, 1943, and estimate that at least 2,500,000 victims were executed and exterminated there by gassing and burning, and at least another half million [died of] starvation and disease, making a total dead of about 3,000,000. This figure represents about 70 percent or 80 percent of all persons sent to Auschwitz as prisoners, the remainder having been selected and used for slave labor in the concentration camp industries. Included among the executed and burnt were approximately 20,000 Russian prisoners of war (previously screened out of Prisoner of War cages by the Gestapo) . . . The remainder of the total number of victims included about 100,000 German Jews, and great numbers of citizens, *mostly* Jewish from Holland, France, Belgium, Poland, Hungary, Czechoslovakia, Greece, or other countries. We executed about 400,000 Hungarian Jews alone at Auschwitz in the summer of 1944.

4. Mass executions by gassing [began] during the summer 1941 and continued until Fall 1944. I personally supervised executions at Auschwitz until the first of December 1943 and know by reason of my

continued duties in the Inspectorate of Concentration Camps . . . that these mass executions continued as stated above. . . .

6. The "final solution" of the Jewish question meant the complete extermination of all Jews in Europe. I was ordered to establish extermination facilities at Auschwitz in June 1941. At that time there were already in the general government three other extermination camps; Belzek, Treblinka and Wolzek. . . . I visited Treblinka to find out how they carried out their exterminations. The Camp Commandant at Treblinka told me that he had [killed] 80,000 in the course of one-half year. He was principally concerned with [killing] all the Jews from the Warsaw Ghetto. He used monoxide gas and I did not think that his methods were very efficient. So when I set up the extermination building at Auschwitz, I used Cyclon B, which was a crystallized Prussic Acid which we dropped into the death chamber from a small opening. It took from 3 to 15 minutes to kill the people in the death chamber . . . We knew when the people were dead because their screaming stopped. We usually waited about one-half hour before we opened the doors and removed the bodies. After the bodies were removed our special commandos took off the rings and extracted the gold from the teeth of the corpses.

7. Another improvement we made over Treblinka was that we built our gas chambers to accommodate 2,000 people at one time, whereas at Treblinka their 10 gas chambers only accommodated 200 people each. The way we selected our victims was as follows: we had two SS doctors on duty at Auschwitz to examine the incoming . . . prisoners. The prisoners would be marched by one of the doctors who would make spot decisions as they walked by. Those who were fit for work were sent into the Camp. Others were sent immediately to the extermination plants. Children of tender years were [always] exterminated since by reason of their youth they were unable to work. Still another improvement we made over Treblinka was that at Treblinka the victims almost always knew that they were to be exterminated and at Auschwitz we endeavored to fool the victims into thinking that they were to go through a delousing process. Of course, frequently they realized our true intentions and we sometimes had riots and difficulties due to that fact. Very frequently women would hide their children under the clothes but of course when we found them we would send the children in to be exterminated. We were required to carry out these exterminations in secrecy

but of course the foul and nauseating stench from the continuous burning of bodies [spread through] the entire area and all of the people living in the surrounding communities knew that exterminations were going on at Auschwitz. . . .

I understand English as it is written above. The above statements are true; this declaration is made by me voluntarily and without compulsion; after reading over the statement, I have signed and executed the same at [Nuremberg], Germany on the fifth day of April 1946.

Review Questions

1. Why were war crimes trials held in Nuremberg, Germany?
2. Who was Rudolf Höss?
3. According to Höss, what was the purpose of camps like Auschwitz?
4. What did Höss mean by the term "final solution"?
5. How did the doctors at Auschwitz determine who would live and who would die?
6. a. Why did Höss refer to the methods of extermination used at Auschwitz as "improvements"?
   b. What does this tell you about the way the Nazis viewed the execution of millions of people?

18 The Last Days of Hitler and His Third Reich

After imposing dictatorship on Germany in 1933, Hitler vowed that what he called the Third German Empire (Third Reich) would last "a thousand years." Yet by the spring of 1945, after almost six years of war, the Third Reich was approaching extinction. The armies of the Allied Powers were closing in on Germany from west and east.

The following document is taken from the memoirs of Alexander Stahlberg, a German general. As German armies reeled under the attacks of the Allies, Stahlberg recorded the disarray within German ranks, marked by open defiance of Hitler's wishes. Like many German officers, Stahlberg believed it would be better for Germany to surrender to U.S. and British troops approaching from the west than to the Soviets who were hammering Germany from the east. Germans expected the Soviets to be unforgiving because of the immensely destructive German invasion that had caused so much suffering in Russia during the war. Also, many Germans feared the harsh nature of Soviet communism.

April 1945

[Looking back], events in Germany at that time seem unreal.

The British and American Armies have long since crossed the Rhine [in western Germany] and [have advanced deeply] into our country. In many places our troops are no longer offering any resistance. Elsewhere German units are still fighting the Allies with self-sacrificial devotion. It is almost incomprehensible that many German divisions in the West should be resisting as fiercely as others in the East. Again and again, vital bridges and strategically important viaducts are being blown up in the West to delay the Allies. Surely the most important thing now is who reaches Berlin first [the United States and Britain, closing in from the west, or the Soviet

Union, advancing from the east]. After all, what matters now is the future of Germany after Hitler. . . .

On 13 April, . . . we hear of the death of the American President, Franklin D. Roosevelt, but none of us feels that his death will alter the course of events in Germany now. . . .

The Field Marshal asks me to find out by telephone where the Army Group headquarters responsible for North Germany is now [located]. On the morning of 19 April, he drives with me to Hamburg. . . . [W]e find the Headquarters of Army Group North-West, in a big old house. . . .

Two Field Marshals now stand before the situation map. . . .

Suddenly the door opens and the Reich Minister for Armaments and Munitions, Albert Speer, stands before us. He has come from Berlin, he says, and spoken to the Führer [leader—Hitler's title] "for the last time." We sit down and listen tensely.

He had flown to Hamburg to persuade the Gauleiter [provincial governor] Karl Kaufmann there, against the Führer's orders, not to have the bridges across the Elbe [in southern and western Germany] blown up. The two Field Marshals listen, dumbfounded. "Against the Führer's orders . . . ?" Speer confirms, "Yes, against!" The Field Marshal and Commander-in-Chief of the Army Group—the only person with military responsibility here—hears the news after the Gauleiter of Hamburg! So chaos has already spread through the chain of command.

Speer describes his last visit to the underground bunker at the Berlin Reich Chancellery: in the office a trembling, wasted wreck of a sick man [Hitler] sits under the portrait of Frederick the Great,[1] scarcely listening to his visitor. He is clutching the bundle of writing and drawing [tools] from the desk tray in front of him in one hand and driving them incessantly into the table top, until the points are broken and the table top deeply punctured. Beside him lies an issue of the *Völkischer Beobachter* [newspaper], now only a few pages long. It lies open at the final part in the series of "Personal reports by Frederick the Great[1] from the Seven Years' War."[2] Only one book, a

[1]**Frederick the Great**—Frederick II, king of Prussia from 1740 to 1786, revered by German nationalists for expanding and strengthening the German state

[2]**Seven Years' War**—major war (1756–1763) in which Prussia, allied with Britain, fought a powerful alliance that included France, Austria-Hungary, and Russia

volume of Thomas Carlyle's *The History of Friedrich II of Prussia, Called Frederick the Great,* lies nearby. . . .

Speer speaks of the situation around Berlin: they are now expecting the city to be encircled [by the Soviet Union's Red Army] in a matter of days. He asks the Field Marshals if they think it possible that [General Walther] Wenck could push through from the southwest as far as the capital. No answer.

Speer reports frankly that the Führer has ordered him to ensure that all major factories in the German Reich are destroyed before the arrival of the enemy. . . . [H]e has been traveling from factory to factory for weeks now, urging the directors not to carry out the order. The two Field Marshals remain silent, shaking their heads. . . .

[Later,] we are unaware that . . . Speer is already on his way back to Berlin—after all, he has only just told us that he has been with Hitler "for the last time." He certainly had the courage to speak up [frankly] against Hitler in front of two Field Marshals, but he had not dared to say that he wanted to revisit Hitler that very day, to "see him once again." So Albert Speer is not yet free of his lord and master, who sits in his underground bunker, surrounding himself to the last with "Frederick the Great," revealing that the tyrant [Hitler] has never understood, but only "used" and hence abused, Prussia and her great king. . . .

[On May 1, 1945,] I switch on my radio to [hear] the first notes of the second movement of Bruckner's Seventh Symphony on the Hamburg radio. "Very solemnly and very slowly" the tubas and violas join in. . . . It does me good to be listening to this symphony again after all this time.

Suddenly I am seized with suspicion. Why are they broadcasting Bruckner's Seventh today? When the movement ends I know the answer: in an emotional voice the speaker announces:

"It is reported from the Führer's headquarters that our Führer, Adolf Hitler, died this afternoon for Germany at his command post in the Reich Chancellery, fighting to his last breath against Bolshevism. On 30 April the Führer named Grand Admiral [Karl] Dönitz as his successor."

The radio report that Stahlberg heard made it sound as though Hitler went down fighting. In reality, he committed suicide rather than face capture by the Red Army of the Soviet

Union. The man he appointed to succeed him, Admiral Karl Dönitz, tried to arrange for Germany to surrender solely to the western Allies. That effort was rebuffed, and Dönitz then agreed to Germany's unconditional surrender on May 7, 1945.

After the war, both Dönitz and Albert Speer were tried for war crimes by the special court at Nuremberg. Both were convicted. Dönitz, who had commanded Germany's navy, served ten years in prison. Speer, who had overseen Germany's use of slave labor, served 20 years.

Review Questions

1. Why was General Stahlberg concerned over which Allied nation reached Berlin first?
2. Why did Hitler want German bridges, viaducts, and factories destroyed?
3. Why did Albert Speer try to persuade others to disobey Hitler's orders?
4. a. How did the German radio's account of Hitler's death differ from the truth?
   b. Why do you think the German people were not told the truth about Hitler's death?
5. What was Admiral Dönitz's role in Germany's surrender?
6. What happened to Speer and Dönitz after the war?

A Hiroshima Boy Finds His Mother

Nuclear weapons have been used in wartime only on two occasions. The first was when the U.S. dropped an atomic bomb on the Japanese city of Hiroshima on August 6, 1945. The second came three days later, when a U.S. plane bombed another Japanese city, Nagasaki.

U.S. President Harry S Truman said the bombings saved the lives of untold thousands of U.S. and other Allied military personnel by convincing Japan that further resistance was futile. Without the bomb, Truman said, Allied forces would have had to invade the Japanese homeland. Judging from the fighting that had gone before, the toll in lives lost would have been extremely heavy on both sides.

The bombs that fell on Hiroshima and Nagasaki achieved the desired effect. They so demoralized the Japanese leadership that on August 14, 1945, Japan agreed to surrender unconditionally. The bombs had killed at least 100,000 people in the two cities. The after-effects of radiation from the bombs took many more lives and left many people severely disabled.

The document that follows is by Tadataka Kuribayashi, who was a child in 1945 and had been evacuated from Hiroshima along with other children. His mother and father remained in Hiroshima. On the day of the bombing, Kuribayashi was in a town nearby. He felt the shock and saw the nuclear cloud rising from the devastated city. Kuribayashi recounts his reunion with his mother four weeks later at a rescue center near Hiroshima.

I looked for Mother with my teacher. It was a big room with tens of tatami mats, and the spaces between A-bomb survivors lying on futon [mats] produced a forlorn atmosphere. We took one round, but couldn't find her. While I took the second round, looking into the face of each person, I was astonished to find Mother, lying on her face and exhausted. She was a small person, but she looked even smaller. Suppressing the [shakiness] of my voice, I called her quietly. There was no answer. I called her again. Then she noticed and slightly raised her head. . . .

When Mother told me about the death of Father, I was not so surprised. I might have been somewhat ready to hear the news. Deprived of a flush of hope, I imagined my father being burned to death in agony. My heart was wrung. . . . Mother told me to take the cloth off her back. I found brown burns all over her back. Because of the burns, she couldn't lie on her back. Why does my mother, as innocent as a person could be, have to be tortured like this? I could not suppress the anger I felt. From that day, I took care of her for 2 nights and 3 days. However, the only medicine provided was mercurochrome. . . . When Mother arrived at the center, she was fine and even washed other people's clothes, but when I got there she couldn't even move her body.

She was engaged in building-demolition work near the Tsurumi Bridge when she was exposed to the flash. She couldn't do anything for Mrs. Takai, who was immediately burned to death in front of her, and climbed the Hijiyama Hill in a hurry with her back burned. From the hill, she looked at the city, which was a hell on earth. . . . The terrible gas [radiation] which entered to the depth of her body gradually damaged her bones and organs. She had completely lost her appetite. . . .

At lunch-time on 4 September, the third day, Mother started to writhe in pain. Her unusual action completely upset me. All I could do was to absentmindedly look at my suffering Mother. After suffering for 30 minutes, she regained her calmness. However, it was the last calmness, the sign of the end of life. I continued calling her name, clinging to her body. Tears welled up in the eyes of my speechless Mother and tears rolled down her cheek. I wondered if the tears were from the sorrow of eternal parting between mother and child or from an anxiety about my future. I shall never forget the tears of my Mother I saw on that day.

Review Questions

1. What are the only two cities ever to have suffered wartime attack with nuclear weapons?

2. Why did the use of atomic bombs bring World War II to an end?
3. a. What were the immediate effects of dropping atomic bombs on Japan?
   b. What were the aftereffects of dropping atomic bombs on Japan?
4. Why was Tadataka separated from his mother and father?
5. What happened to Tadataka's parents?
6. How was the use of atomic bombs on Japan different from an action that might usually be expected to occur during a war?

Write a well-organized essay that includes an introduction, several paragraphs, and a conclusion. Use evidence from at least ***four*** *documents from the unit in the body of the essay. Support your response with relevant facts, examples, and details. Include additional outside information.*

Historical Context

The years 1900 through 1945 marked a period representing both the greatest hope and deepest despair for humankind.

Task: Using the documents and questions in the unit, along with your knowledge of global history, write an essay in which you:

- Describe **one** example of hope and **one** example of despair that took place during the period 1900 through 1945
- Show how **each** example affected a specific group of people
- Describe **one** outcome for each of the two examples you have given

The World Since 1945

The United Nations Universal Declaration of Human Rights

In its charter, adopted in 1945, the United Nations stated that one of its primary goals was fostering respect for human rights "without distinction as to race, sex, language, or religion." In large measure, the UN set this goal in response to the violations of human rights that had been committed during the 1930s and in World War II. It also was an attempt to right the wrongs of colonialism and the exploitation of Africans, Asians, and women throughout the world. In 1948, the UN General Assembly undertook to define fundamental rights by adopting the Universal Declaration of Human Rights.

This document is sometimes called "an international bill of rights." Unlike the U.S. Bill of Rights, the Universal Declaration is not a legally binding document. It cannot necessarily be enforced in courts. It is an expression of moral judgment that gets its force from the fact that it was adopted without a single negative vote and represents a broad consensus about the meaning of human rights.

Article 1

All human beings are born free and equal in dignity and rights. They are endowed with reason and conscience and should act toward one another in a spirit of brotherhood.

Article 2

Everyone is entitled to all the rights and freedoms set forth in this Declaration, without distinction of any kind, such as race, color, sex, language, religion, political or other opinion, national or social origin, property, birth or other status. . . .

Article 3

Everyone has the right to life, liberty, and security of person.

[Articles 4 and 5 itemize different aspects of the general right stated in Article 3. Article 4 prohibits slavery. Article 5 prohibits torture and cruel or unusual punishment.]

Article 6

Everyone has the right to recognition everywhere as a person before the law.

[Article 7 states the equality of all persons before the law. Article 8 discusses the right to justice in national courts. Article 9 prohibits arbitrary arrest and punishment. Article 10 states an accused person's right to a fair trial. Article 11 asserts that a person must be presumed innocent until proved guilty in a public trial. It also states that a person cannot be held guilty for an act committed before the act was constituted a penal offense. Article 12 asserts that law should protect a person's privacy, honor, and reputation.]

Article 13

1. Everyone has the right to freedom of movement and residence within the borders of each state.
2. Everyone has the right to leave any country, including his own, and to return to his country.

[Article 14 addresses people's right to go to another country for asylum from persecution. Article 15 prohibits depriving people of their nationality or denying them the right to change their nationality if they so wish.]

Article 16

1. Men and women of full age . . . have the right to marry and to found a family. They are entitled to equal rights as to marriage, during marriage, and at its dissolution.
2. Marriage shall be entered into only with the free and full consent of the intending spouses.
3. The family is the natural and fundamental group unit of society and is entitled to protection by society and the state.

Article 17

1. Everyone has the right to own property alone as well as in association with others.

2. No one shall be arbitrarily deprived of his property.

Article 18

Everyone has the right to freedom of thought, conscience, and religion. . . .

> [Article 19 extends the right stated in Article 18 to the right to freedom of opinion and expression.]

Article 20

1. Everyone has the right to freedom of peaceful assembly and association.

2. No one may be compelled to belong to an association.

Article 21

1. Everyone has the right to take part in the government of his country, directly or through freely chosen representatives.

2. Everyone has the right of equal access to public service in his country.

3. The will of the people shall be the basis of the authority of government; this will shall be expressed in periodic and genuine elections which shall be by universal and equal suffrage and shall be held by secret vote. . . .

Article 22

Everyone, as a member of society, has the right to social security and is entitled to realization . . . of the economic, social, and cultural rights indispensable for his dignity and the free development of his personality.

> [Article 23 addresses (1) the right to work, to have free choice of employment, and to have protection against unfavorable work conditions and against unemployment; (2) the right to equal pay for equal work; (3) the right to wages or

supplemental income that allows a dignified lifestyle; (4) the right to form and join trade unions. Article 24 states the right to reasonable limitation on working hours.]

Article 25

1. Everyone has the right to a standard of living adequate for the health and well-being of himself and of his family, including food, clothing, housing, and medical care and necessary social services. . . .

2. Motherhood and childhood are entitled to special care and assistance. All children . . . shall enjoy the same social protection.

Article 26

1. Everyone has the right to education. Education shall be free, at least in the elementary and fundamental stages. Elementary education shall be compulsory. Technical and professional education shall be made generally available. . . .

2. Education shall be directed to the full development of the human personality and to the strengthening of respect for human rights and fundamental freedoms. . . .

3. Parents have a prior right to choose the kind of education that shall be given to their children.

Article 27

1. Everyone has the right freely to participate in the cultural life of the community, to enjoy the arts, and to share in scientific advancement and its benefits.

2. Everyone has the right to the protection of the moral and material interests resulting from any scientific, literary, or artistic production of which he is the author.

Article 28

Everyone is entitled to a social and international order in which the rights and freedoms set forth in this declaration can be fully realized.

Article 29

1. Everyone has duties to the community. . . .

2. In the exercise of his rights and freedoms, everyone shall be subject only to such limitations as are determined by law solely for the purpose of securing due recognition and respect for the rights and freedoms of others. . . .

3. These rights and freedoms may in no case be exercised contrary to the purposes and principles of the United Nations.

> [Article 30 prohibits states, groups, or persons from interpreting any of the articles of the declaration in such a way as to destroy any of the rights and freedoms that it asserts.]

Review Questions

1. How does the Universal Declaration say all human beings should behave or act toward one another?
2. What three basic rights does the declaration guarantee to all people?
3. According to the declaration, what is the main responsibility of a government toward each member of society?
4. How did the Holocaust and other crimes of war lead to the writing and adoption of the Universal Declaration of Human Rights?

Winston Churchill Describes the "Iron Curtain"

When former British Prime Minister Winston Churchill visited the United States in 1946, World War II had been over for less than a year. Much of Europe still lay in ruins. The people of Britain and of many other European countries were struggling to rebuild shattered homes and industries. Hunger and want were widespread. Most people were tired of war and ready to forget about international problems—but not Churchill.

In a speech at Westminster College in Fulton, Missouri, in March 1946, Churchill warned Western democracies to remain on guard. He accused leaders of the Soviet Union of seeking "indefinite expansion of their power and doctrines." And he introduced the term "iron curtain" to describe the boundary between zones of Western influence and Soviet influence in Europe. Churchill's "iron curtain" speech was an early warning about what soon became known as the cold war.

. . . A shadow has fallen upon the scenes so lately lighted by the Allied victory. Nobody knows what Soviet Russia and its Communist international organization intend to do in the immediate future, or what are the limits, if any, to their expansive . . . tendencies. . . .

From Stettin in the Baltic to Trieste in the Adriatic, an iron curtain has descended across the continent. Behind that line lie all the capitals of the ancient states of Central and Eastern Europe. . . . [A]ll these famous cities and the populations around them lie in what I must call the Soviet sphere, and all are subject in one form or another, not only to Soviet influence but to a very high . . . measure of control from Moscow. . . . The Communist parties, which were very small in all these Eastern states [countries] of Europe, have been raised to . . . power far beyond their numbers and are seeking everywhere to obtain totalitarian control. Police governments are prevailing in nearly every case, and so far, except in Czechoslovakia, there is no true democracy.

An attempt is being made by the Russians in Berlin to build up a quasi-Communist party in their zone of occupied Germany by showing special favors to groups of left-wing German leaders. . . .

. . . Whatever conclusions may be drawn from these facts—and facts they are—this is certainly not the liberated Europe we fought to build up. Nor is it one which contains the essentials of permanent peace.

In front of the iron curtain which lies across Europe are other causes for anxiety. . . . [I]n a great number of countries, far from the Russian frontiers and throughout the world, Communist fifth columns[1] are established and work in complete unity and absolute obedience to the directions they receive from the Communist center. Except in the British Commonwealth and in the United States where communism is in its infancy, the Communist parties or fifth columns constitute a growing challenge and peril to . . . civilization. . . .

I do not believe that Soviet [leaders] desire war. What they desire is . . . the indefinite expansion of their power and doctrines. But what we have to consider here today while time remains, is the permanent prevention of war and the establishment of conditions of freedom and democracy as rapidly as possible in all countries. Our difficulties and dangers will not be removed . . . by mere waiting to see what happens; nor will they be removed by a policy of appeasement. . . .

From what I have seen of our Russian friends and Allies during the war, I am convinced that there is nothing . . . for which they have less respect than for weakness, especially military weakness. For that reason the old doctrine of a balance of power is unsound. We cannot afford, if we can help it, to work on narrow margins, offering temptations to a trial of strength. If the Western democracies stand together in strict adherence to the principles of the United Nations charter, their influence for furthering those principles will be immense and no one is likely to molest them. If, however, they become divided or falter in their duty, and if these all-important years are allowed to slip away, then indeed catastrophe may overwhelm us all. . . .

---

[1]**fifth column**—a group within a country that works secretly on behalf of another country or cause

Review Questions

1. What did Winston Churchill mean when he stated "a shadow has fallen upon the scenes so lately lighted by the Allied victory"?
2. Why did Churchill declare that much of Eastern Europe was behind an "iron curtain"?
3. a. What did Churchill mean by "appeasement"?
   b. Why was Churchill against appeasing the Soviet Union?
4. How did Churchill feel that Western democracies should behave toward the Soviet Union?

The Cold War Nuclear Arms Race

After World War II ended in 1945, two new superpowers—the United States and the Soviet Union—emerged. The United States led the democracies of the West against the Soviet Union, its, allies, and its satellite countries. Since the hostility between the Western democracies and the Eastern Communist states never erupted into a shooting, or hot, war, the conflict was called the *cold war*.

Soviet leaders were committed to spreading the Communist form of government. Both before and during the cold war era, the Soviet Union made inroads into Central Europe and even into Latin America. Several Asian and African countries adopted Communist regimes.

The United States and the Soviet Union fought each other's influence with propaganda, international conferences and military alliances, economic aid, and spying. Both built up powerful arsenals of both conventional and nuclear weapons. At first, the United States enjoyed an overwhelming advantage in weapons. It alone had the atomic bomb. By 1949, however, the Soviets also had the bomb. In the 1950s, both nations developed the even deadlier hydrogen bomb. Each side continued to improve on and increase its stockpile of nuclear weapons, until they were roughly equal in destructive power. This contest to build the most destructive weapons became known as the *arms race*.

People began to argue that the arms race made nuclear war unlikely. It ensured that neither side would benefit from attacking the other. If one side launched the first bomb, the other would instantly retaliate, and both would be destroyed. The phrase "mutually assured destruction" (MAD) summed up this argument. MAD expresses the irony that cooperation could spring from so deadly a source. The argument, however, proved accurate. In the 1960s, the United States and the Soviet Union began to hold arms-control conferences to keep the balance of nuclear power stable.

In spite of arms-control agreements between the two powers, many people still feared the dangerous radioactive fallout that resulted from nuclear testing. James Arthur Wood's 1950 cartoon expresses the pressure that ordinary people felt at being caught in the rivalry between the two superpowers.

The U.S.-Soviet nuclear arms race ©*Corbis*

Review Questions

1. Why was the confrontation between the United States and the Soviet Union known as the cold war?
2. How did the cold war lead the U.S. and the Soviet Union into an arms race for nuclear superiority?
3. Why did some people feel that the nuclear arms race would actually prevent a nuclear catastrophe?
4. How did the cartoon by James Arthur Wood reflect the fears of many people who lived through the cold war?

The Space Race I: The First Space Flight

On April 12, 1961, a Russian cosmonaut (space pilot) named Yuri Gagarin became the first human to soar into space. He made one complete orbit of the Earth in a spacecraft called *Vostok I*. It was a proud moment for Soviet space engineers and a disturbing one for U.S. leaders. The latter were playing catch-up in what people were calling "the space race."

As far as the public was concerned, the "race" had started three and a half years before, on October 4, 1957, when the Soviet Union launched *Sputnik I*—the first artificial satellite to be put into earth orbit. Early in 1959 an unmanned Soviet space vehicle passed close to the moon and went into orbit around the sun. U.S. leaders were shocked by these challenges to what most Americans had assumed was U.S. superiority in all areas of technology. Especially disturbing during this time of the cold war was the thought that the same Soviet rockets that launched space vehicles could be adapted to carry nuclear weapons around the world for strikes against U.S. targets.

After the Gagarin flight in 1961, the United States bounced back to win "the space race." In May 1961 U.S. astronaut Alan B. Shepard, Jr., rode into space and returned, although he did not orbit the Earth. A few weeks later, President John F. Kennedy announced that the United States was committing itself to the goal of landing an astronaut on the moon "before this decade is out."

The document that follows is an account of Gagarin's pioneering space flight.

9:11 Moscow time. Gagarin had left Earth's atmosphere. The second stage[1] had separated and fallen away. Temperature and velocity fell sharply. There were silent handshakes 200 miles below

[1]**stage**—a booster rocket that enabled the *Vostok* and other spacecraft to accelerate and escape the earth's gravitational pull

[at the Baikonur space center]. In the cabin Gagarin felt the sudden release as his [flight path] altered and he fell into the huge swinging curve that was to take him around the world. He was in orbit.

Gagarin had counted from the moment of separation. Now his words came through clearly . . . "18 . . . 19 . . . 20 . . . this is Vostok. Last stage gone. . . ." He pulled his body toward the cabin window and the dim light beyond. "I can see the Earth in a haze. Feeling fine." He added, after a second look, "How beautiful. . . . "

Now he was able to move for the first time, and he loosened his straps. Instantly his body parted from the seat and he was floating, still held down by the straps, but completely relaxed. He loosened the nylon bonds still further and unclipped his face mask. Ground control asked him how he was. "Fine . . ." he repeated.

Already he had been in a state of zero gravity, in flight, longer than any man had ever experienced. . . . He reached down and switched on the globe navigator. This was a space-age instrument straight from science fiction. No man had ever used the whole globe as his chart before now. It was revolving, slowly, as his position altered in relation to Earth. A cross in the center indicated the exact spot below him. Another switch, and the spot was pulled up into sharp magnification. He was tracing his own invisible equator around the earth; Siberia, the Pacific . . . into darkness, for he was now moving into the shadowed part of the globe. Through the porthole, though, he could just make out the outline of islands and streamers of white and grey cloud.

He repeated the instrument readings every three or four minutes; after each came a calm confirmation from Earth. . . .

Minutes went by, and as he hurtled on toward his second dawn of the day he strained his eyes to watch it; watching it as no one had ever watched a sunrise. . . . This little porthole was Man's first unclouded window on the Universe. . . .

Vostok sailed on, and Gagarin sang. . . . Through his headphones he heard an appreciative chuckle. "When you're through singing, we've got a professional," and clearly, with only a trace of [static] to heighten the effect, came the nostalgia-charged lyrics of "Moscow Nights," a honey-sweet hit tune that throbs with emotion. Gagarin knew it well; Moscow Radio plays it every day, but it had never been played like this before. . . .

The south Atlantic slid into view. Just 188 miles down there, heaving on an ice-cold sea, a Russian tracking ship was stationed, its radar antennae probing skyward for its countryman riding the biggest sea of all.

Gagarin . . . felt for the feeding tube; he hadn't had breakfast. . . .

Time: 10:15. He reported: "Over Africa," and then, in reply to a query, "Standing up well to weightlessness." At 10:16, as the minute hand of the chronometer passed zero plus sixty-nine [minutes since takeoff], the red panel light glowed to give notice of descent in ten minutes. He was 8,000 km. from the landing ground. Swiftly he checked his instruments again, reported once more that all was well and that there were no abnormalities. Control confirmed this, asking if he now wanted to make any alteration in the flight plan. . . .

In front of him the magic eye globe was still revolving in its socket, and he pushed the switch for magnification. A glass strip, etched with a tiny white triangle, moved slowly toward a thick red line. When the two met, that was the exact moment for the firing of the retro-rockets. The area inside the triangle would be the landing place, Smelovka. . . .

Gagarin . . . strapped himself back into the seat, released a catch to let it down into the fully reclining position, and waited. . . .

Even firmly strapped in, Gagarin felt the atmosphere around him in the cabin change, almost imperceptibly. The sensation of weightlessness left him. The brakes had fired with a shattering roar and he watched, awed, as white tongues of flames streaked past the porthole. . . . The solar thermometers in the cabin and on Earth shot up to register a fantastic 4,000° C.; the skin [of the space capsule] was hotter than a bar of molten steel, but the two refrigeration units, the cooling system and the air regeneration equipment pumped steadily on.

Overload was greater than on the way up; the pressure was painful in the extreme. Every muscle and nerve was being hammered by vibration. Instruments began to swim in front of his eyes, but through it all the clock was visible. . . .

Time: 10:27. There were twenty-eight minutes to go. On the TV screens Gagarin's face retreated in profile until it was almost flat. The nose was pushed in, the eye sockets grew larger, and shadowy. Every bone in his face was sharply outlined by dead-white skin. Speech was impossible, though he could just hear the reassuring voice of the controller through the screeching of the engine, telling him that all was well.

The pressure was slowly lifted. After one and a half minutes he was warned by orange lights and radio to prepare for landing. "Above target, on course, para-brakes," called control, and Gagarin felt a push in the chest as the parachutes, a huge cluster of them, billowed out high above the capsule. . . . As he floated down gently, he could see from his window the multicolored squares of familiar farmland rushing up to meet him; familiar because this was near Saratov, his old training base. . . .

Two women working in the fields were staring at the sky. The dot grew larger, changing from black to white. Parachutist, one whispered. Alarmed but determined, they ran toward the object as it drifted over the trees and hit the earth in the middle of a long, stubbly field. As they ran a hatch opened and a head emerged, followed by a body in a sky-blue suit. . . . [T]he spaceman grinned and called: "Hello, give me a hand."

Review Questions

1. Identify:
   a. *Vostok I*
   b. Yuri Gagarin
2. a. Why were many Americans concerned that Russia was ahead of the United States in the space race?
   b. How did President John F. Kennedy respond to Yuri Gagarin's flight into space?
3. What new scientific instrument did Gagarin use on his flight?
4. Approximately how long did Gagarin's flight into space last?

The Space Race II: A Walk on the Moon

On February 20, 1962, less than a year after Gagarin's flight, astronaut John H. Glenn, Jr., became the first American to orbit the earth. Glenn's craft, *Friendship 7*, made three orbits in a five-hour period. Seven years later, after much testing and more Earth-orbits by U.S. astronauts, the U.S. space program managed to meet President Kennedy's deadline with months to spare. On July 20, 1969, the Apollo 11 mission placed two U.S. astronauts on the moon. They were Neil A. Armstrong and Colonel Edwin E. (Buzz) Aldrin, Jr. A third astronaut, Lieutenant Colonel Michael Collins, remained in orbit around the moon in the spaceship *Columbia* while Armstrong and Aldrin descended in a lunar module (or LM) named *Eagle*. The dramatic moment when Armstrong first set foot on the moon was telecast live in the United States and 42 other nations. The United States thus showed its ability to meet and surpass the Soviet lead in space technology.

This document is from a book by Aldrin. The excerpt begins with the descent of the lunar module, which was out of radio contact with mission control in Houston while it swung behind the moon.

The moon rolled by silently outside my window. The craters were slowly becoming more distinct as we descended. There wasn't much to do except monitor the instruments and wait for AOS (acquisition of signal). As we got closer, the moon's color changed from beige to bleached gray. The hissing crackle of Houston's signal returned to our earphones. "*Eagle,* Houston," Charlie Duke called through the static. "If you read, you're go for powered descent. Over."

Neil nodded, his tired eyes warm with anticipation. I was grinning like a kid. We were going to land on the moon. . . .

We were just 700 feet above the surface when Charlie gave us the final "go." . . .

Neil . . . wasn't satisfied with the terrain. . . . We scooted across the boulders. At 200 feet our hover slid toward a faster descent rate. . . .

The low-fuel light blinked. . . .

Thirty feet below the LM's gangly legs, dust that had lain undisturbed for a billion years blasted sideways in the plume of our engine.

"Thirty seconds," Charlie announced solemnly. . . .

I stared out at the rocks and shadows of the moon. It was as stark as I'd ever imagined it. A mile away, the horizon curved into blackness.

"Houston," Neil called, "Tranquility Base here. The *Eagle* has landed." . . .

I reached across and shook Neil's hand, hard. We had pulled it off. Five months and ten days before the end of the decade, two Americans had landed on the moon. . . .

Suiting up for the moon walk took us several hours. Our PLSS [portable life-support system] backpacks looked simple, but they were hard to put on and tricky to operate. They were truly our life-support systems, with enough oxygen, cooling water, electrical power, and radio equipment to keep us alive on the moon and in constant contact with Houston (via a relay in the LM) for four hours. On Earth, the PLSS and spacesuit combination weighed 190 pounds, but here it was only 30. Combined with my own body weight, that brought me to a total lunar-gravity weight of around 60 pounds.

Seven hours after we touched down on the moon, we depressurized the LM, and Neil opened the hatch. My job was to guide him as he backed out on his hands and knees onto the small porch. He worked slowly, trying not to jam his backpack on the hatch frame. When he reached the ladder attached to the forward landing leg, he moved down carefully. . . .

The surface was a very fine-grain powder. "I'm going to step off the LM now." . . .

From my window I watched Neil move his blue lunar overshoe from the metal dish of the footpad to the powdery gray surface.

"That's one small step for . . . man, one giant leap for mankind." . . .

One of the first things Neil did on the surface was take a sample of the lunar soil in case we had to terminate our moon walk early.

Now he started working with his scoop and collection box while I set up the metal foil "window shade" of the solar wind collector. The moon was like a giant sponge that absorbed the constant "wind" of charged particles streaming outward from the sun. Scientists back on Earth would examine the collector to learn more about this phenomenon and, through it, the history of the solar system. . . .

Of all the jobs I had to do on the moon, the one I wanted to go the smoothest was the flag raising. Bruce [McCandless in Houston] had told us we were being watched by the largest television audience in history. . . . Just beneath the powdery surface, the subsoil was very dense. We succeeded in pushing the flagpole in only a couple of inches. It didn't look very sturdy. But I did snap off a crisp West Point salute once we got the banner upright. . . .

Bruce told us that President Richard Nixon wanted to speak to us. . . . The president said, "For one priceless moment, in the whole history of man, all the people on this Earth are truly one." . . .

Time was moving in spasms. We still had many tasks to accomplish. Some seemed quite easy and others dragged on. It took me a long time to erect the passive seismometer (the "moonquake" detector). . . .

Our liftoff was powerful. Nothing we'd done in the simulators had prepared us for this amazing swoop upward in the weak lunar gravity. Within seconds we had pitched forward a sharp 45 degrees and were soaring above the crater fields.

"Very smooth," I called, "very quiet ride." It wasn't at all like flying through Earth's atmosphere. Climbing fast, we finally spotted the landmark craters we'd missed during the descent. Two minutes into the ascent, we were batting along at half a mile per second.

Columbia was above and behind us. Our radar and the computers on the two spacecraft searched for each other and then locked on and communicated in a soundless digital exchange.

Four hours after Neil and I lifted off from the Sea of Tranquility, we heard the capture latches clang shut above our heads. . . . Soon Mike [Collins] would unseal the tunnel so that Neil and I could pass the moon rocks through and then join Mike in *Columbia* for the long ride back.

Review Questions

1. Identify:
   a. *Columbia*
   b. *Eagle*
2. How many years elapsed between Yuri Gagarin's space flight and the first landing of human beings on the surface of the moon?
3. a. How much did astronaut Edwin Aldrin weigh on the moon with all his space equipment?
   b. Why did Aldrin weigh less on the moon than he did on Earth?
4. Explain the meaning of the following statements in the document:
   a. "That's one small step for . . . man, one giant leap for mankind."
   b. "For one priceless moment, in the whole history of man, all the people on this Earth are truly one."
5. How would you describe the difference between Gagarin's space trip in 1961 and the U.S. moon flight in 1969?
6. How was the space race just one area of competition between the United States and the Soviet Union?

Asian and African Countries Call for an End to Colonialism

When World War II ended in 1945, much of Asia and most of Africa were under the rule of European imperialist powers. (The Philippines was under the rule of the United States.) Then began a process known as decolonization. The Philippines became independent in 1946, India and Pakistan in 1947. Other nations soon did also—Burma (now Myanmar), Ceylon (now Sri Lanka), Indonesia, and more.

In 1955, these newly independent nations—along with such nations as Thailand and China, which had not been colonies—held a conference at Bandung, Indonesia, to talk about common interests and concerns. Indonesia's President Sukarno referred to the gathering as "the first international conference of colored peoples in the history of mankind." Twenty-nine countries, representing more than half the world's population, sent delegates. Major leaders who attended included Sukarno, Premier Zhou En-lai of China, and Prime Minister Jawaharlal Nehru of India.

Since the Bandung Conference occurred at the height of the cold war, it caused quite a stir. U.S. leaders viewed the gathering with deep misgivings—and so did the leaders of the Soviet Union. Many in the U.S. saw the event as a sign of rising Chinese Communist influence in the developing world. Nonetheless, many delegates to the conference were strongly opposed to communism. They considered the Soviet Union's domination of Eastern Europe and central Asia to be an example of colonialism. In the end, the conference condemned "colonialism in all its manifestations [forms]."

The documents that follow touch on the theme of anti-colonialism. The first is from Sukarno's speech to the conference's opening session. The second is excerpted from the conference's closing statement. The third is a Western observer's understanding of the conference.

A. Sukarno's Speech

All of us, I am certain, are united by more important things than those which superficially divide us. We are united, for instance, by a common detestation of colonialism in whatever form it appears. We are united by a common detestation of [racism]. And we are united by a common determination to preserve and stabilize peace in the world. . . .

We are often told, "Colonialism is dead." Let us not be deceived or even soothed by that. I say to you, colonialism is not yet dead. How can we say it is dead, so long as vast areas of Asia and Africa are unfree?

And, I beg of you, do not think of colonialism only in the classic form which we of Indonesia, and our brothers in different parts of Asia and Africa, knew. Colonialism has also its modern dress, in the form of economic control, intellectual control, actual physical control by a small but alien community within a nation. It is a skillful and determined enemy, and it appears in many guises. It does not give up its loot easily. Wherever, whenever and however it appears, colonialism is an evil thing, and one which must be eradicated from the earth. . . .

B. Closing Statement

The Asian-African Conference discussed the problems of dependent peoples and colonialism and the evils arising from subjection of peoples to alien . . . domination and exploitation. The Conference agreed:

First, in declaring that colonialism in all its [forms] is an evil which should speedily be brought to an end;

Second, in affirming that the subjection of peoples to alien . . . domination and exploitation constitutes a denial of fundamental human rights, is contrary to the Charter of the United Nations, and is [a bar] to the promotion of world peace and cooperation;

Third, in declaring its support of the cause of freedom and independence for all such peoples; and

Fourth, in calling upon the powers concerned to grant freedom and independence to such peoples.

One of those who attended the Bandung Conference as a journalist and observer was Richard Wright, the African

American novelist, author of *Black Boy* and other well-known works. Wright attended the conference hoping to gain a new understanding of the political stirrings in Asia and Africa and the changing nature of world politics. The following excerpt is from his 1956 book *The Color Curtain: A Report on the Bandung Conference*.

C. Richard Wright on the Conference

The results of the [discussion] of the delegates at Bandung would be, of course, addressed to the people and the statesmen of the Western powers, for it was the moral notions—or lack of them—of those powers that were in question here; it had been against the dominance of those powers that these delegates and their populations had struggled so long. After two days of torrid public speaking and four days of discussions in closed sessions, the Asian-African Conference issued a [statement]. It was a sober document, brief and to the point, yet it did not hesitate to lash out, in terse legal prose, at racial injustice and colonial exploitation.

I repeat and underline that the document was addressed to the West. . . . It was my belief that the delegates at Bandung, for the most part, though bitter, looked and hoped toward the West. . . . The West, in my opinion, must be big enough, generous enough, to accept and understand that bitterness. The Bandung communiqué was no appeal, in terms of sentiment or ideology, to Communism. Instead, it carried exalted overtones of the stern dignity of ancient and proud peoples who yearned to rise and play again a role in human affairs.

Review Questions

A. Sukarno

1. Why did Sukarno refer to both colonialism and racism in his opening statement?
2. What were the common bonds that united all the delegates to the conference?
3. What group did Sukarno mean when he spoke of "a small but alien community within a nation"?

B. Closing Statement

1. a. How did the closing statement of the conference use Sukarno's opening statement?
   b. Why did the delegates refer to the charter of the United Nations?
2. How might the delegates have used the United Nations Universal Declaration of Human Rights to support their arguments against colonialism?

C. Richard Wright

1. Why did Richard Wright feel that the closing statement of the conference was directed toward Western nations?
2. Do you think Wright's interpretation was correct?

Nasser Takes Over the Suez Canal

The Suez Canal Crisis of 1956 was a landmark event of the cold war years. It resulted in a sharp drop in British and French influence in the Middle East. It also represented a stormy chapter in the history of Arab-Israeli relations.

Egypt in the 1950s was just emerging from a long period of dominance by European powers. French engineers under Ferdinand de Lesseps had built the Suez Canal in the 1860s, and in 1875 Britain took over principal ownership of the canal company. To protect this "lifeline to India," the British soon began to rule Egypt in fact if not in name. In 1952, Egyptian nationalists overthrew King Farouk, who had cooperated with the British. Egyptian Army officer Gamal Abdel Nasser became premier of a new Egyptian republic in 1953, and later its president. He hoped to bring other Arab nations together with Egypt under his own leadership. Nasser was a sharp critic of colonialism and of Israel, and he won wide popularity in the Arab world.

With the cold war at its height, Nasser sought and received military aid from the Soviet bloc in 1955. The United States countered by offering to finance the building of a High Dam at Aswan on the Nile River. This was a project to produce large amounts of electricity, which Nasser counted on to build up Egyptian industry. But when Nasser continued to oppose U.S. policy on international issues, the United States took back its offer on July 19, 1956.

One week later, Nasser announced that he was nationalizing the Suez Canal. That is, he was taking it away from its British and French owners and making it the property of the Egyptian government. He wanted the revenue from the canal to finance the building of the High Dam. Also, he wanted to diminish the British and French role in the region and teach "the imperialists" (Western countries) a lesson.

The following document is by Mohamed Hassanein Heikal, the editor of Egypt's leading newspaper at the time and a close associate of Nasser. It describes Nasser's calculations, including the reactions he expected from other nations and how he evaluated the odds for and against success.

[On the night of July 20, 1956,] Nasser sat down and made his estimation of what would happen if he nationalized the Suez Canal. . . . [I]t was based on everything that had happened between himself and Eden[1] since their dinner seventeen months before, set in the context of the whole history of Anglo-Egyptian relations.

President Nasser told me all about it over the telephone. His [evaluation] covered [these] points, which, according to the notes I made at the time, were as follows:

1. Eden will behave in a violent way.
2. The violence will take the form of military action. . . .
3. The possibility of violence will be 80 percent. It depends on how many troops the British have ready for quick intervention. . . .
4. Most probably Eden will try to pull France with him, or maybe France is going to pull Eden. But certainly France may participate in any action against us.
5. The United States will remain silent, giving their blessing under the table. . . .
6. The position of Russia will be decisive. . . . If we tell them, will that mean asking their permission?. . .
8. The possibilities of the success of intervention. . . . Landing, occupying the Canal? . . . Possible. We need to reinforce Eastern Command. . . .
14. Would Israel take the chance alone and attack Syria or Jordan? . . .

Everything depended on the reports of British strength. Nasser waited impatiently for those reports to come in. . . .

Until . . . [July 24] he had told no one about his plans. But at the opening of [an oil-pumping station on that day] he heard Mahmoud Younes, the engineer in charge of the pipeline, talking, and decided to choose him to head the nationalization project. . . .

Nasser told him what he had in mind and asked him to prepare a complete plan for the takeover of the Canal administration, to cope with any trouble, and to keep the Canal running. He wanted this plan the following day.

That night the President had enough information to convince him that the British did not have a sufficiently powerful force in the area to [support] an invasion and that it would take them two months to assemble such a force. The President said: "All I need is

---

[1]**Eden**—Anthony Eden, the British prime minister

one month, so this is long enough for me." The President was to make a speech on July 26 . . . so when Younes appeared with his completed plans for the takeover of the Canal administration, Nasser told him to go to Ismailia[2] and listen on the radio to the speech he was going to make in Alexandria on that evening.

Younes was to listen for President Nasser to mention the name de Lesseps, the French builder of the Canal. That was the code word for Younes to put the plan into action.

The President was so worried that Younes and his team would miss it that he kept on repeating the Frenchman's name. . . .

Younes moved immediately when he heard that name the first time. . . . [A]t the word "de Lesseps" he switched off the set and took over the Ismailia headquarters of the Suez Canal Company at gunpoint. . . .

The governor of the Eastern District . . . [and Younes] took over the Canal installations while the police occupied the Company's offices in Cairo.

It was a well-planned and well-executed operation. By the time the President had finished reading his declaration of nationalization, the Canal had been taken over. . . .

The people went wild with excitement. The Canal had always stood as a monument to the exploitation of Egypt. Thousands of Egyptians had died digging it. The Suez Canal Company was a state within a state. It had its own [codes] and its own flag. . . . [T]he wildest dream of most Egyptians had been that we might not renew the concession when it ran out in 1968. And now Nasser had nationalized it. It belonged to Egypt.

In response to nationalization, British Prime Minister Anthony Eden secretly planned with France and Israel to attack Egypt. Three months after the canal takeover, Israeli forces invaded from the east. Claiming a need to protect the canal, Britain and France bombed Egyptian sites and sent paratroopers to seize the canal. But the Soviet Union and the United States vigorously opposed the attack. The United Nations Security Council ordered a cease-fire and a

[2]**Ismailia**—town at southern end of Suez Canal where the Universal Suez Canal Company had offices

withdrawal of the attacking forces. In the end, Egypt kept the canal and Britain and France were humiliated. Nasser became a hero to many Arab nationalists.

Review Questions

1. Explain the meaning of the term "nationalization."
2. How did the cold war competition between the Soviet Union and the United States lead Nasser to nationalize the Suez Canal?
3. What reaction to the nationalization of the Suez Canal did Nasser expect from Britain, France, and the United States?
4. What did Mohamed Hassanein Heikal mean when he referred to the Suez Canal Company as a "state within a state"?
5. Why did most Egyptians enthusiastically support the nationalization of the Suez Canal?
6. What did Britain, France, and Israel do after Egypt nationalized the canal?

8 Quotations From Chairman Mao

During the mid-1960s, China went through a period of turmoil known as the "Great Proletarian Cultural Revolution." It was Communist Party Chairman Mao Zedong's way of reviving the revolutionary enthusiasm of the Chinese people. (An attempt at modernization in the 1950s had failed.) Authorities shut down schools and universities. They sent young people into the countryside to work with the peasants and "learn from the masses." They also sent Communist Party members and leaders into the countryside. Mao declared the goals of his "cultural revolution" were to fight bureaucracy and eliminate outworn ways of thinking. But he mainly wanted to make sure that China continued on a path of "uninterrupted revolution" toward a Communist future.

Mao was already the subject of nationwide hero worship. Many idolized him as the leader of the 1949 Communist revolution, which overthrew the Chinese Nationalists. In the late summer and fall of 1966, Mao's image became even more powerful. A small, red-covered booklet called "Quotations From Chairman Mao" found its way to millions of Chinese readers. People carefully studied the book of sayings in search of guidance and certainty in a time of change. Groups of students known as the Red Guards staged mass demonstrations in which they waved their copies of the "Little Red Book" in the air. The Red Guards were Mao's "shock troops." They often charged through towns and cities attacking or humiliating people they accused of being enemies of communism. In 1968, when the turmoil finally became too great, Mao called a halt to the "cultural revolution."

The passages that follow are from Mao's "Little Red Book." It is a collection of passages from Mao's writings and speeches over the years.

If there is to be revolution, there must be a revolutionary party. Without a revolutionary party, without a party built on the Marxist-

Leninist revolutionary theory [that is, based on the writings of Marx and Lenin] and in the Marxist-Leninist revolutionary style, it is impossible to lead the working class and the broad masses of the people in defeating imperialism . . . .

History shows that wars are divided into two kinds, just and unjust. All wars that are progressive are just, and all wars that [slow] progress are unjust. We Communists oppose all unjust wars that [slow] progress, but we do not oppose progressive, just wars. Not only do we Communists not oppose just wars, we actively participate in them. As for unjust wars, World War I is an instance in which both sides fought for imperialist interests; therefore, the Communists of the whole world firmly opposed that war. The way to oppose a war of this kind is to do everything possible to prevent it before it breaks out and, once it breaks out, to oppose war with war, to oppose unjust war with just war, whenever possible. . . .

Every Communist must grasp the truth: "Political power grows out of the barrel of a gun."

There is an ancient Chinese fable called "The Foolish Old Man Who Removed the Mountains." It tells of an old man who lived in northern China long, long ago and was known as the Foolish Old Man of North Mountain. His house faced south and beyond his doorway stood the two great peaks, Taihang and Wangwu, obstructing the way. With great determination, he led his sons in digging up these mountains hoe in hand. Another graybeard, known as the Wise Old Man, saw them and said derisively, "How silly of you to do this! It is quite impossible for you few to dig up these two huge mountains." The Foolish Old Man replied, "When I die, my sons will carry on; when they die, there will be my grandsons, and then their sons and grandsons, and so on to infinity. High as they are, the mountains cannot grow any higher and with every bit we dig, they will be that much lower. Why can't we clear them away?". . . He went on digging every day, unshaken in his conviction. God was moved by this, and he sent down two angels, who carried the mountains away on their backs.

Today, two big mountains lie like a dead weight on the Chinese people. One is imperialism, the other is feudalism. The Chinese Communist Party has long made up its mind to dig them up. We must persevere and work unceasingly, and we, too, will touch God's heart. Our God is none other than the masses of the Chinese people. If they stand up and dig together with us, why can't these two mountains be cleared away?

We must affirm anew the discipline of the [Communist] party, namely:

1. the individual is subordinate to [under the direction of] the organization;
2. the minority is subordinate to the majority;
3. the lower level is subordinate to the higher level; and
4. the entire membership is subordinate to the Central Committee.

Whoever violates these articles of discipline disrupts party unity. . . .

A man in China is usually subjected to the domination of three systems of authority [political authority, clan authority, and religious authority]. . . . As for women, in addition to being dominated by these three systems of authority, they are also dominated by the men (the authority of the husband). These four authorities—political, clan, religious, and masculine—are the four thick ropes binding the Chinese people, particularly the peasants. [T]he peasants have overthrown the political authority of the landlords in the countryside. . . . [That was] the backbone of all the other systems of authority. With that overturned, the clan authority, the religious authority, and the authority of the husband all begin to totter [collapse]. . . .

As to the authority of the husband, this has always been weaker among the poor peasants because, out of economic necessity, their womenfolk have to do more manual labor than the women of the richer classes and therefore have more say and greater power of decision in family matters. With the increasing [failure] of the rural economy in recent years, the basis for men's domination over women has already been undermined. With the rise of the peasant movement, the women in many places have now begun to organize rural women's associations; the opportunity has come for them to lift up their heads, and the authority of the husband is getting shakier every day. In a word, the [old] feudal-patriarchal system is tottering with the growth of the peasants' power.

Review Questions

1. What was Mao's goal for the cultural revolution?
2. What was Mao's purpose in circulating his "Little Red Book"?
3. How did Mao distinguish "just wars" from "unjust wars"?
4. Why do you think Mao referred to ancient Chinese sayings and stories?
5. a. How did Mao feel about the relationship of the individual to the larger group?
   b. To what extent was Mao's view of the individual similar to or different from that found in the United States and other democratic nations?
6. According to Mao, how had the Chinese revolution affected the role and status of women in China?

Nkrumah Seeks Independence for Ghana

The first African colony to gain its freedom after World War II was the British-ruled Gold Coast, which became the independent nation of Ghana in 1957. Under the leadership of Kwame Nkrumah (pronounced KWA-may en-KROO-mah), Ghana was a strong link in the nonaligned movement for many years. (Nonaligned countries supported neither the United States nor the Soviet Union in the cold war.) Nkrumah played a leading role in Ghana's drive for independence. As leader of the Convention People's Party, he campaigned for local self-rule. He spent time in British jails. When Britain permitted Ghana to elect a colonial legislature, Nkrumah and his party won wide support. In this document, taken from Nkrumah's autobiography, he describes the day in 1949 when he announced his plan for a new political party.

On Sunday, June 12, 1949, . . . before an audience of about sixty thousand people, I announced the formation of the Convention People's Party. It was without doubt the largest rally ever held in Accra [capital of the Gold Coast and later of Ghana] . . . It was a great day and my heart felt very full as I stood up to [receive] the deafening cheers of welcome from an excited crowd. . . .

I reminded the people that our land was our own and that we did not want to continue to live in slavery and under exploitation and oppression; that it was only under full self-government that we would be in a position to develop the country so that our people could enjoy the comforts and [advantages] of modern civilization. I explained to them the necessity for backing our demand for "self-government now" with a program of positive action employing legitimate agitation, newspaper and political educational campaigns, and the application of strikes, boycotts and noncooperation based on the principle of nonviolence. I advised against diplomacy and deception as I pointed out to them that the British, as past masters themselves of diplomatic [tactics], would far prefer to have from us frankness and firmness. A policy of [cooperation] and appeasement would get us nowhere in our struggle for immediate self-government. . . .

I wanted to know there and then the wishes of the people assembled there. . . .

"[M]ay I break away from any leadership which is faltering and [trembling] before imperialism and colonialism and throw in my lot with the chiefs and people of this country for full self-government NOW?"

The unanimous shouts of approval from that packed arena was all that I needed to give me my final spur. I was at that moment confident that whatever happened, I had the full support of the people. . . .

Then, on behalf of the Convention Youth Organization, in the name of the chiefs, the people, . . . the Labor Movement, our valiant ex-servicemen, the youth movement throughout the country, the man in the street, our children, and those yet unborn, the new Ghana that is to be, . . . and in the name of God Almighty and humanity, I declared to the crowd the birth of the Convention People's Party which would, from that day forward, carry on the struggle for the liberation of our dear Ghana . . . , until full self-government was won for the chiefs and people of the country.

The applause which had been tumultuous eventually died away and a deep silence followed. It was a most touching moment for each one of us there. We had decided to take our future into our own hands, and I am sure that in those few minutes everyone became suddenly conscious of the burden we had undertaken. But in the faces before me I could see no regret or doubt, only resolution.

Review Questions

1. a. Why did Kwame Nkrumah want "self-government now" for Ghana?
   b. What program did he propose to achieve this goal?
2. a. Why was Nkrumah against a policy of cooperation and appeasement with Britain?
   b. What did Nkrumah propose instead?
3. What was to be the major goal of Nkrumah's Convention People's Party?

10 The Gulag: Solzhenitsyn on Soviet Prison Camps

Drawing on his experiences in Soviet prison camps in the decade after 1945, the Russian writer Aleksandr Solzhenitsyn wrote a series of novels and exposés that earned him international literary fame—and exile from the Soviet Union.

Solzhenitsyn fell victim of the Soviet system while serving as an officer with the Red Army in 1945. Soviet authorities intercepted a letter to a friend in which Solzhenitsyn sharply criticized Joseph Stalin, the Soviet dictator. As a result, he was confined in prison camps for eight years, then sent into forced exile. In 1956, he was allowed to settle in central Russia and became a teacher of mathematics.

Solzhenitsyn began writing about his experiences and about the massive Soviet system of prison camps that stretched from Siberia in the east to the westernmost edges of Soviet territory. His novel *One Day in the Life of Ivan Denisovich* (1962) described life in the prison camps. It was published in the Soviet Union and won wide attention. In the mid-1960s, however, the Soviet government began to limit freedom of expression, and it became harder for Solzhenitsyn to get his later works published. Like many other Soviet writers, he quietly circulated self-published works, often in the form of carbon copies of typed pages. When he was awarded the Nobel Prize for Literature in 1970, Solzhenitsyn declined to travel to the awards ceremony in Sweden. He feared that he would not be allowed to return to his homeland.

This document is from Solzhenitsyn's *The Gulag Archipelago*, first published in France in 1973. ("Gulag" is the acronym by which Soviet bureaucrats referred to the system of prison camps.) Solzhenitsyn uses the metaphor of an archipelago—a group of islands surrounded by water—for the camps scattered across Soviet territory. In this excerpt, Solzhenitsyn describes the transport of prisoners in special train cars with details from his own early days in the system.

Soviet leaders reacted with fury to *The Gulag Archipelago*. In February 1974 they charged Solzhenitsyn with treason and then expelled him from the Soviet Union. For many years he lived in the United States, in Vermont. After the collapse of the Soviet Union, he was able to return to Russia in 1994.

. . . At the big stations the loading and unloading [of the prisoners] takes place far, far from the passenger platform and is seen only by switchmen and roadbed inspectors. . . .

And you, hurrying along the platform with your children, your suitcases, and your string bags, are too busy to look closely: Why is that second baggage car hitched onto the train? There is no identification on it, and it is very much like a baggage car—and the gratings have diagonal bars, and there is darkness behind them. But then why are soldiers, defenders of the Fatherland, riding in it, and why, when the train stops, do two of them march whistling along on either side and peer down under the car? . . . [T]his was a railroad car for prisoners. . . .

An ordinary passenger might have a difficult time *boarding* a train at a small way station—but not getting off. Toss your things out and jump off. This was not the case with a prisoner, however. . . .

[T]he convoy guards . . . come out with their overcoats on and knock their gunstocks on the floor. That means they are going to unload the whole car.

First the convoy forms up in a circle at the car steps, and no sooner have you dropped, fallen, tumbled down them, than the guards shout at you deafeningly in unison from all sides (as they have been taught): "Sit down, sit down, sit down!" This is very effective when several voices are shouting it at once and they don't let you raise your eyes. It's like being under shellfire, and involuntarily you squirm, hurry (and where is there for you to hurry to?), crouch close to the ground, and sit down, having caught up with those who disembarked earlier.

"Sit down!" is a very clear command, but if you are a new prisoner, you don't yet understand it. When I heard this command on the switching tracks in Ivanovo, I ran, clutching my suitcase in my arms (if a suitcase has been manufactured out in freedom and not in camp, its handle always breaks off and always at a difficult moment), and set it down on end on the ground and without looking around to see how the first prisoners were sitting, sat down on the suitcase. After all, to sit down right on the ties, on the dark oily sand, in my officer's coat, which was not yet so very dirty and which still had uncut flaps! The chief of the convoy—a ruddy mug, a good Russian face—broke into a run, and I hadn't managed to grasp what he wanted and why until I saw that he meant, clearly, to plant his sacred boot in my cursed back but something restrained him. However, he didn't spare his polished toe and kicked the suitcase and smashed in the top. "Sit down!" he gritted by way of explanation. Only at that point did it dawn on me that I towered over the surrounding [prisoners], and without even having the chance to ask: "How am I supposed to sit down?" I already understood how, and sat down in my precious coat, like everybody else, just as dogs sit at gates and cats at doors. . . .

And forcing prisoners to sit down was also a [planned] maneuver. If you are sitting on your rear end on the ground, so that your knees tower in front of you, then your center of gravity is well back of your legs, and it is difficult to get up and impossible to jump up. And more than that, they would make us sit as tightly massed together as possible so that we'd be in each other's way. And if all of us wanted to attack the convoy together, they would have mowed us down before we got moving.

They had us sitting there to wait for the Black Maria (it transports the prisoners in batches, you couldn't get them all in at once), or else to be herded off on foot. They would try to sit us down someplace hidden so that fewer free people would see us, but at times they did make the prisoners sit right there awkwardly on the platform or in an open square. . . . And it is a difficult experience for the free people: we stare at them quite freely and openly with a totally sincere gaze, but how are they supposed to look at us? With hatred? Their consciences don't permit it. . . . With sympathy? With pity? Be careful, someone will take down your name and they'll set you up for a prison term too; it's that simple. And our proud free citizens . . . drop their guilty heads and try not to see us at all, as if the place were empty. The old women are bolder than the rest. They believe in God. And they would break off a piece of bread from their meager loaf and throw it to us. . . . [A]nd the convoy guards would immediately work the bolts of their rifles—pointing them at the old woman, at kindness, at the bread: "Come on, old woman, run along."

And the holy bread, broken in two, was left to lie in the dust while we were driven off.

Review Questions

1. What was the Soviet Gulag?
2. Why was Solzhenitsyn a prisoner in the Gulag?
3. Why were Soviet state prisoners kept far from the passenger platforms of the larger railroad stations?
4. a. How did ordinary citizens react when they saw the prisoners? Why do you think so?
   b. Why did Solzhenitsyn say the old women were "bolder than the rest"?

The Cuban Missile Crisis: A Warning From Khrushchev

The Cuban missile crisis of October 1962 was one of the most frightening times in the cold war. A U.S. spy plane flying high above Cuba photographed Soviet nuclear missile bases under construction there. The bases meant that the Soviet Union was seeking to shorten the time it would take for its nuclear warheads to reach U.S. targets. Cuba is only 90 miles off the coast of Florida, and midrange missiles based there could strike a large part of the United States. In a dramatic television address on October 22, President John F. Kennedy demanded that the Soviet Union remove the missiles. He imposed a naval blockade (he called it a "quarantine") aimed at preventing Soviet ships from carrying any more missiles to Cuba.

This document is a letter to President Kennedy by Soviet Premier Nikita Khrushchev. Its uncompromising tone stirred fears of a showdown, perhaps involving an exchange of nuclear strikes. However, both sides eased their positions. Khrushchev ordered Soviet ships to stop and wait. Kennedy promised that U.S. forces would not invade Cuba if the missiles were removed. Kennedy also said that he would remove U.S. nuclear missiles based in Turkey not far from Soviet borders. On October 28, Khrushchev announced that he would stop building bases in Cuba and withdraw the missiles.

His Excellency
Mr. John F. Kennedy
President of the United States of America
Washington

Dear Mr. President,

. . . Imagine, Mr. President, what if we were to present to you such an ultimatum [demand] as you have presented to us by your actions. How would you react to it? I think you would be outraged at such a move on our part. And this we would understand.

Having presented these conditions to us, Mr. President, you have [challenged us]. Who asked you to do this? By what right have you done this? Our ties with the Republic of Cuba, as well as our relations with other nations, regardless of their political system, concern only the two countries between which these relations exist. And, if it were a matter of quarantine [isolating people, goods, or places infected with some danger to prevent the infection from spreading] as mentioned in your letter, then, as is customary in international practice, it can be established only by states agreeing between themselves, and not by some third party. Quarantines exist, for example, on agricultural goods and products. However, in this case we are not talking about quarantines, but rather about much more serious matters, and you yourself understand this.

You, Mr. President, are not declaring a quarantine, but rather issuing an ultimatum, and you are threatening that if we do not obey your orders, you will then use force. Think about what you are saying! And you want to persuade me to agree to this! What does it mean to agree to these demands? It would mean for us to conduct our relations with other countries not by reason, but by yielding to tyranny. You are not appealing to reason; you want to intimidate us.

No, Mr. President, I cannot agree to this, and I think that deep inside, you will admit that I am right. I am convinced that if you were in my place you would do the same. . . .

Th[e] Organization [of American States] has no authority or grounds whatsoever to pass resolutions like those of which you speak in your letter. Therefore, we do not accept these resolutions. International law exists, generally accepted standards of conduct exist. We firmly adhere to the principles of international law and strictly observe the standards regulating navigation on the open sea, in international waters. We observe these standards and enjoy the rights recognized by all nations.

You want to force us to renounce the rights enjoyed by every sovereign state; you are attempting to [make laws concerning] questions of international law; you are violating the generally accepted standards of this law. All this is due not only to hatred for the Cuban people and their government, but also for reasons having to do with the election campaign in the USA. What morals, what laws can justify such an approach by the American government to international affairs? Such morals and laws are not to be found, because the actions of the USA in relation to Cuba are outright piracy. This, if you will, is the madness of a [shrinking] imperialism. Unfortunately, people of all nations, and not least the American people themselves, could suffer heavily from madness such as this, since with the appearance of modern types of weapons, the USA has completely lost its former inaccessibility [unreachable global position].

Therefore, Mr. President, if you weigh the present situation with a cool head without giving way to passion, you will understand that the Soviet Union cannot afford not to decline the [tyrannical] demands of the USA. When you lay conditions such as these before us, try to put yourself in our situation and consider how the USA would react to such conditions. I have no doubt that if anyone attempted to dictate similar conditions to you—the USA, you would reject such an attempt. And we likewise say—no.

The Soviet government considers the violation of the freedom of navigation in international waters and air space to constitute an act of aggression propelling humankind into the abyss of a world nuclear-missile war. Therefore, the Soviet government cannot instruct captains of Soviet ships bound for Cuba to observe orders of American naval forces blockading this island. Our instructions to Soviet sailors are to observe strictly the generally accepted standards of navigation in international waters and not retreat one step from them. And, if the American side violates these rights, it must be aware of the responsibility it will bear for this act. To be sure, we will not remain mere observers of pirate actions by American ships in the open sea. We will then be forced on our part to take those measures we deem necessary and sufficient to defend our rights. To this end we have all that is necessary.

Respectfully, /s/ N. Khrushchev
N. Khrushchev
Moscow
24 October 1962

Review Questions

1. Why did President John F. Kennedy order a naval blockade ("quarantine") of Cuba?

2. What did Soviet Premier Nikita Khrushchev mean when he said that President Kennedy was "not declaring a quarantine, but rather issuing an ultimatum"?
3. Why did Khrushchev refuse to cooperate with the United States?
4. What did Khrushchev mean when he stated, "with the appearance of modern types of weapons, the USA has completely lost its former inaccessibility"?
5. How did the Cuban missile crisis end?

Standing Up for Freedom in Tiananmen Square

The Communist government of China has traditionally been authoritarian. It has used propaganda to justify its policies and prison labor camps to enforce them. In spite of these measures, Chinese leaders have not always been able to control the people.

In the late 1980s, a worldwide movement for greater political freedom took place. Eastern European countries began to free themselves from Communist dominance. Chinese leaders, seeing that this movement was gaining followers in China, banned political demonstrations. They stopped the reforms that had allowed for somewhat freer economic activity.

By 1988, the Chinese people began to react against the new political restrictions and economic regulations. University students began to make demands for greater freedom.

On May 17, 1989, a peaceful demonstration took place in Tiananmen Square in Beijing. Other citizens flocked to support the students until more than a million people had gathered in the square.

Threatened by the large numbers of protesters, Chinese leaders declared martial law. When soldiers and tanks arrived to clear the square, the unarmed protesters stood their ground. The photograph on page 344 demonstrates their courage. Here, a single man stands blocking a file of tanks.

For two weeks, the army hesitated to attack the defenseless people. Early on June 4, however the tanks entered the square. The soldiers killed hundreds of the protesters. After the attack on the square, police tracked down and arrested many of those who had escaped. They were put on trial and sent to prison. In spite of the disapproval of democratic countries, the Chinese government made its policies even more repressive.

Man confronting tanks in Tiananmen Square, May 1989 © Stuart Franklin, Magnum Photos, Inc.

Review Questions

1. How did the collapse of communism in Eastern Europe influence the leaders of Communist China?
2. How did the Chinese people react to the imposition of new political restrictions?
3. How does the photograph illustrate the bravery of the protesters?
4. What was the result of the demonstration in Tiananmen Square?

Václav Havel on Responsibility and Democracy

With startling rapidity, Communist control over the countries of Eastern Europe crumbled away during 1989 and 1990. One of the countries that reestablished democratic government in that period was Czechoslovakia, which had been under Communist rule since 1948.

In 1968, Czech leaders had tried to establish a more democratic form of government, but Soviet troops led an invasion to block the changes. Soviet leaders and their Eastern European allies succeeded in restoring hard-line Czechoslovak Communists to power.

At the time of the 1968 events, Václav Havel (VAHT-slahff HAH-vul) was a playwright who took an active part in reform efforts. After 1968, his plays ridiculing Communist Party officials and exploring moral issues drew unfavorable attention from the authorities, and his works were banned. Havel became a prominent spokesperson for human rights, which drew even more government attention. He spent four years in prison for his activities. In 1989, as democratic reforms began in other nations of Eastern Europe, Czechoslovaks took to the streets in mass demonstrations. Havel was among the protest leaders. Bowing to popular pressure, in December 1989, the Communist government agreed to form a coalition government with the opposition. By this "peaceful revolution," democracy returned to Czechoslovakia.

Havel was chosen as acting president until binding elections could be held later. On January 1, 1990, three days after taking office, he addressed the nation (or, as he says, "nations"—the Czech and Slovak peoples). These excerpts are from his address.

For forty years on this day you heard, from my predecessors, variations on the same theme: how our country flourished, how many million tons of steel we produced, how happy we all were, how we trusted our government, and what bright [prospects] were unfolding before us.

I assume you did not propose me for this office so that I, too, would lie to you.

Our country is not flourishing. The enormous creative and spiritual potential of our nations is not being used sensibly. Entire branches of industry are producing goods that are of no interest to anyone, while we are lacking the things we need. A state that calls itself a workers' state humiliates and exploits workers. Our [out-of-date] economy [wastes] what little energy we have available. A country once proud of its educational standards now spends so little on education that it ranks seventy-second in the world. We have contaminated [poisoned] the soil, rivers, and forests [left] to us by our ancestors, and today we have the most polluted environment in Europe. Adults in our country die earlier than [do adults] in most other European countries. . . .

But all this is still not the main problem. The worst thing is that we live in a contaminated moral environment. We fell morally ill because we got used to saying something different from what we thought. We learned not to believe in anything, to ignore each other, to care only for ourselves. Concepts such as love, friendship, compassion, humility, and forgiveness lost their depth and dimensions, and for many of us they came to represent only psychological peculiarities, or to resemble long-lost greetings from ancient times, a little ridiculous in the era of computers and spaceships. Only a few of us were able to cry aloud that the powers that be ought not to be all-powerful. . . . The previous regime—armed with its arrogant and intolerant ideology—reduced man to a force of production and nature to a tool of production. . . . It reduced gifted and [independent] people to nuts and bolts of some monstrously huge, noisy, and stinking machine, whose real meaning is not clear to anyone. It could do no more than slowly but [relentlessly] wear itself out, along with its nuts and bolts.

When I talk about contaminated moral atmosphere, I am not talking just about the gentlemen [who once ruled]. I am talking about all of us. We had all become used to the totalitarian system and accepted it as an unalterable fact of life, and thus we helped to [keep] it [going]. In other words, we are all—though naturally to differing extents—responsible for the operation of totalitarian machinery. None of us is just its victim: we are all also its co-creators.

Why do I say this? It would be quite unreasonable to understand the sad [inheritance] of the last forty years as something alien, something [left] to us by some distant relative. On the contrary, we must accept this legacy as a sin we committed against ourselves. If we accept it as such, we will understand that it is up to us all, and up to us alone, to do something about it. We cannot blame the previous rulers for everything, not only because it would be untrue but also because it could blunt the duty each of us faces today, that is, the obligation to act independently, freely, reasonably, and quickly. Let us make no mistake: the best government in the world, the best parliament, and the best president in the world cannot achieve much on their own. And it would also be wrong to expect a general remedy to come from them alone. Freedom and democracy require participation and therefore responsible action from us all.

If we realize this, then all the horrors the new Czechoslovak democracy has inherited will cease to appear so terrible. If we realize this, hope will return to our hearts. . . .

On January 1, 1993, Czechoslovakia peacefully divided into two countries—the Czech Republic and the Slovak Republic. Havel had opposed the split. He was later elected president of the Czech Republic.

Review Questions

1. Why did Václav Havel use the plural "nations" in his New Year's address?
2. Why did Havel feel that Czechoslovak citizens had become "morally ill"?
3. What challenge did Havel make to the people of Czechoslovakia?
4. How did Czechoslovakia change on January 1, 1993?

Argentina's "Dirty War": Mothers of the Plaza de Mayo

Argentina was one of many Latin American countries that shifted from elected government to military rule in the second half of the 20th century. In 1976, in the midst of economic crisis and political turmoil, Argentine military officers overthrew the elected president. Argentina became a brutal military dictatorship. Government-backed "death squads" abducted, tortured, and murdered Argentines and foreigners who were suspected of supporting leftist revolutionary groups. An estimated 13,000 to 15,000 people were killed in this "dirty war." Many of those abducted were later found dead. But many more just disappeared for good.

As the number of the "disappeared" mounted, mothers and other relatives of the missing took to the streets to demand an accounting. These protesters risked arrest and torture themselves, but they persisted. Every Thursday afternoon, women gathered at the Plaza de Mayo in downtown Buenos Aires for silent marches and other forms of protest. Called *madres de la Plaza de Mayo* ("Mothers of the Plaza de Mayo"), these women helped to draw international attention to the dirty war. In time, the United States, Britain, and other foreign governments began to put pressure on Argentine military leaders to respect human rights and end the dirty war. But it was Argentina's defeat by Britain in the Falkland Islands War of 1982 (after Argentina invaded the British-ruled islands off the coast of South America) that finally brought an end to military rule and the dirty war. Humiliated by the defeat, the military allowed elections and a return to democracy.

In this excerpt, two of the "mothers of the disappeared" talk of their experiences.

Dora de Bazze: . . . My son was in his fifth year of medical school when he was kidnapped, married with a young child. . . . We were driving in the car when, three streets from my house, we stopped at some traffic lights and three or four cars surrounded us. One went up on the pavement at the side of us. Hugo only had time to say "Mamá . . . ," and stopped. There was a man pointing a machine gun at his head through the car window and on my side another one with a machine gun pointed at me. They pulled out my son and I shouted like a madwoman and they dragged me out and threw me on the ground, stamping on my glasses and one of them holding me down with his boot, an army boot, and a machine gun at my face. From the ground I saw them tie my son's hands and put a hood over his head.

It was one in the afternoon, in the middle of a street at the side of the hospital in Palermo where there was always a lot of people. It all happened very quickly. They put Hugo in the back seat of a car and one of them got into my son's car and drove it away with three or four others following behind. One, a Ford Falcon, went on ahead down the wrong side of the street with its sirens going.

I stood there in the street shouting and a young woman came running up to me. Apparently she was a doctor. She had a badge with her name on which said Dr. somebody, but at the time it didn't occur to me to remember it. She said, "Don't run after them because they'll kill you too." I just stood there, three streets from my house, but so shocked and confused I felt like I was in another world. . . .

Aida de Suárez: They started to call us *las locas* [the madwomen]. When the foreign embassies began to ask questions about the disappearances, because they didn't only take Argentines they took all nationalities, and the foreign journalists began to ask about us, they [Argentine officials] used to say, "Don't take any notice of those old women, they're all mad." Of course they called us mad. How could the armed forces admit they were worried by a group of middle-aged women? And anyway we were mad. When everyone was terrorized, we didn't stay at home crying—we went to the streets to confront them directly. We were mad, but it was the only way to stay sane.

Dora de Bazze: I was detained many times, like a lot of the Mothers. Once they came and took eighty or a hundred women, herding us into a bus like sheep, pushing us and hitting us with their [clubs]. In the police station we had to go in one at a time to speak to the chief. "What were you doing in the square?" "I'm looking for my son." "Sign here to say you won't go to the square on

Thursdays again." "I'm not signing anything because I'm going to the square next Thursday. Put yourself in my place. If you lost a child, wouldn't you do the same?" "You have to sign it anyway." The next Thursday they took us again. It was like that. A psychological war. We were never afraid. On the contrary, we used to shout at them, "Aren't you ashamed? Take off your uniforms, you lousy vermin! Don't you realize the people don't want you. . . .?"

I remember the first day we carried a banner. Nobody took banners to the square because it was very dangerous. One day I made a big one out of some material I had in the house and I painted on "*Dónde están los detenidos-desaparecidos*? [Where are the detained-disappeared people?]—*Madres de Plaza de Mayo*" and we put two broomsticks in the sides to hold it up. My daughter was terrified that day in case they took me. I rolled it up, wrapped it in brown paper as if it was something I'd just bought and took it on the [subway]. I had to be very careful because they watched all those places. I wasn't afraid at all. When I got to Plaza de Mayo I told the Mothers I had a banner to unroll. Everyone was happy—"Let's open it!" There were a lot of *milicos* [military agents] that day so I hid behind some other Mothers and opened it. There was a tourist bus passing and they were all looking, pointing their fingers at us. The milicos came and kicked us. . . . [A]nd we kicked them back. A journalist took a photo which came out in Holland, but it wasn't printed here. It was a tremendous thing. Thirty or forty Mothers shouting "*Dónde están nuestros hijos?*" [Where are our sons?] and the milicos all lined up in front of us with [clubs] and machine guns and behind them the tear gas trucks.

A national fact-finding commission learned in the 1980s that over 340 detention centers, located all over Argentina, had held the "disappeared." There, the abducted were subject to brutal treatment and painful death. All along, however, the military denied that the centers existed and that the "disappeared" were still in the country.

Review Questions

1. To what does the term "dirty war" refer?
2. Who were the "disappeared"?

3. How did the mothers whose children had disappeared respond to their loss?
4. Why did the Argentinean officials say that the mothers were [mad] "old women"?
5. How did the women's actions gain international attention?
6. How did the war between Argentina and Great Britain over the Falkland Islands end the "dirty war"?

Unit VII Document-Based Question

*Write a well-organized essay that includes an introduction, several paragraphs, and a conclusion. Use evidence from at least **four** documents from the unit in the body of the essay. Support your response with relevant facts, examples, and detail. Include additional outside information.*

Historical Context

World War II brought major shifts in global power, which changed international relationships and contributed to the emergence of newly independent nations and an increased concern for human rights. As the world continues to make advances in communications, science, and technology, people throughout the world are realizing that they truly live in a "global village."

Task: Using the documents and questions in the unit, along with your knowledge of global history, write an essay in which you:

- Describe **two** changes that took place during the years following World War II
- Show how **each** of the two changes illustrated the extent to which conditions had changed since before World War II
- Show how **one** of the changes you selected indicates that the nations of the world were becoming increasingly interdependent

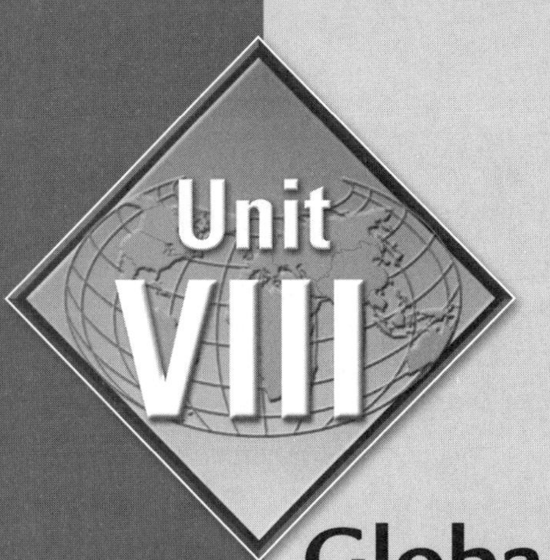

Global Connections and Interactions

A Choice Between Death and Death: A Haitian View of Globalization

Globalization is the process by which all the nations of the world are being drawn into a single, worldwide economic system. Since World War II, world leaders have cooperated in promoting freer trade among nations. For example, more than 140 nations have joined the World Trade Organization in support of its goal of cutting tariffs and other barriers to free trade. As a result, some workers and producers have faced increasingly stiff competition in a global marketplace.

Supporters of globalization say that it lowers prices for consumers, promotes economic efficiency, and raises standards of living. But not everyone benefits equally. Those who are hardest hit are often the poorest people, whether in rich countries or in poor countries.

Haiti is the poorest country in the Americas. During the 18th century, when Haiti was a colony of France, its sugar plantations sent a rich stream of profits back to France. During the 1790s, the African slaves who worked those plantations rose up in revolt. They eventually ousted the French, creating an independent republic in 1804. Troubled by decades of political unrest and misrule, Haiti has only recently emerged from dictatorship. In its first democratic election in 1990, voters elected as president a leftist former Roman Catholic priest, Jean-Bertrand Aristide. Ousted by a military coup seven months later, Aristide went into exile. A U.S.-led military intervention restored him to power in 1994 and he served out the rest of his term, turning over leadership to another elected president in 1995. Five years later, Aristide won a second term.

In the following document, from a book Aristide wrote before his second victorious campaign, the Haitian leader tells of his misgivings about globalization.

A morgue worker is preparing to dispose of a dozen corpses. One living soul lifts himself off of the table, shakes his head and declares, "I am not dead!" To which the morgue worker answers, "Yes you are. The doctors say that you are dead, so lie down."

In today's global marketplace, trillions of dollars are traded each day via a vast network of computers. In this market no one talks, no one touches. Only numbers count.

And yet today this faceless economy is already five times larger than the real, or productive, economy.

We know other marketplaces. On a plain high in the mountains of Haiti, one day a week thousands of people still gather. This is the marketplace of my childhood in the mountains above Port Salut. The sights and the smells and the noise and the color overwhelm you. Everyone comes. If you don't come you will miss everything. . . . [People] share trade, and laughter, gossip, politics, and medical and child-rearing tips. A market exchange, and a human exchange.

We are not against trade, we are not against free trade, but our fear is that the global market intends to [destroy] our [Haitian] markets. We will be pushed to the cities, to eat food grown on factory farms in distant countries, food whose price depends on the daily numbers game of the first market. "This is more efficient," the economists say. "Your market, your way of life, is not efficient," they say. But we ask, "What is left when you reduce trade to numbers, when you erase all that is human?". . .

Globalization, the integration of world markets, has promised to "lift all boats," rich and poor, to bring a global culture of entertainment and consumer goods to everyone—the promise of material happiness. And indeed, since 1980 most third world countries [developing nations] have embraced [accepted] globalization. They have opened their economies to the world, lowered tariffs, embraced free trade, and allowed goods and services from the industrialized world to flow in. It seems the world is brought closer together. In fact the gap . . . has never been larger.

What happens to poor countries when they embrace free trade? In Haiti in 1986 we imported just 7,000 tons of rice, the main staple food of the country. The vast majority was grown in Haiti. In the late 1980s Haiti [accepted] . . . free-trade policies [backed] by the international lending agencies and lifted tariffs on rice imports. Cheaper rice immediately flooded in from the United States where the rice industry is subsidized [government supported]. . . . Haiti's farmers could not possibly compete. By 1996 Haiti was importing 196,000 tons of foreign rice at the cost of $100 million a year. Haitian rice production [almost stopped]. Once the dependence on foreign rice was complete, import prices began to rise, leaving Haiti's population, particularly the urban poor, completely at the whim of rising world grain prices. And the prices continue to rise.

What lessons do we learn? For poor countries free trade is not so free, or so fair. Haiti, under intense pressure from international lending institutions, stopped protecting its domestic agriculture while subsidies to [another country's] rice industry increased. A hungry nation became hungrier. . . .

The choices that globalization offers the poor remind me of a story. Anatole, one of the boys who had lived with us at *Lafanmi Selavi*,[1] was working at the national port. One day a very powerful businessman offered him money to [damage] the main unloading forklift at the port. Anatole said to the man, "Well, then, I am already dead." The man, surprised by the response, asked, "Why?" Anatole answered, "because if I sneak in here at night and do what you ask they will shoot me, and if I don't, you will kill me." The dilemma [problem] is, I believe, the classic dilemma of the poor; a choice between death and death. Either we enter a global economic system, in which we know we cannot survive, or, we refuse, and face death by slow starvation. With choices like these, the urgency of finding a third way is clear. We must find some room to maneuver, some open space simply to survive. We must lift ourselves up off the morgue table and tell the experts we are not yet dead.

Review Questions

1. a. What is "globalization"?
   b. How does free trade sometimes cause problems for workers and producers?
2. How does Jean-Bertrand Aristide describe the impact of globalization and the global market on Haiti?
3. a. How have most third world countries responded to globalization?
   b. Why does Aristide believe these third world nations have followed the trend toward globalization?
4. How does Aristide use the example of the Haitian rice industry to show the bad effects of globalization?
5. a. Why does Aristide believe globalization offers Haiti "a choice between death and death"?
   b. How does Aristide believe Haiti should deal with the dilemma that globalization presents?

[1] ***Lafanmi Selavi***—a center for street children, founded in 1986 by Aristide

The Era of Globalization

In his book *The Lexus and the Olive Tree* (1999), *New York Times* columnist Thomas L. Friedman explores the nature and consequences of globalization. His title draws attention to a contrast he thinks is important. On the one hand, there is modern, globalized industry. It uses robots and high technology to produce cars like the Lexus, and sells them all over the world while largely ignoring national borders. On the other hand, there is the traditional world of communities and nations, of borders and local traditions, of nationalism and age-old feuds. For Friedman, this world is symbolized by the olive tree, firmly rooted in one place. The tensions between these two worlds are the subject of Friedman's book, from which the following document is taken.

Today's era of globalization, which replaced the Cold War, is a similar international system, with its own unique attributes.

To begin with, the globalization system, unlike the Cold War system, is not static, but a dynamic ongoing process: globalization involves the inexorable [unstoppable] integration of markets, nation-states and technologies to a degree never witnessed before—in a way that is enabling individuals, corporations and nation-states to reach around the world farther, faster, deeper and cheaper than ever before, and in a way that is also producing a powerful backlash from those brutalized or left behind by this new system.

The driving idea behind globalization is free-market capitalism—the more you let market forces rule and the more you open your economy to free trade and competition, the more efficient and flourishing your economy will be. Globalization means the spread of free-market capitalism to virtually every country in the world. Globalization also has its own set of economic rules—rules that revolve around opening, deregulating and privatizing [selling state-owned businesses to private enterprises] your economy.

Unlike the Cold War system, globalization has its own dominant culture, which is why it tends to be homogenizing [makes everything similar]. In previous eras, this sort of cultural homogenization happened on a regional scale—the Hellenization of the Near East and the Mediterranean world under the Greeks, the Turkification of Central Asia, North Africa, Europe and the Middle East by the Ottomans, or the Russification of Eastern Europe and parts of Eurasia under the Soviets. Culturally speaking, globalization is largely, though not entirely, the spread of Americanization—from Big Macs to iMacs to Mickey Mouse—on a global scale.

Globalization has its own defining technologies: computerization, miniaturization, digitization, satellite communications, fiber optics and the Internet. And these technologies helped to create the defining perspective of globalization. If the defining perspective of the Cold War was division, the defining perspective of globalization is "integration." The symbol of the Cold War was a wall [the Berlin wall], which divided everyone. The symbol of the globalization system is the World Wide Web, which unites everyone. The defining document of the Cold War system was "The Treaty." The defining document of the globalization system is "The Deal."

Review Questions

1. Explain the symbolism of the Lexus and the olive tree in the title of Thomas Friedman's book.
2. How does Friedman compare the era of globalization with the Cold War era?
3. Why does Friedman say that globalization is largely the spread of Americanization?
4. How has technology aided in the development of globalization?

3 What Is the World Trade Organization?

Created in 1995, the World Trade Organization (WTO) works to facilitate trade among nations. It is the successor to the General Agreement on Tariffs and Trade, which was formed at the end of World War II to encourage international trade. The WTO's supporters favor increasing trade as a way to boost the economies of both exporting and importing countries. And, indeed, trade has increased rapidly under the WTO, as it did under its predecessor GATT. Critics, however, argue that the rules of GATT and the WTO have tended to favor large multinational corporations over smaller businesses and to promote globalization at the expense of workers and the environment.

The following document is the World Trade Organization's explanation of its purposes and structure.

[T]he World Trade Organization (WTO) is the only international organization dealing with the global rules of trade between nations. Its main function is to ensure that trade flows as smoothly, predictably and freely as possible. . . .

At the heart of the system—known as the multilateral trading system [involving more that one nation or party]—are the WTO's agreements, negotiated and signed by a large majority of the world's trading nations, and ratified in their parliaments. These agreements are the legal ground-rules for international commerce. Essentially, they are contracts, guaranteeing member countries important trade rights. They also bind governments to keep their trade policies within agreed limits to everybody's benefit. . . .

Organization

The WTO's overriding objective is to help trade flow smoothly, freely, fairly and predictably.

It does this by:

- administering trade agreements
- acting as a forum for trade negotiations
- settling trade disputes
- reviewing national trade policies
- assisting developing countries in trade policy issues, through technical assistance and training programs
- cooperating with other international organizations.

Structure. The WTO has more than 130 members, accounting for over 90 percent of world trade. Over 30 others are negotiating membership.

Decisions are made by the entire membership. This is typically by consensus [general agreement]. A majority vote is also possible but it has never been used in the WTO, and was extremely rare under the WTO's predecessor, GATT. The WTO's agreements have been ratified in all members' parliaments. . . .

Secretariat. The WTO Secretariat, based in Geneva, has around 500 staff and is headed by a director-general. It does not have branch offices outside Geneva. Since decisions are taken by the members themselves, the Secretariat does not have the decision-making role that other international bureaucracies [have].

The WTO Agreements

The WTO's rules—the agreements—are the result of negotiations between the members. The current set were the outcome of the 1986–1994 Uruguay Round of negotiations which included a major [rewriting] of the original General Agreement on Tariffs and Trade (GATT).

GATT is now the WTO's principal rule-book for trade in goods. The Uruguay Round also created new rules for dealing with trade in services, relevant aspects of intellectual property, dispute settlement, and trade policy reviews. The complete set runs to some 30,000 pages consisting of about 60 agreements . . . made by individual members in specific areas such as lower customs duty rates and services market-opening.

Through these agreements, WTO members operate a nondiscriminatory trading system that spells out their rights and their obligations. Each country receives guarantees that its exports will be treated fairly and consistently in other countries' markets. Each promises to do the same for imports into its own market. The system also gives developing countries some flexibility in implementing their commitments.

[Three omitted sections describe how the WTO deals with trade in goods, services, and intellectual properties.]

Dispute Settlement. . . . Countries bring disputes to the WTO if they think their rights under the agreements are being infringed [intruded on]. Judgments by specially appointed independent experts are based on interpretations of the agreements and individual countries' commitments.

The system encourages countries to settle their differences through consultation [discussion]. Failing that, they can follow a carefully mapped out, stage-by-stage procedure that includes the possibility of a ruling by a panel of experts, and the chance to appeal the ruling on legal grounds. . . .

Review Questions

1. What is the World Trade Organization (WTO), and what is its main objective?
2. Outline some of the ways the WTO promotes trade between nations.
3. What are the rights and obligations of member nations, according to the WTO agreements?
4. How does the WTO resolve trade disputes among member nations?

China Opens Its Doors to World Trade

Western democracies have used economic sanctions (prohibited the sale or purchase of goods from another nation) to force those nations to recognize their citizens' human rights. In the 1980s and 1990s, sanctions aided black South Africans in their struggle against apartheid. In protest against the white South African government, several nations passed laws prohibiting their nations' businesses from trading with South African businesses. The resulting damage to South Africa's economy helped persuade the government to abandon apartheid.

After the 1989 massacre in Tiananmen Square, many people felt that the United States should impose sanctions on China. Since the 1970s, the U.S. had accepted Chinese goods at the lowest available tariff. This advantage is called *most favored nation* (MFN) status. It must be renewed every year.

When Bill Clinton became U.S. president in 1993, he signed an order requiring China to improve its human rights policy before he awarded it MFN status. Many opposed this order. They pointed out that restricting trade with China would cause American businesses to lose jobs and contracts. They claimed that doing business with Western democracies would eventually loosen the Chinese government's grip on its economy and people. Then too, such foreign products as satellite dishes and newspapers would help the Chinese people get information about the benefits of democracy.

Clinton listened to these advisers. In 1994, he awarded MFN status to China. In the early 21st century, China received the status of regular trading partner, in spite of limited improvements in its human rights policy.

The cartoon by Tony Auth on page 364 illustrates the argument that China's trade with the United States is a weapon against the Communist government. It draws a parallel between free trade and an incident in Western history early in the classical era. Warring Greeks, pretending to give up their siege of the city of Troy, left a large wooden horse at the city's gates, supposedly as a peace offering. Greek soldiers were hiding in the horse, however. The Trojans dragged the horse inside their gates. When they left, the Greeks emerged, opened Troy's gates, and let in the rest of their army. The Greeks caught the Trojans by surprise and defeated them. The cartoon's point is that the various businesses represented by the "horse" would bring changes to the Chinese economy. Once the Chinese people experienced economic freedom, they would demand more political rights. The repressive Communist government would either grant these rights or collapse.

AUTH ©2000 *The Philadelphia Inquirer.* Reprinted with permission of UNIVERSAL PRESS SYNDICATE.

Review Questions

1. What are economic sanctions?
2. Why did some Americans favor economic sanctions against China in the 1990s?
3. Briefly retell the story of the Trojan horse.
4. How might trade with the United States and the rest of the free world act as a "Trojan horse" against China?

The Environment: The Greenhouse Effect and Global Warming

In the last decades of the 20th century, scientists began sounding warnings about *global warming*—a slow upward creep in average world temperatures. According to their theory, this warming is mainly due to human activities, especially the use of carbon-based fuels like wood, coal, and gasoline.

Here is how global warming is assumed to work: As industries, households, and cars and trucks burn fuel, a variety of gases are released into the atmosphere. Those gases include carbon dioxide, nitrous oxide, and others. The gases create a *greenhouse effect*. They act much like the glass in a greenhouse. The glass allows heat from the sun to pass into the greenhouse in the daytime while limiting heat loss at night. And it is not just the burning of fuel that creates greenhouse gases. Also implicated are water vapor and gases known as halocarbons, used in air conditioners, refrigerators, aerosol cans, and aluminum production.

While the anticipated effects of global warming are large, some countries—for example, in northern Europe—might welcome milder winters and warmer summers. But low-lying countries like Bangladesh in South Asia and island nations in the Pacific might see large areas flooded by rising sea levels. And, in other countries, regions that now receive only limited rainfall might get even less rainfall in the future, and deserts may expand into what have been agricultural areas.

Concerns such as these led the United Nations to examine ways of fighting global warming. It called an international meeting of nations, called the Conference on Environment and Development, in 1992. Nicknamed the Earth Summit, the conference was held in Rio in 1992. The attending nations reached an agreement that they called the United Nations Framework Convention on Climate Change. The agreement was ratified (officially approved) by more than 180 nations, including the United States.

The purpose of the convention is to get the world's nations to cooperate in reducing the amounts of greenhouse gases in the earth's atmosphere. The focus is on six key anthropogenic, or human-caused, gases. By far the most important of these is carbon dioxide, or CO_2.

The framework convention assumes that there are two ways to reduce greenhouse gases. One is to limit the production of gases by factories, homes, and vehicles. The other is to create conditions that help to remove gases already in the air. For example, growing trees absorb greenhouse gases as they grow. Therefore, the convention aims to promote the well-being of existing forests and the planting of new forests where possible. Places where greenhouse gases are absorbed are called sinks.

Another key idea underlying the convention is that the rules for industrial nations should be tougher than rules for developing nations, since the industrial nations produce the most greenhouse gases today. The developing nations of Asia, Africa, and Latin America have fewer industries and fewer vehicles and therefore contribute less to the problem. Yet, because of their locations and their poverty, they can expect to face the most damaging consequences of global warming.

Every year or so, the nations (called "parties") that have signed the convention send delegates to a Conference of the Parties to work out further rules for dealing with global warming.

The document below is an excerpt from the convention.

Article 2 Objective

The ultimate objective of this Convention . . . is to achieve . . . stabilization of greenhouse gas concentrations in the atmosphere at a level that would prevent dangerous anthropogenic [human-caused] interference with the climate system. Such a level should be achieved within a time-frame sufficient to allow ecosystems [systems in which living organisms are dependent on each other and on their environments] to adapt naturally to climate change, to ensure that food production is not threatened and to enable economic development to proceed in a sustainable manner [one that can be kept up].

Article 3 Principles

. . . [T]he Parties shall be guided . . . by the following:

1. The Parties should protect the climate system for the benefit of present and future generations of humankind. . . .

2. The specific needs and special circumstances of developing country Parties, especially those that are particularly vulnerable [exposed] to the adverse effects of climate change, and of those Parties, especially developing country Parties, that would have to bear a disproportionate or abnormal burden under the Convention, should be given full consideration.

3. The Parties should take precautionary measures to anticipate, prevent or minimize the causes of climate change and [lessen] its adverse effects. . . .

4. The Parties have a right to, and should, promote sustainable development. . . .

5. The Parties should cooperate to promote a supportive and open international economic system that would lead to sustainable economic growth and development in all Parties, particularly developing country Parties, thus enabling them better to address the problems of climate change. . . .

Article 4 Commitments

1. All Parties . . . shall:

(a) Develop, periodically update, publish and make available to the Conference of the Parties . . . national inventories [itemized lists] of anthropogenic emissions by sources and removals by sinks of greenhouse gases. . . .

(b) [Work] . . . to . . . [limit] climate change by addressing anthropogenic emissions by sources and removals by sinks of greenhouse gases, and [develop] measures to facilitate adequate adaptation to climate change;

(c) Promote and cooperate in the development, application and . . . [spread] . . . of technologies, practices and processes that control, reduce or prevent anthropogenic emissions of greenhouse gases . . . ;

(d) Promote sustainable management, and promote and cooperate in the conservation and enhancement, as appropriate, of sinks and reservoirs of all greenhouse gases . . . , including living matter, forests and oceans as well as other terrestrial [earthly], coastal and marine ecosystems; . . .

2. The developed country Parties . . . commit themselves specifically as provided for in the following:

Each of these Parties shall adopt national policies and take corresponding measures on the [lessening] of climate change, by limiting its anthropogenic emissions of greenhouse gases and protecting and enhancing its greenhouse gas sinks and reservoirs. These policies and measures will demonstrate that developed countries are taking the lead in modifying longer-term trends . . . ;

3. The developed country Parties . . . shall provide new and additional financial resources to . . . developing country Parties . . . ;

4. The developed country Parties . . . shall also assist the developing country Parties that are particularly vulnerable to the adverse effects of climate change in meeting costs of adaptation to those adverse effects.

5. The developed country Parties . . . shall . . . promote . . . the transfer of, or access to, environmentally sound technologies and know-how to other Parties, particularly developing country Parties, to enable them to [carry out] the provisions of the Convention. . . .

7. The extent to which developing country Parties will effectively [carry out] their commitments under the Convention will depend on the effective [performance] by developed country Parties of their commitments under the Convention related to financial resources and transfer of technology and will take fully into account that economic and social development and poverty eradication are the first and overriding priorities of the developing country Parties.

The framework convention of 1992 alarmed many people. They feared it would impose costly new burdens on businesses and individuals, especially in developed nations. The fact that the convention gave special treatment to developing nations also caused concern in developed nations.

Controversy grew as a 1997 Conference of the Parties approached in Kyoto. There, the delegates planned to write an amendment, or protocol, to the 1992 convention. The purpose of the protocol was to describe specific steps for nations to take to reduce global warming.

The Kyoto Conference decided that the burden of reducing emissions of greenhouse gases should be placed almost entirely on the industrial nations at first. Developing nations were asked to adopt voluntary targets for reducing their own emissions, while the targets for 38 industrial nations were declared to be binding.

Under the terms of the December 1997 Kyoto Protocol, the industrial nations were required to cut their average greenhouse-gas emissions for the period 2008–2112 to 5.2 percent below the level of 1990. For the United States, the required reduction was 7 percent; for the European Union, 8 percent; and for Japan, 6 percent.

Like the framework convention of 1992, the Kyoto Protocol was a treaty that had to be ratified (formally approved) before it could take effect. By 2002, most of the world's nations had ratified the Kyoto Protocol. A major, and perhaps decisive, exception was the United States. In 2001, the U.S. government announced that it would not adhere to the requirements of the Kyoto Protocol because they would endanger the nation's economic development and growth in the 21st century. The fate of the Kyoto Protocol remained in doubt.

Review Questions

1. What is global warming, and why is it of such concern to the world's nations?
2. a. What are environmental "sinks"?
   b. How do these sinks protect the environment from harmful greenhouse gases?
3. What two ways of reducing greenhouse gases are supported by the 1992 UN framework convention?
4. Why is it difficult both to promote economic growth and to protect against harmful climate change?
5. a. Why might developed nations be expected to take the lead in solving the problem of greenhouse gas emissions?
   b. How were the developed nations expected to help the developing nations?

Fourth World Conference on Women I: A Woman Observer Reports

In September 1995, almost 50,000 women and men from all over the world converged on Beijing, China, for the United Nations Fourth World Conference on Women. The meeting was a follow-up to earlier UN conferences on women held at Mexico City in 1975; Copenhagen, Denmark, in 1980; and Nairobi, Kenya, in 1985.

The conference consisted of two parts. One was a meeting of more than 5,000 government delegates from 189 nations. That was the official meeting, held in downtown Beijing. The other was a meeting of representatives from some 2,100 nongovernmental organizations, or NGOs, held in the nearby county of Huairou. The NGOs ranged from international human rights and religious organizations to groups of feminist educators and gay/lesbian rights advocates. All the NGOs had a common goal: to make known their own concerns and recommendations for the "Platform for Action" being drawn up by the official governmental delegates.

Joan Chittister, a Benedictine sister and lecturer from Pennsylvania, attended the Beijing and Huairou meetings as a peace advocate and writer for the *National Catholic Reporter*. The following document contains passages from her book *Beyond Beijing: The Next Step for Women* (1996).

August 30, 1995

The opening event was a [display of skill] of Chinese organization, creativity, scope and sheer weight of numbers. At one point in the show, we estimated that there were at least 3500 performers on the field at once. . . .

[T]he event was a milestone in my own experience of womanhood. No Olympic Games could possibly capture the spirit that [spread through] this massive outpouring of womanhood. I had been in military [spectaculars], in football playoffs, in some of the largest church ceremonies in the world. In all of them, in most of life, I and others like me were the minority, the other, the onlookers at events that really belonged to men, that were directed by men and staffed by men. Here, the stands were full of women, thousands and thousands of women. The performers, by and large, were women, the symphony orchestra of Beijing that filled the arena with bright and brilliant music from every continent on earth was a women's orchestra with a woman conductor, the speakers were all women, the roars of the crowd were women's roars. This was my world and it was a real one. . . .

The sheer improbability of it all caught me completely off guard. I saw with my own eyes what concerns men about the women's movement: the fact of the matter is that these women really could run the world. . . .

On the other hand, the stadium was also dotted with men, plainclothes security men we were all now sure, keeping sentry [guard] over the dangers of untamed ideas. . . .

August 31, 1995

Huairou, the site of the NGO Forum, is about 60 km [37 miles] outside of Beijing. . . .

The streets teemed with women from every part of the world. African [women] swept by in bright colors and turbans, Asian women in silk wrap-arounds, Muslim women in *chadors*, Westerners in shorts and slacks. These were the women who were going to agree on a Platform of Action for all the women of the world? I'll believe it when I see it. . . .

September 4, 1995

You could read all your life and never get as much in a professional degree as you can get just talking to women on the streets here [in Beijing]. They are financial planners, social engineers, government ministers, theologians, philosophers, doctors, scientists, sociologists. They are all doing something to reshape life as we know it so that women can come to know life as men know it—in all its fullness, with all its security, all its opportunity, all its potential. The woman next to me at lunch [started] a woman's bank. The woman next to me in line organizes women in barrios [poor urban districts] in South America to pressure governments into developing sanitation projects in these areas. The woman sitting next to me in the peace tent has written textbooks for children on the effects of militarism. A woman in the cab with us writes stories about the lack of adoption facilities in Asia and the effects of female infanticide on social structure.

It's an exciting thing, this conference. It is like a second-hand ticking away before the dynamite blows in a match factory. All the poor of the world—colored, landless and female—are rising up out of the slime of the earth to claim their birthrights. It is an age-old conflict, this quest of the deprived for their human inheritance. And in the end, in the long, dark, withering end, the deprived, history records, always, always eventually win. . . .

September 7, 1995

The two experiences—the [NGO] Forum and the Conference—are beginning to come together now. The things we heard in Huairou now have echoes here [in Beijing]. These NGO delegates want action from the governments of the world on economic issues. They want the protection of girl-children through international law. They want the elimination of the gender-gap in education. They want health care for women. They want protection from abuse. NGO delegates on every delegation, NGO experts on every issue, track every working group, every amendment, every political compromise and report back to the larger body daily. They keep a running [account] on what items of the Platform for Action are in question, or being debated, or are in danger of being lost. Then, every day the group [separates] to do more work, talk to more delegates, provide more materials, go to more hearings with the NGO agenda firmly in mind. It goes on from early morning until late, late at night. This is not your average professional convention. This is serious business. This will determine what the family of nations will say that being a woman is all about. . . .

September 12, 1995

These days in Beijing have been a . . . study in contrasts, a [see-saw] of experiences that ranged from the very difficult to the very exhilarating, the very exciting to the very sobering. I am, for instance, looking at some of the world's most tragically illiterate women on the streets of Beijing. At the same time, I am looking at some of the most professionally literate women in the world in the Conference Center across town. All these women are in the same city at the same time. They are all watching one another, evaluating one another, talking about one another. They are all trying to make the world a better place for their daughters. They are each of them from incredibly different worlds and the same world at the same time. It is like a human face split down the middle and painted a different color on each side. Only together are they womanhood, part of it in the light, the rest of it in darkness yet. . . .

September 14, 1995

Sometimes it sounds as if the Platform has the universal support it will take to change the world overnight. At other times, it sounds as if the world—and the women's movement—is splitting apart at the seams right in front of our faces. The briefings have been one long cry for mutual support. Handicapped women asked for access. Tibetan women asked for freedom from China. [Rural] women asked for intellectual property rights. Women in war zones pleaded for pressure groups to decry the militarization of the world. Lesbians begged for protection from civil discrimination. If you cannot help us, every group entreated the assembly, at least do us no harm. Don't barter us away, in other words. Don't sell out our rights for yours. . . .

September 17, 1995

I am someplace over who-knows-where on my way to Chicago. . . . I am on my way back to spend the rest of my life watching to see if anybody but me and the 40,000 other women who went to Beijing were serious about the Fourth UN Conference on Women. The daughters of our tears depend on us.

Review Questions

1. Why did Joan Chittister describe the opening event of the women's conference as different from any she had ever experienced?

2. Why did Chittister believe that the women at the conference were trying to "reshape life as we know it"?
3. Describe the demands of the nongovernmental organization (NGO) delegates.
4. Why did Chittister describe her time in Beijing as "a study in contrasts"?
5. What did Chittister mean when she wrote, "The daughters of our tears depend on us"?

Fourth World Conference on Women II: Platform for Action

After almost two weeks of discussion and debate, of writing and rewriting, the governmental delegates in Beijing adopted by consensus a lengthy Platform for Action. It highlighted 12 areas of concern to women and made recommendations about what steps governments and international agencies should take to advance women's rights and improve women's lot. The recommendations were just that—recommendations; they were not formal obligations or duties that governments had to accept or reject. Delegates set a series of follow-up sessions to assess progress on the Beijing goals. The first such meeting was held in 2000 in New York.

Below are two documents. The first contains passages from the Platform for Action.

Platform for Action (excerpts)

. . . 9. The objective of the Platform for Action, which is in full conformity [agreement] with the purposes and principles of the Charter of the United Nations and international law, is the empowerment of all women. The full realization of all human rights and fundamental freedoms of all women is essential for the empowerment of women. . . . [I]t is the duty of States, regardless of their political, economic and cultural systems, to promote and protect all human rights and [basic] freedoms. The [putting into effect] of this Platform . . . is the sovereign responsibility of each State. . . .

26. The growing strength of the nongovernmental sector [NGOs], particularly women's organizations and feminist groups, has become a driving force for change. Nongovernmental organizations have played an important advocacy role in advancing legislation or [ways] to ensure the promotion of [rights for] women. . . .

44. . . . Governments, the international community and civil society, including nongovernmental organizations and the private

sector, are called upon to take action in the following [critical] areas:

- The persistent and increasing burden of poverty on women
- Inequalities and inadequacies in and unequal access to education and training
- Inequalities and inadequacies in and unequal access to health care and related services
- Violence against women
- The effects of armed or other kinds of conflict on women, including those living under foreign occupation
- Inequality in economic structures and policies, in all forms of productive activities and in access to resources
- Inequality between men and women in the sharing of power and decision-making at all levels
- Insufficient mechanisms at all levels to promote the advancement of women
- Lack of respect for and inadequate promotion and protection of the human rights of women
- Stereotyping of women and inequality in women's access to and participation in all communication systems, especially in the media
- Gender inequalities in the management of natural resources and in the safeguarding of the environment
- Persistent discrimination against and violation of the rights of the girl child

The Platform for Action goes on to make a series of recommendations regarding each of the listed "critical areas." This second document is from a United Nations summary of some of those recommendations.

Summary of Recommendations

Women's Rights as Human Rights. The Platform takes the 1979 [United Nations] Convention on the Elimination of All Forms of Discrimination against Women, which recognizes violence against women as a human rights problem, one step further by asserting women's right "to have control over and decide freely and responsibly on matters related to their sexuality, including sexual and reproductive health, free of [compulsion], discrimination and violence."

Right to Inherit. Traditional legal structures in many societies discriminate against women inheriting land and property. The Platform calls for a change in these structures by "enacting as appropriate, and enforcing legislation that guarantees equal rights to succession and ensures equal right to inherit, regardless of the sex of the child."

Reviewing Laws on Illegal Abortion. The Platform asks nations to "consider reviewing laws containing punitive measures against women who have undergone illegal abortion."

Role of the Family. The Platform points out the importance of the family as the basic unit of society and recognizes the "social significance of maternity, motherhood and the role of parents in the family and in the upbringing of children." Furthermore, it notes that maternity should not [stand in the way of] the full participation of women in society.

Culture and Religion. Traditional interpretations of religious texts often marginalize [treat as unimportant] the role of women in society. However, according to the Platform, religion can "contribute to fulfilling women's and men's moral, ethical and spiritual needs and to realizing their potential in society."

Rape as a War Crime. Rape, according to the Platform, is a war crime, and in some cases, an act of genocide. Those guilty of such a crime "must be punished" whenever possible.

Review Questions

1. What is the Platform for Action?
2. a. What is the objective of the platform?
   b. How does the platform define "empowerment" for women?
3. Choose one of the areas in the summary of the platform, in which governments are called upon to take action.
   a. Identify one nation where you believe that concern should be addressed, explaining the need for recommendations in that country.
   b. Discuss some of the difficulties that might be encountered in following the platform's recommendations in the nation you selected.

8 HIV/AIDS: United Nations Declaration of Commitment

In June 2001, the United Nations General Assembly issued a statement called the Declaration of Commitment on HIV/AIDS (human immunodeficiency virus/acquired immunodeficiency syndrome). The declaration is a call to the world's governments and private industries to fund the billions of dollars needed to fight AIDS on a global scale. AIDS is no longer viewed as simply a medical problem but as a global epidemic that has political, economic, and human rights implications.

The declaration is exceptional because of the unprecedented honesty with which it addresses the issue of HIV/AIDS. The UN had been silent on this subject since the outbreak of AIDS in the early 1980s. The declaration is an attempt to rally all the UN's member nations to rise above the cultural stereotyping and prejudice that have contributed to this global crisis.

Much of the leadership behind the UN's effort has come from African nations, where more than three-quarters of the world's 40 million HIV-infected people live. In Africa, Islam, and many animist religions, have opposed either sex education or the use of condoms as a way of preventing the disease. Cultural biases have also prevented essential services and educational programs from reaching such stigmatized groups as homosexuals, intravenous drug users, and prostitutes.

The Declaration of Commitment is linked to the earlier UN Platform for Action, drawn up at the 1995 world conference on women. (See documents 6 and 7.) This earlier document calls for the empowerment of women so that they have control over matters related to their own sexuality. The 2001 declaration states that women and girls are "disproportionately affected [have a higher risk for] HIV/AIDS." The declaration also echoes Joan Chittister's hope that women would "come to know life as men know it, in . . . all its potential," and with full enjoyment of all human rights. Both the Declaration of Commitment and the Platform for Action were inspired by the UN's 1948 Universal Declaration of Human Rights. The Declaration of Human

Rights asserts that all people have the right to a standard of living high enough to provide adequate health care and security for themselves and their families (Unit VII, Document 1).

Like the Platform for Action, the Declaration of Commitment contains only recommendations. It is not enforceable. The declaration does call for a global fund to fight AIDS, with developed nations paying a proportionately larger share. It also seeks to help developing countries whose limited resources, overburdened public health systems, and inadequate government organization make fighting the AIDS epidemic extremely difficult or nearly impossible.

Leadership by governments in combating HIV/AIDS is essential, and their efforts should be complemented by the full and active participation of civil society, the business community, and the private sector. . . .

Prevention must be the mainstay of our response.

By 2003, establish time-bound national targets . . . to reduce by 2005 HIV prevalence among young men and women aged 15–24 in the most affected countries by 25 percent and by 25 percent globally by 2010, and to . . . challenge gender stereotypes and attitudes, and gender inequalities in relation to HIV/AIDS. . . .

By 2005, ensure that a wide range of prevention interventions which take account of local circumstances, ethics, and cultural values is available in all countries, . . . including information, education, and communication in languages most understood by communities and respectful of cultures, aimed at reducing risk-taking behavior and encouraging responsible sexual behavior, including abstinence and fidelity; expanded access to essential commodities, including male and female condoms and disposable syringes; harm-reduction efforts related to drug use; expanded access to voluntary and confidential counseling and testing; safe blood supplies; and early and effective treatment of transmissible infections. . . .

By 2003, ensure that national strategies . . . are developed . . . to strengthen health-care systems and address factors affecting the provision of HIV-related drugs; [including] affordability and pricing . . .; and technical and health care systems capacity. . . .

By 2003, enact . . . measures to eliminate all forms of discrimination against, and to ensure the full enjoyment of all human rights and fundamental freedoms by, people living with HIV/AIDS; . . . to ensure their access to [among other things] education, inheritance, employment, health care, social and health services, prevention, support, treatment, information, and legal protection while respecting their privacy and confidentiality; and develop strategies to combat stigma and social exclusion connected with the epidemic.

By 2005, bearing in mind the context and character of the epidemic and that globally women and girls are disproportionately affected by HIV/AIDS, develop and accelerate the implementation of national strategies that promote the advancement of women and women's full enjoyment of all human rights; promote shared responsibility of men and women to ensure safe sex; empower women to have control over and decide freely and responsibly on matters related to their sexuality to increase their ability to protect themselves from HIV infection. . . .

By 2003, develop and/or strengthen national strategies . . . to promote and protect the health of those identifiable groups which currently have high or increasing rates of HIV infection . . . as indicated by such factors as . . . poverty, sexual practices, drug-using behavior, livelihood, institutional location, disrupted social structures, and population movements forced or otherwise. . . .

By 2005 . . . reach an overall target of annual expenditures on the epidemic of between U.S. $7 billion and U.S. $10 billion in low- and middle-income countries . . . and take measures to ensure that needed resources are made available, particularly from donor countries and also from national budgets, bearing in mind that resources of the most affected countries are seriously limited. . . .

Urge the developed countries that have not done so to strive to meet the target of . . . 0.15 percent to 0.20 percent of gross national product as official development assistance for least developed countries, as agreed, as soon as possible, taking into account the urgency and gravity of the HIV/AIDS epidemic. . . .

Review Questions

1. How does the Declaration of Commitment view the fight against AIDS as not just a medical problem but a human rights issue as well?

2. What measures outlined in the declaration also show its commitment to prevention as the primary strategy in the war against AIDS?
3. Among the many goals outlined in the declaration, which do you think are the most important? Explain your reasons.
4. How does the declaration attempt to take into account the different cultures, ethics, and values of the world's nations?
5. a. Why do many developing countries have great difficulties in meeting the challenge of the AIDS epidemic?
   b. What role does the declaration see for developed nations in the global effort against AIDS?

Unit VIII Document-Based Question

*Write a well-organized essay that includes an introduction, several paragraphs, and a conclusion. Use evidence from at least **four** documents in the unit in the body of the essay. Support your response with relevant facts, examples, and details. Include additional outside information.*

Historical Context

By the start of the 21st century, the world's nations had become more interdependent than at any other time in history. As a result, the decisions made by developed nations had an increasing impact on both the people in the developing nations and on the earth's environment.

Task: Using the documents and questions in the unit, along with your knowledge of global history, write an essay in which you:

- Discuss the impact of globalization on developing nations
- Discuss the relative responsibilities of developed and developing nations to take steps to protect both the human rights of people in the developing nations and the earth's environment
- Evaluate the extent to which the world's nations should balance the need for economic growth with the need to protect both the human rights of the people who are at great risk and the environment

Acknowledgments

Unit I The Ancient World

3 From *History Begins at Sumer: Thirty-nine Firsts in Recorded History*, by Samuel Noah Kramer. Copyright © 1956 by Samuel Noah Kramer. Reprinted by permission of the University of Pennsylvania Press.

5 From *The Epic of Gilgamesh*, Maureen Gallery Kovacs, trans., with an Introduction and Notes. Copyright © 1985, 1989 by the Trustees of the Leland Stanford Junior University. With the permission of Stanford University Press, www.sup.org.

8 From *The Torah: The Five Books of Moses*. Copyright © 1962 by the Jewish Publication Society of America. Reprinted by permission of the Jewish Publication Society, Philadelphia, Pa.

12 From B. Tierney, ed., *Western Societies: A Documentary History*, vol. 1. New York, Alfred A. Knopf. Copyright © 1984. Reprinted by permission of The McGraw-Hill Companies.

14 From James Henry Breasted, ed., *Ancient Records of Egypt*, vol. 2, University of Chicago Press, 1906.

17 From *Chinese Poems*, Arthur Waley, trans. London, G. Allen & Unwin, 1946. Reprinted by permission of the Arthur Waley Estate.

20 From *Plutarch: Selected Lives and Essays*, Louise Ropes Loomis, trans. Roslyn, New York, Walter J. Black, Inc., 1951.

25 Reprinted by permission of the publishers and the Trustees of the Loeb Classical Library from *Dio Cassius: Volume VIII*, Loeb Classical Library Volume L 176, translated by Earnest Carey on the basis of the version of Herbert B. Foster, 1905–1906, pp. 83–85, Cambridge, Mass.: Harvard University Press, 1925. The Loeb Classical Library ® is a registered trademark of the President and Fellows of Harvard College.

28 From *Suetonius: The Twelve Caesars*, Robert Graves, trans. New York: Penguin Books, 1957. Reprinted by permission of Carcanet Press, Ltd.

32 Copyright Scala/Art Resource. Reproduced by permission of Art Resource.

34 From *The Bhagavad-Gita*, Barbara Stoler Miller, trans. New York, Columbia University Press. Copyright © 1986. Reprinted with the permission of the publisher.

37 From *The Dhammapada*, John Richards, trans. Copyright © John Richards. Reprinted by permission.

41 From *The Analects of Confucius*, Arthur Waley, trans. George Allen & Unwin, 1958. Reprinted by permission of the Arthur Waley Estate.

44 From *Holy Bible, New Living Translation*, copyright © 1996 by Tyndale Charitable Trust. All rights reserved. For more information on the New Living Translation, visit www.newlivingtranslation.com.

47 From *The Koran*, N. J. Dawood, trans. Penguin Classics. 1956. 5th revised ed. 1996. Copyright N. J. Dawood, 1958, 1959, 1966, 1968, 1974, 1990.

Unit II Expanding Zones of Encounter and Exchange

53 Copyright Scala/Art Resource. Reproduced by permission of Art Resource.

56 From *East Asia History Sourcebook*. http: www.fordham.edu. halsall/eastasia/781/nestorian.html.

58 From Anthony C. Yu, trans. and ed., Ch'eng-en Wu, *The Journey to the West*, vol. 1. University of Chicago Press. © 1977 by the University of Chicago.

61 From Arthur J. Arberry, *Avicenna on Theology* ("Wisdom of the East" series). London, John Murray Publishers, Ltd. Reprinted by permission.

64 From James Henry Robinson, ed., *Readings in European History*, vol. 1. Boston: Ginn & Co., 1904.

68 From *Medieval Sourcebook*. http://fordham.edu/halsall/source/will1-lawsb.html.

71 Excerpt from *The Tale of Genji*, by Lady Murasaki, translated by Arthur Waley. Copyright 1929. Reprinted by permission of Houghton Mifflin Co. All rights reserved.

74 From *Sources of Japanese Tradition*, R. Tsunada, et al, eds. © 1958. Reprinted by permission of Columbia University Press.

76, 78 From Nizam al-Mulk, *The Book of Government, or Rules for Kings*, Hubert Darke, trans. Routledge & Kegan Paul, 1960. Reprinted by permission of Bibliotheca Persica.

81, 87 From James Harvey Robinson, ed., *Readings in European History*, vol. 1. Boston: Ginn & Co., 1904.
84 From *The Alexiad of the Princess Anna Comnena*, Elizabeth A. S. Dawes, trans. London: Routledge & Kegan Paul, 1967.

Unit III Global Interactions

93 From J. C. Hall, "The Hojo Code of Judicature," in *Transactions of the Asiatic Society of Japan*, 1906.
96 From Daidoji Yuzan, *Budoshohinshu: The Code of the Warrior*, A. L. Sadler, trans. Boston: Charles E. Tuttle Co., Inc., 1988.
98 From Wm. T. de Bary, et al, eds., *Sources of Chinese Tradition*, vol. 1. © 1960 by Columbia University Press. Reprinted by permission of the publisher.
101 From Milton Rugoff, ed., *The Great Travelers*, © 1960. Reprinted by permission of Routledge (UK).
104, 107 From pp. 193, 195–196 of *They Came to Japan: An Anthology of European Reports on Japan, 1543–1640*, edited by Michael Cooper. Michigan Classics in Japanese Studies, Number 15 (Ann Arbor: Center for Japanese Studies, The University of Michigan, 1995; original: The University of California Press, 1965). Used by permission.
109 From Frederic Austin, ed. *A Source Book of Medieval History*. New York: Cooper Square Publishers, 1972. (First published 1907.)
117 From Thomas Aquinas, *Summa theologiae*, David Burr, trans. At http://www.najbill.vt.edu/history/burr/Aquinas2.html. Reprinted by permission.
121 From *The Divine Comedy of Dante Alighieri: Inferno*, by Allen Mandelbaum, copyright © 1980 by Allen Mandelbaum. Used by permission of Bantam Books, a division of Random House, Inc.
124 From Giovanni Boccaccio, *The Decameron*, vol. 1. London, J. M. Dent & Sons, Ltd., 1930, 1955.
127 From Charles W. Colby, ed., *Selections from the Sources of English History*. London: Longmans, Green, 1920.
130 Copyright The Frick Collection, New York.
132 From *Georgio Vasari, Lives of the Artists*, vol. 1., George Bull, trans. Copyright © George Bull, 1965. Penguin Classics, 1965.
135, 137 From J. H. Robinson, ed., *Readings in European History*. Boston, Ginn & Co., 1906.

Unit IV The First Global Age

143 Extracted with the permission of Simon & Schuster from *Popol Vuh*, by Dennis Tedlock. Copyright © 1985, 1996 by Dennis Tedlock.
148 From *Parker on the Iroquois: The Constitution of the Five Nations*, edited by William N. Fenton. Syracuse University Press, Syracuse, New York, 1981.
153 From *The Travels of Ibn Battuta*, ed. C. Defrenery and B. R. Sanguinetti; trans. A. R. Gibb. London: The Hakluyt Society, 1994. Reprinted by permission.
158 From *Admiral of the Ocean Sea: Life of Christopher Columbus*, by Samuel Eliot Morrison. Copyright © 1942 by Samuel Eliot Morrison; copyright © renewed 1970 by Samuel Eliot Morrison. By permission of Little, Brown & Company, Inc.
161 (A) From *The Broken Spears*, by Miguel Leon-Portilla. © 1962, 1990 by Miguel Leon-Portilla. Expanded and updated edition © 1992 by Miguel Leon-Portilla. Reprinted by permission of Beacon Press, Boston. (B) From Hernan Cortés, *Letter to Emperor Charles V, 1520*, in Harry J. Carroll, Jr., et al, *The Development of Civilization: A Documentary History of Politics, Society, and Thought*, vol. 1. Scott, Foresman & Co., 1961.
169 The great temple of Tenochtitlán, reconstructed by Ignacio Marquina, from descriptions of Spanish conquerors and existing Aztec manuscripts. Courtesy Department of Library Services, American Museum of Natural History. Negative number 32657.
171 From Agustin de Zárate, *The Discovery and Conquest of Peru*, J. M. Cohen, trans. Baltimore: Penguin Books, 1958. Copyright © 1968, 2002 the estate of J. M. Cohen.
174 Hans Holbein, the Younger, Portrait of merchant Georg Gisze. AKG Picture Library, London.
176 From John Newton, *Thoughts Upon the Slave Trade*, London, 1788.
180 From Olaudah Equiano, *The Interesting Narrative of the Life of Olaudah Equiano, or Gustavas Vassa, the African: Written by Himself*. London, 1789.

Unit V An Age of Revolutions

187 From Nicolas Copernicus, "On the Revolutions of the Heavenly Bodies," James Fieser, trans. Reprinted by permission.

190 Reprinted by permission of the Instituto e Museo de Storia della Scienza, Florence, Italy. www.imiss.fi.it>

193 From *Second Treatise of Government,* by John Locke, Peardon, T. P., trans. © Reprinted by permission of Pearson Education, Inc., Upper Saddle River, N.J.

197 From Samuel Edwards, *The Divine Mistress.* New York: David McKay Co., Inc., 1970.

199 Fall of the Bastille. Contemporary watercolor. Paris: Musée Carnavalet. AKG Picture Library, London.

201 Reprinted with permission from the *New Encyclopaedia Britannica,* 15th Edition. © 1980 by Encyclopaedia Britannica, Inc.

204 From Adam Smith, *An Inquiry Into the Nature and Causes of the Wealth of Nations: Selections.* Bobbs-Merrill Co., Inc. 1961.

207 Newcomen's steam engine, 1775; modified by R. Trevithick. Mary Evans Picture Library, London.

210 From *Leeds Intelligencer,* June 13, 1786. Quoted in J. F. C. Harrison, *Society and Politics in England 1780–1960.* Harper & Row, Publishers, 1965.

213 From Great Britain, *Parliamentary Papers,* 1842, Vol. XIV. http://www.fordham.edu, halsall.

215 From *Leipzig Illustrite Zeitung,* 27 March 1847. Mary Evans Picture Library, London.

217 From Karl Marx and Frederick Engels, *Manifesto of the Communist Party.* New York: International Publishers, 1948.

222 From Lisa Knapp, ed. and trans., *Dostoyevsky as Reformer: The Petrashevsky Case.* © 1987 Ardis Publishing, Dana Point, Ca.

227 National Photo Archive, Dublin, Ireland.

230 From *The Zionist Idea: A Historical Analysis and Reader.* Published by the Jewish Publication Society, Philadelphia, Pa. Used by permission.

233 From *Zapata and the Mexican Revolution,* by John Womack, Jr. Copyright © 1968 by John Womack, Jr. Used by permission of Alfred A. Knopf, a division of Random House, Inc.

Unit VI A Half-Century of Crisis and Achievement

239 Address to Congress, January 8, 1918. *Supplement to the Messages and Papers of the Presidents Covering the Second Administration of Woodrow Wilson.* Also: http://www.fordham.edu/halsall/moc/1918wilson.html.

242 From Leon Stein, *The Balfour Declaration.* New York: Simon & Schuster, 1961.

245 From the Covenant of the League of Nations. Quoted in Leland M. Goodrich, *The United Nations.* New York: T. Y. Crowell, 1959. Also at http://acusd.edu/gen/text/versaillestreaty/veroo1.html.

248 From Harry Kessler, *In the Twenties: The Diaries of Harry Kessler.* Reprinted by permission of Suhrkamp Verlag, Frankfort am Main, Germany.

253 From Emma Goldman, *My Disillusionment in Russia.* New York: T. Y. Crowell, 1971.

257 From *Gandhi's Autobiography: The Story of My Experiments With the Truth,* by M. K. Gandhi. Washington, D.C.: Public Affairs Press, 1948.

261 From *The Basic Writings of Sigmund Freud,* trans. and ed. by A. A. Brill. New York: Random House, 1938. Reprinted by permission of the A. A. Brill Estate.

264 From Karl Jung, *Freud and Psychoanalysis.* Copyright © 1961 by Princeton University Press. Reprinted by permission of Princeton University Press.

266 From Helen Dukas and Banesh Hoffman, *Albert Einstein: The Human Side.* Copyright © 1979 by the Estate of Albert Einstein. Reprinted by permission of Princeton University Press.

268 Excerpts from *Homage to Catalonia,* by George Orwell, copyright 1952 and renewed 1980 by Sonia Brownell Orwell, reprinted by permission of Harcourt, Inc.

273 Museo Nacional Centro de Arte Reina Sofia, Madrid, Spain. Copyright © 1999 by John Bigelow Taylor/Art Resource, New York.

275 By permission of the Estate of David Low.

277 (A) From Iris Chang, *The Rape of Nanking, The Forgotten Holocaust of World War II.* New York: Basic Books, 1997. (B) Diary of John Rabe, at http://missouri.edu/~ischool/nanking/Terror/terror 03.htm.

280 Reproduced from the collections of the Library of Congress.

282 From *Alicia: My Story,* by Alicia Appleman-Jurman, copyright © 1988 by Alicia Appleman-Jurman. Used by permission of Bantam Books, a division of Random House, Inc.

286 Excerpt from *Night,* by Elie Wiesel, translated by Stella Rodway. Copyright © 1960 by MacGibbon & Kee. Copyright renewed © 1988 by The Collins Publishing Group. Reprinted by permission of Hill and Wang, a division of Farrar, Straus and Giroux, LLC.

290 Affidavit of Rudolf Franz Ferdinand Hoess, Office of United States Chief of Counsel for the Prosecution of Axis Criminality, Nurnberg, Germany, April 8, 1946.

293 From Alexander Stahlberg, *Bounden Duty: The Memoirs of a German Officer 1932–1945,* trans. Patrick Crampton, 1990. Reprinted by permission of Salamander Books, London.

297 From Tadataka Kuribayashi, *My Experience of the Atomic Bomb.* Japan, 1966. Accessed at http://www.csi.ad.jp/ABOMB/RERF/setb-4.html.

Unit VII The World Since 1945

303 Accessed at http://www.un.org/Overview/rights.html.

308 *Modern History Sourcebook.* http://www.fordham.edu.halsall/mod/churchhill-iron.html.

311 Cartoon by James Arthur Wood. © Corbis. Reprinted by permission.

313 From Wilfred Burchett and Anthony Purdy, *Cosmonaut Yuri Gagarin: First Man in Space.* London: Anthony Gibbs and Phillips, 1961.

317 From *Men From Earth,* by Buzz Aldrin and Malcolm McConnell, copyright © 1989 by Research and Engineering Consultants, Inc., and Malcolm McConnell. Used by permission of Bantam Books, a division of Random House, Inc.

321 (A) From *Africa-Asia Speaks from Bandung.* Jakarta: Indonesian Ministry of Foreign Affairs, 1955. (B) From Carlos P. Romulo, *The Meaning of Bandung.* Chapel Hill, N.C., 1956. (C) From *The Color Curtain* © 1956 by Richard Wright. Reprinted by permission of John Hawkins & Associates, Inc.

325 From *The Cairo Documents,* by Mohamed Heikal, copyright © 1971, 1972, 1973 by Mohamed Heikal and *The Sunday Telegraph.* Used by permission of Doubleday, a division of Random House, Inc.

329 From *Quotations From Chairman Mao,* ed. Stuart R. Schram. New York: Frederick A. Praeger, 1968.

333 From Kwame Nkrumah, *Ghana: The Autobiography of Kwame Nkrumah.* New York: Thomas Nelson & Sons, 1957.

335 From *The Gulag Archipelago 1918–1956; An Experiment in Literary Investigation, I-II,* by Alexandr I. Solzhenitsyn. Copyright © 1973 by Alexandr I. Solzhenitsyn. English language translation copyright © 1973, 1974 by Harper & Row, Publishers, Inc. Reprinted by permission of HarperCollins Publishers, Inc.

339 From Cold War International History Project, Woodrow Wilson International Center for Scholars. At http://cwihp.si.edu.cwihplib.nsf.

343 Copyright © Stuart Franklin, Magnum Photos, Inc. D89-128/04 FRS8994OK001.

345 From *The Art of the Impossible,* by Václav Havel, trans. by Paul Wilson, copyright © 1997 by Václav Havel and Paul Wilson. Used by permission of Alfred A. Knopf, a division of Random House, Inc.

348 From Jo Fisher, *Mothers of the Disappeared.* Cambridge, Mass.: South End Press, 1989. Reprinted by permission.

Unit VIII Global Connections and Interactions

355 From Jean-Bertrand Aristide, *Eyes of the Heart: Seeking a Path for the Poor in the Age of Globalization.* Copyright © 2000 Jean-Bertrand Aristide. Monroe, Maine: Common Courage Press.

358 Excerpt from "Tourist with an Attitude," from *The Lexus and the Olive Tree: Understanding Globalization,* by Thomas L. Friedman. Copyright © 1999 by Thomas L. Friedman. Reprinted by permission of Farrar, Straus and Giroux, LLC.

360 http://www.wto.org/english/thewto_e/whatis/ Reprinted by permission of the World Trade Organization.

363 Cartoon by Tony Auth, *The Philadelphia Inquirer,* May 19, 2000. Reprinted by permission of Universal Press Syndicate.

365 http://unfccc.int/resource/conv/cnv.

370 From Joan Chittister, *Beyond Beijing: The Next Step for Women.* Copyright © Joan Chittister. Kansas City, Mo.: Sheed and Ward, 1996.

375 http://www.un.org/womenwatch/daw/beijing/platform/index.html.

378 http://un.org/ga/aids/coverage/FinalDeclarationHIVAIDS.html.